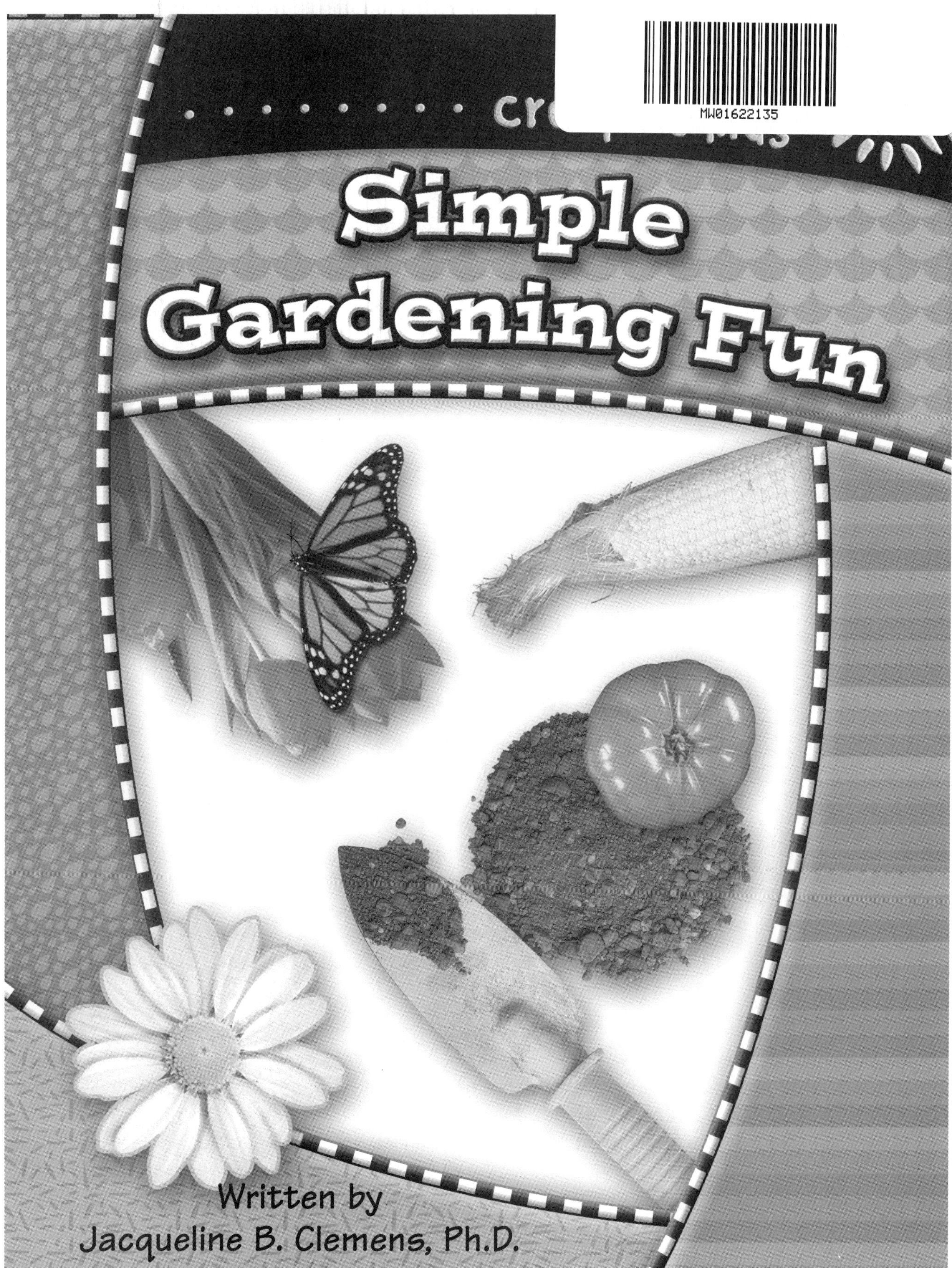
MW01622135
Simple Gardening Fun
Written by
Jacqueline B. Clemens, Ph.D.
Teacher Created Resources

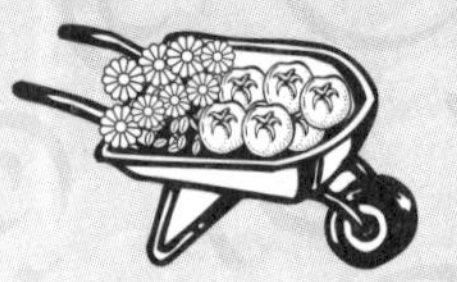
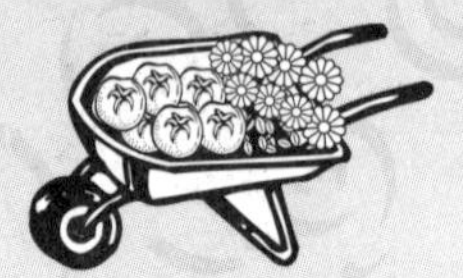

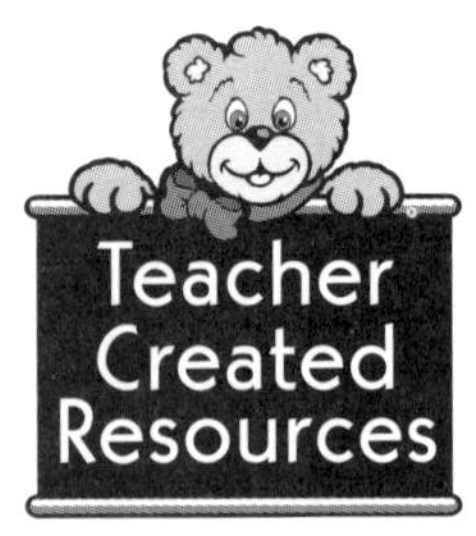

Teacher Created Resources, Inc.

6421 Industry Way

Westminster, CA 92683

www.teachercreated.com

ISBN-1-4206-3194-2

Contributing Author:
Donald L. Coan

Managing Editor:
Karen Goldfluss, M.S. Ed.

Editors:
Marsha Kearns
Lorin Klistoff, M.A.

Cover Artist:
Brenda DiAntonis

Illustrator:
Victoria Ponikvar Frazier

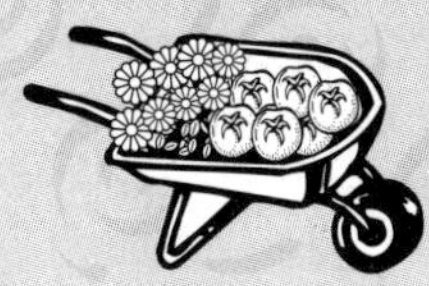

Table of Contents

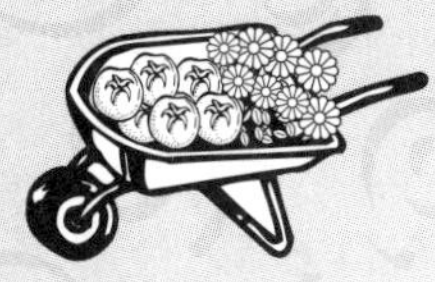

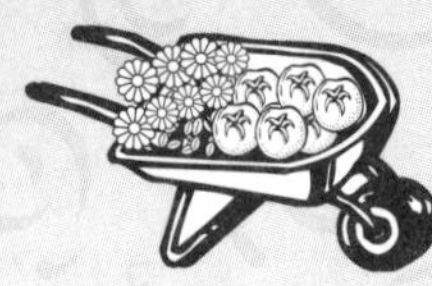

Table of Contents

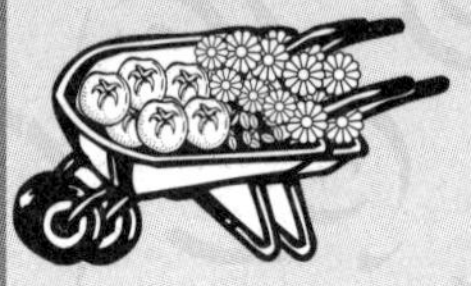

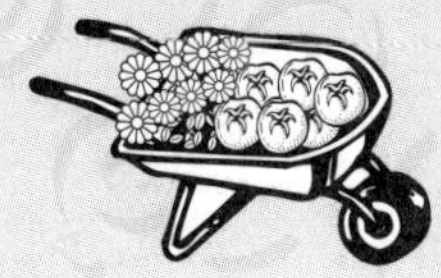

Introduction

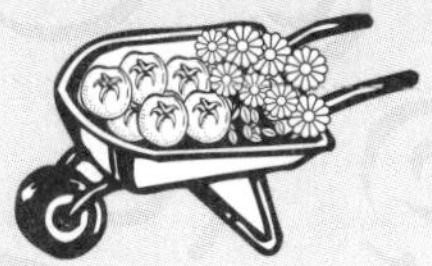

Simple Gardening Fun offers a myriad of helpful gardening tips, recipes, and activities for parents, teachers, and group leaders to use with preschool through middle school children. Satisfaction in gardening comes not only from harvesting the fruits—and vegetables—of your labors but also from the process of planning, preparation, and planting. Eight main sections guide you through the joyous adventure of gardening—and the pleasure of eating what you grow!

Getting Ready to Garden orients you to thinking about gardening before you plant, helps you create a calendar of tasks, and teaches you how seeds sprout.

Successful Gardening offers important gardening tips, shows you how to grow new plants from cuttings and rooting them in water, explores keeping a gardening journal, offers suggestions for gardening with groups of children, reminds you to think about safety, and provides a checklist of considerations for cooking what you grow.

Kinds of Gardens and Gardening Tools describes conventional, container, raised and square-foot, and hydroponic gardens and the tools and equipment you will need for gardening.

Vegetable Gardens presents how to grow and prepare some of your best-liked foods.

Herb Gardens introduces easy-to-grow and fun-to-use plants that are often overlooked.

Flower Gardens teaches you about annuals and perennials, growing flowers from bulbs, and how to create a bird garden.

Cactus, Succulents, and Ferns gives you insight into the strange world of sun-loving cacti and succulents and shade-dwelling ferns.

Have a Garden Party helps you plan for hosting a party that will allow you and your guests to enjoy what you have grown in your garden.

The plant categories, related fun activities, and mouth-watering recipes are organized for easy use.

Materials—lists the main things you will need to plant or complete a recipe or activity

Let's Do It!—leads you step-by step through the gardening process, activity, or recipe

More Ideas—provides alternate ways of doing something that you may want to try

Tidbits—adds a little extra fun or educational information

Learn More—Gives books and materials available in libraries, bookstores, garden centers, and other sources. You might want to also look for gardening books written specifically for the region where you live. Check the Internet for ideas and information. The National Gardening Association sponsors a Web Pals program.

Book Fun—integrates reading into the gardening experience

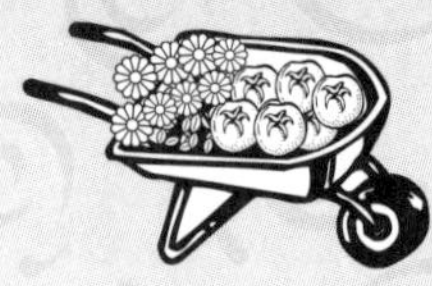

How to Use This Book

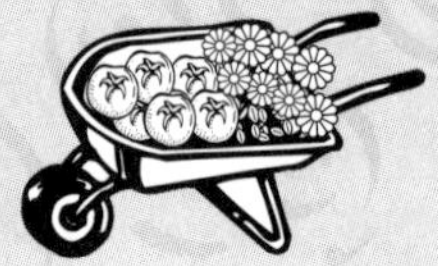

Preview the Book: Page through the book to familiarize yourself with the gardening tips, the types of plants suggested for growing and cooking, and the related activities. Artwork helps clarify such things as materials needed, difficult steps, and finished activities.

Gathering Materials: As you preview the book, note items such as tools and equipment you will need and can begin to assemble before you start gardening. You can grow many of the items used in the related activities, and others can be found in your home, in nature, or in a local nursery, grocery store, or hobby shop. Keep in mind you will always need to plant in a spot where a hose will reach so you can water your plants. You may wish to keep some of these items on hand—craft sticks, construction paper, scissors, tape, glue, paint, brushes, markers, potting soil, and fertilizer.

Storing Materials: Provide a covered area in which you can store tools, equipment, and supplies, including bags of soil, peat, and compost. Make sure you have a cabinet or box into which you can lock away from children potentially harmful chemicals and fertilizers. Remind children that tools are not toys and that they are to ask your permission before they use them. Store tools with sharp points downward.

Getting Started: Carefully read the sections on Getting Ready to Garden, Successful Gardening, and Kinds of Gardens and Gardening Tools before you begin. Refer to these sections as you get children started, and read to them the tips and planning procedures you want them to know and remember. Before you start a planting session, a recipe, or a craft, be sure to check the Materials list to ensure you have what you need to complete your activity. Also, be aware of any allergies the children may have.

Safety Concerns: Read Think About Safety (page 27) frequently, and make children aware of the potential hazards and prevention skills they need to enjoy safe gardening. Make sure you teach children how to recognize and stay away from chemicals, fertilizers, and the poisonous plants shown on page 28. Demonstrate the proper use and storage of all gardening tools and kitchen implements. Don't forget to pay attention to the proper and safe storage of raw and cooked food.

Creating Excitement: Gardening with children is a cooperative activity with built-in excitement. Kids love helping plan a garden, choosing the seeds and plants, preparing the soil and planting, watching plants sprout and bloom, and tending their plants. In addition, they learn what insects and birds visit their garden, develop skills in using tools, and truly understand the connection among all life. Cooking and eating what you grow is a real thrill for kids. Keep in mind that gardening also presents the opportunity for kids to see the cycle of life and death. Children learn that responsibility and hard work often equal success and develop resilience in the face of the inevitable failures. Gardening helps teach kids that, in spite of mistakes and setbacks, life goes on.

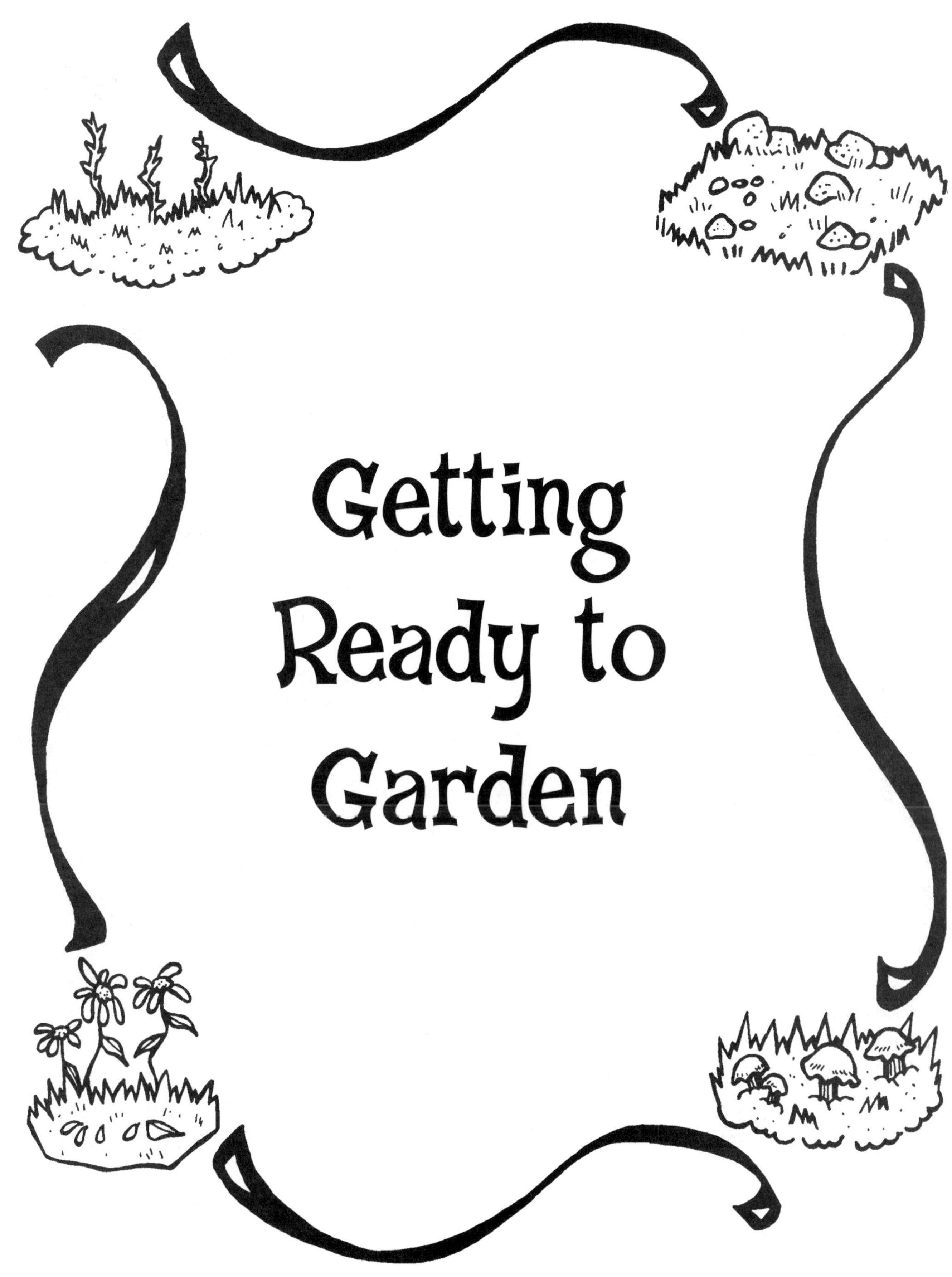

Getting Ready to Garden

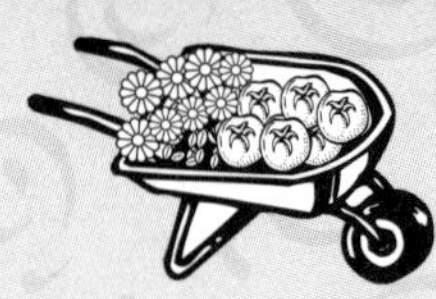

Before You Plant

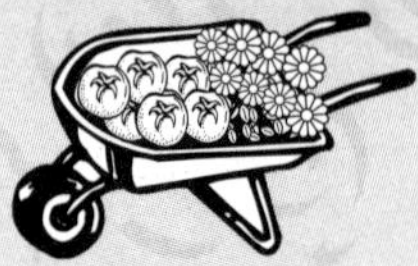

The climate, growing season, available space, and needs of plants will determine the best time and location for planting.

Answer these questions to help you plan your garden:

- Do I want to garden indoors or outdoors?
- Do I have a sunny, well-drained space to plant an outdoor garden?
- Is my space limited so that a raised garden or containers may work best?
- Do I need to terrace a sloped garden area to prevent erosion?
- How much time do I have available to care for the plants after the initial planting is done?
- Do I want to raise vegetables, flowers, herbs, and/or other types of plants?
- Do the plants I want grow best in cool, warm, or hot weather?
- Do I want annuals (plants that live only one growing season) or perennials (plants that come back year after year)?
- What native plants can I choose that will resist disease and pests and reduce maintenance time and costs?

Take advantage of the experts at your local nurseries, garden clubs, and county agricultural extension centers. Use the Internet and your public library to find the answers to your specific gardening questions. Here are a few resources you can use to help you get started on a successful gardening adventure.

Learn More

Bartholomewe, Mel. *Square Foot Gardening.* Emmaus, PA: Rodale Press, 1981.

Growing Ideas. A Journal of Garden-Based Learning. National Gardening Association. 180 Flynn Avenue, Burlington, VT 05401.

Jaffee, Roberts and Appel, Gary. *The Growing Classroom.* Menlo Park, CA: Addison-Wesley Innovative Division, 1990.

"KinderGarden: Children and Horticulture."
URL:http//aggiehorticulture.tamu.edu/kindergarten/kinder.htm

Ocone, Lynn and Eve Pranis. *National Gardening Association Guide to Kids' Gardening.* New York: John Wiley & Sons, 1990. (To order, call National Gardening Association, 1-800-538-7476.)

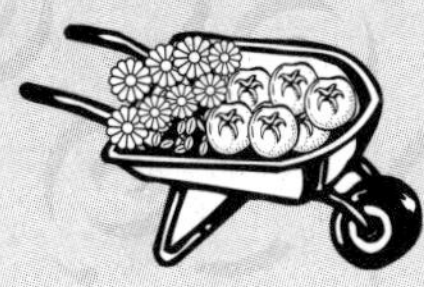

Create a Calendar of Tasks

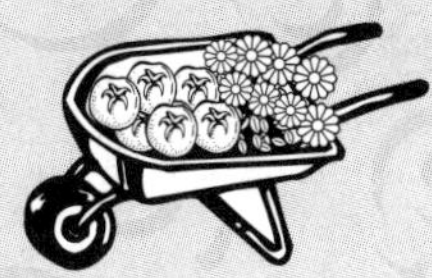

After you answer the basic questions about your garden, involve children in the planning process.

- Visit local nurseries, garden centers, and the library.
- Write for information leaflets and seed catalogs.
- Learn firsthand how seeds sprout (page 16).
- Start a gardening journal (page 23).
- Keep a garden calendar (pages 10–15, enlarge if needed) and use it to list the following:
    - ✓ when to prepare the garden for planting
    - ✓ when to shop for pots, plants, potting soil, and fertilizer
    - ✓ when to plant seeds or seedlings
    - ✓ when to fertilize
    - ✓ when and how to mulch to preserve moisture and reduce weeds
    - ✓ when to trim or prune plants
    - ✓ when to thin, repot, or divide plants
    - ✓ when to harvest
    - ✓ what to do with the fruits (vegetables, herbs, flowers) of your labors
- Weed and prepare soil.
- Add fertilizer.
- Buy seeds.

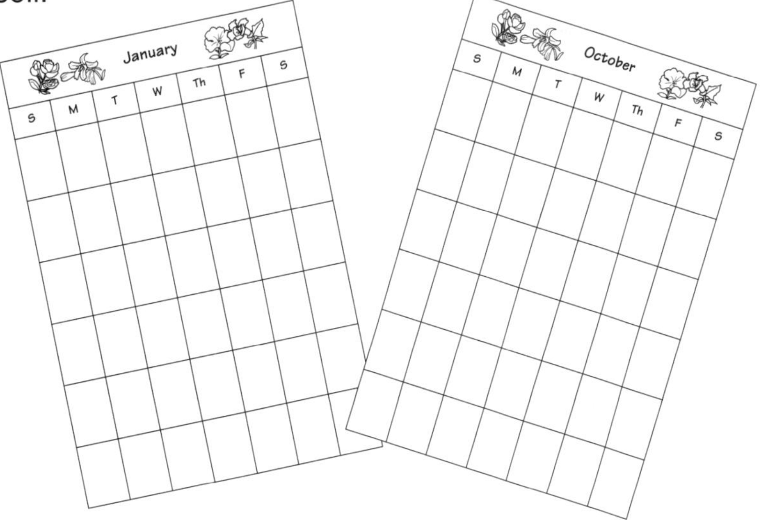

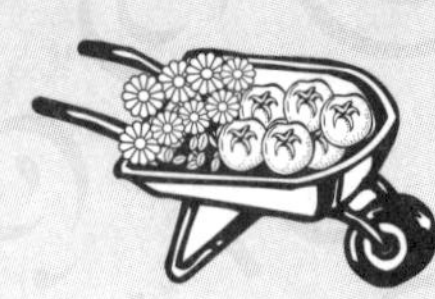

Our Garden Calendar

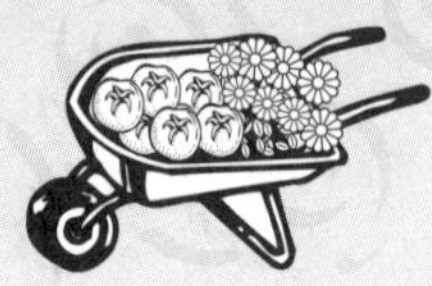

January						
S	M	T	W	Th	F	S

February						
S	M	T	W	Th	F	S

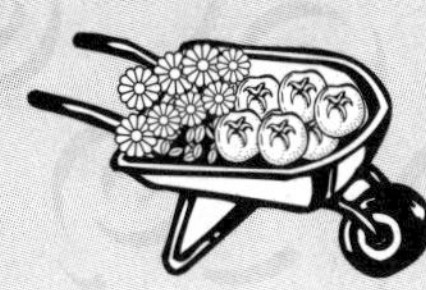

Our Garden Calendar

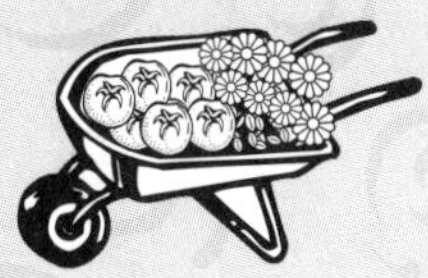

March						
S	M	T	W	Th	F	S

April						
S	M	T	W	Th	F	S

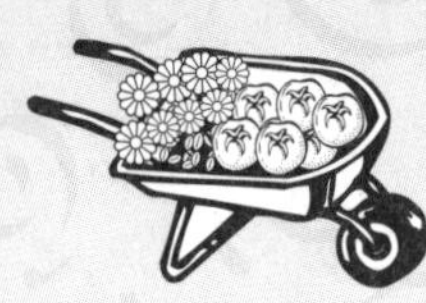

Our Garden Calendar

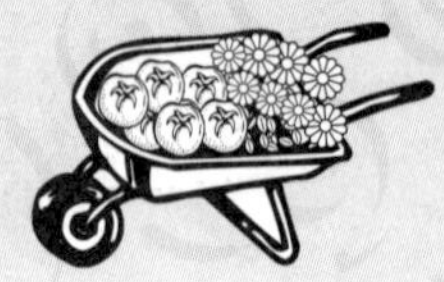

June

S	M	T	W	Th	F	S

May

S	M	T	W	Th	F	S

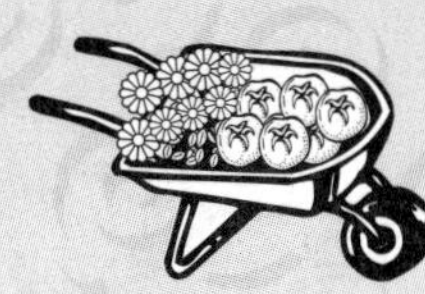

Our Garden Calendar

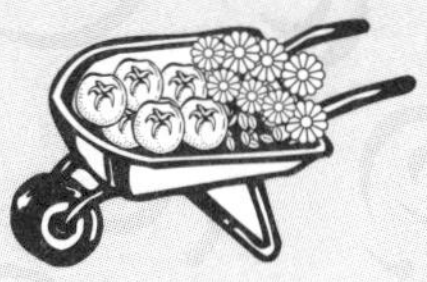

July

S	M	T	W	Th	F	S

August

S	M	T	W	Th	F	S

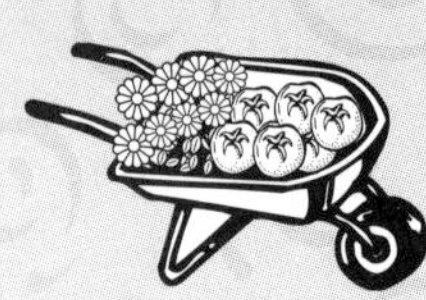

Our Garden Calendar

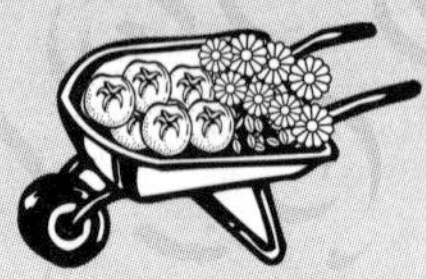

September

S	M	T	W	Th	F	S

October

S	M	T	W	Th	F	S

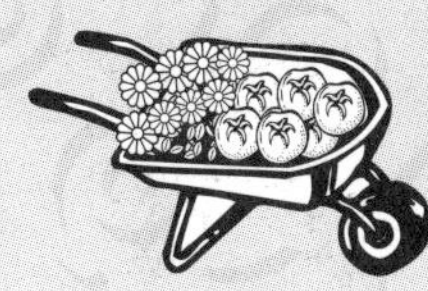

Our Garden Calendar

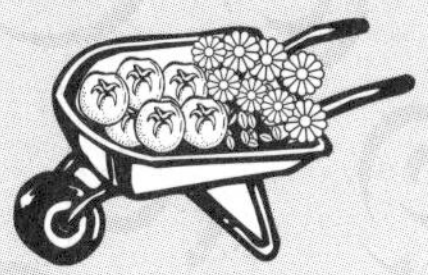

November

S	M	T	W	Th	F	S

December

S	M	T	W	Th	F	S

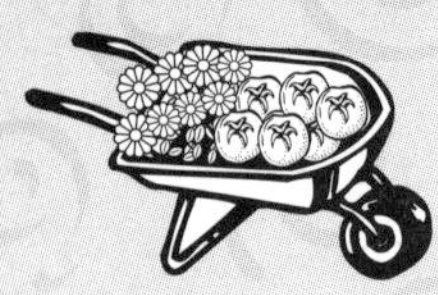

Learn How Seeds Sprout

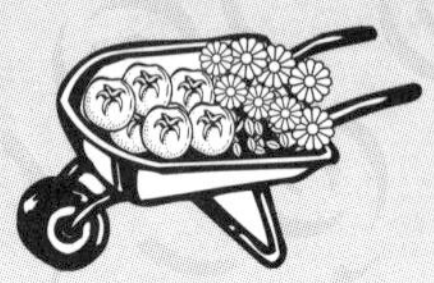

Materials

- 15 dried lima beans
- 15 corn seeds
- 15 other seeds, assorted
- paper towels
- aluminum foil
- water
- fine-tip permanent marker
- ruler

Let's Do It !

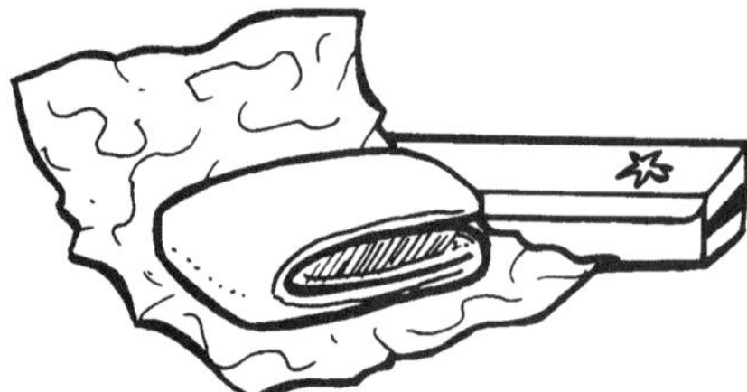

1. Dampen a paper towel. Place 3 lima beans, 3 corn seeds, and several other seeds on the towel. Fold it in thirds. Wrap it in a piece of foil, and fold the ends under to seal it. Set it aside.
2. After four days, unwrap the foil to see what has happened.
3. When the roots are at least $^1/_2$" long, mark a dot on them where the root emerges from the seed covering. Reclose the towel. Dampen the towel if it has dried out. Repeat for several days.
4. Measure the space between the dots to see how much the roots have grown each day.

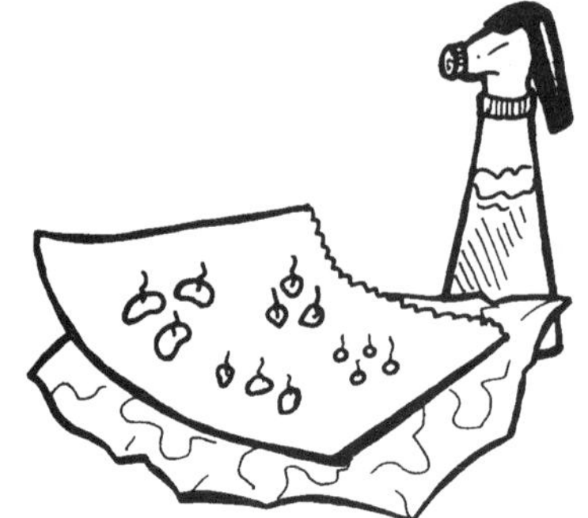

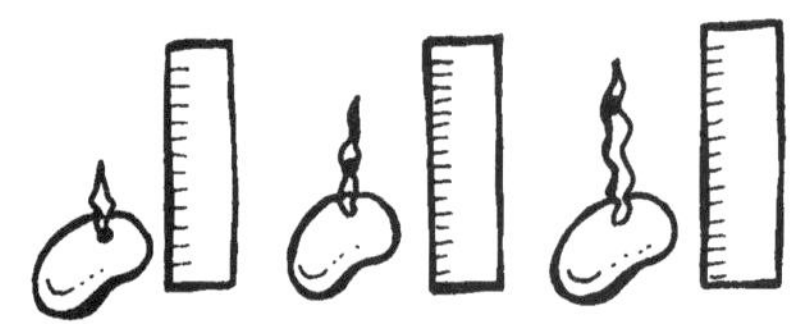

More Ideas

- Provide 4 plastic resealable bags. Place 3 lima beans and 3 corn seeds in each bag. Add $^1/_2$ teaspoon of water to two bags and seal them. Do not add water to the other two bags, and seal them. Put one bag with water and one bag without water in a dark cabinet. Tape the other bags (one with water and one without) to a sunny window. In a week, observe and discuss what happened in all of the bags.

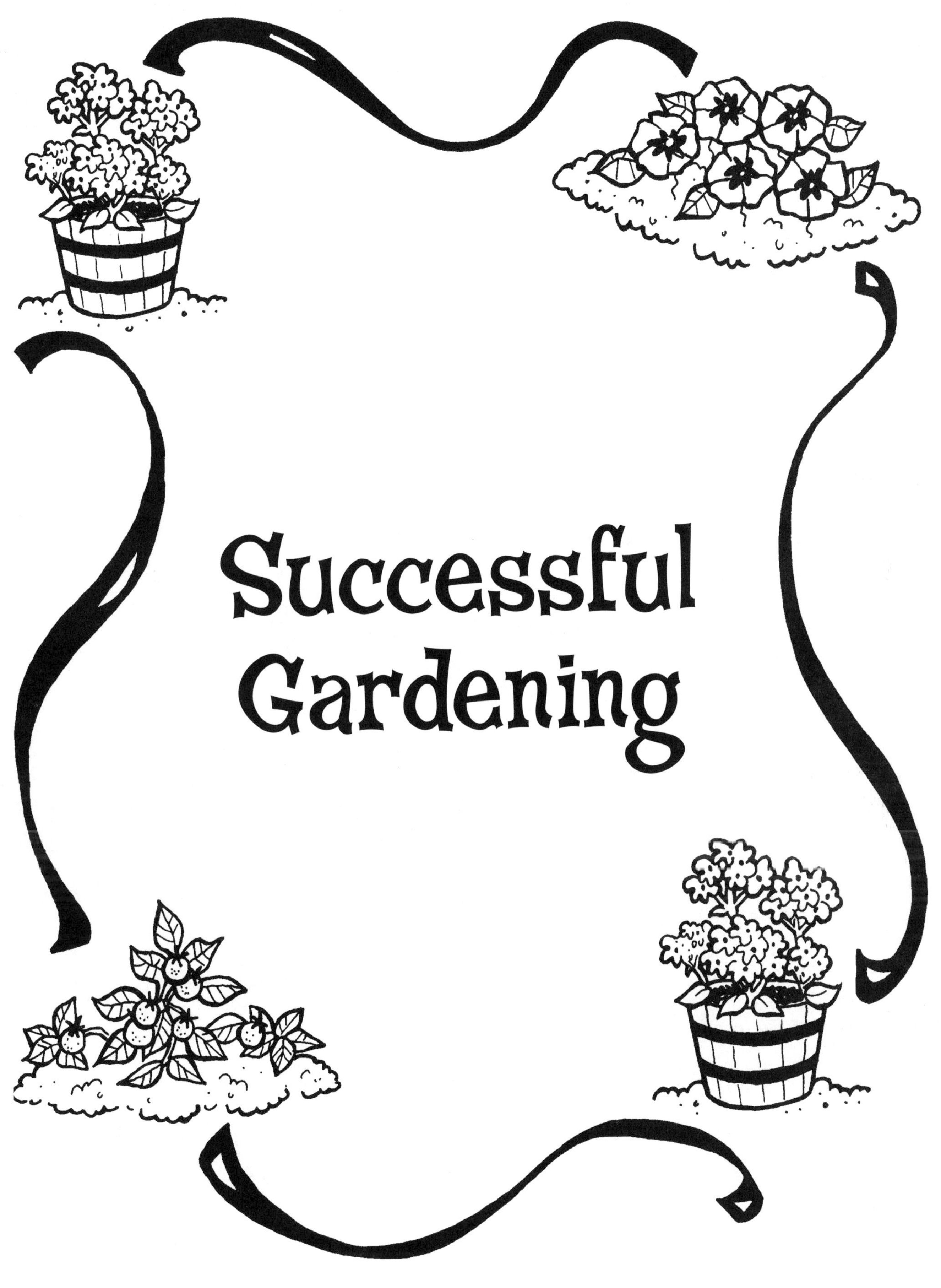

Successful Gardening

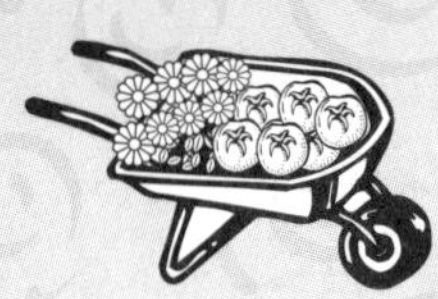

Gardening Tips

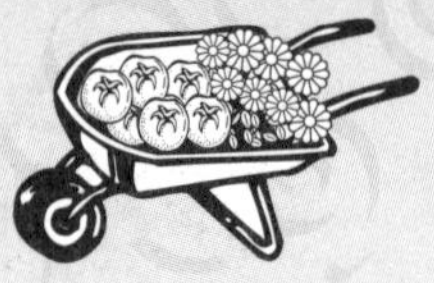

1. Be sure to purchase fresh seeds for best results.
2. To get a head start on gardening for an earlier harvest, purchase seedlings (sets) for plants such as tomatoes, peppers, and sweet potatoes.
3. Make sure a water source is handy to attach a hose or fill watering containers.

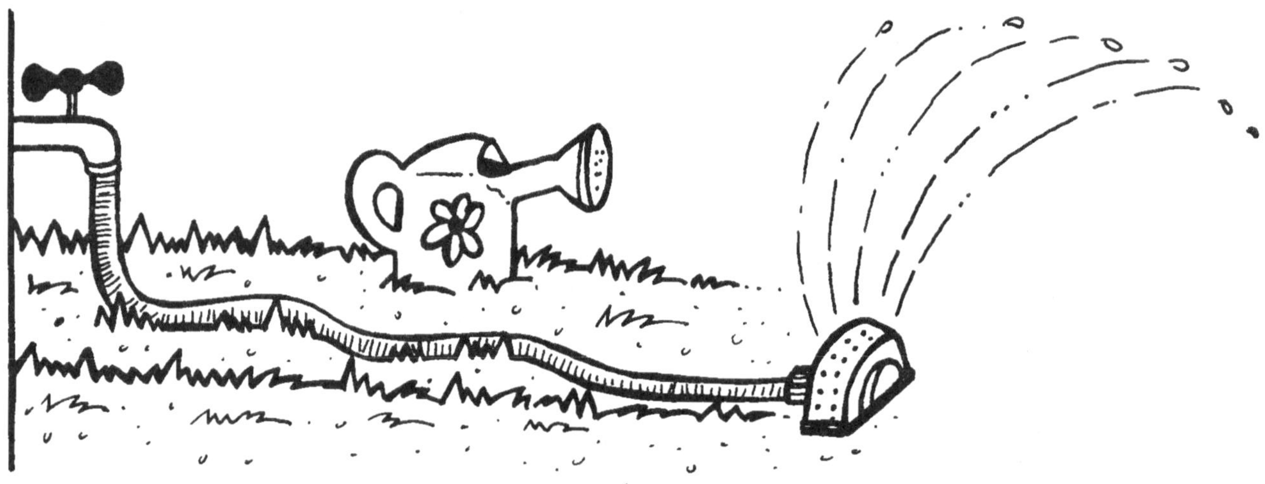

4. Mulch your garden to retain moisture and reduce weeds. After plants are five or six inches tall, spread straw, leaves, or dried grass clippings among the rows and around the plants.
5. Weed your garden weekly. This helps prevent weeds from taking over, robbing the soil of nutrients, and using water your plants need. Teach children how to distinguish between weed leaves and the leaves of vegetables and flowers you plant.
6. Plants need a regular diet of food and water. A balanced fertilizer such as 8-8-8 or 10-10-10, or organic fertilizer such as compost, can be worked into the soil before you plant. Work a side dressing (small amount of fertilizer) into the soil during the growing season if needed.
7. Avoid getting chemical fertilizer on the leaves of plants since it can burn them. Manures should be composted rather than raw.
8. Water newly planted seeds and seedlings every few days until the plants are well established. Thereafter, water plants regularly as needed.

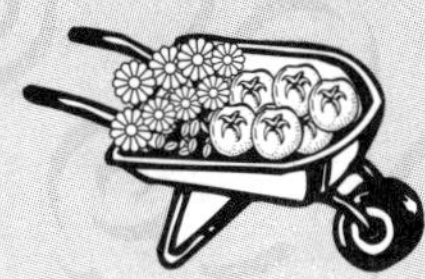

Gardening Tips

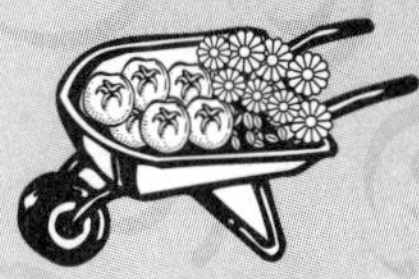

9. Follow the directions for planting, cultivating, and harvesting that come with seeds. Thin seedlings when they are a few inches tall. Crowded plants won't grow well.
10. Many varieties of flowers produce fuller plants with more blooms if you pinch off the center stem when the plants are a few inches tall. This promotes the growth of side branches.
11. Pinch off dead flowers from annuals and perennials to encourage more blossoms.
12. Raised gardens and square-foot gardens are easier to reach and care for than conventional gardens.
13. Maintain a compost pile for recycling dead plants, vegetable peelings, eggshells, coffee grounds, tea leaves, and fireplace ashes. Do not include meat scraps or bones. When the materials have decomposed, work this rich organic matter into the soil.
14. Check your garden area every few days for signs of pests or disease. Consult with local nursery staff about safe ways to keep problems under control.
15. Ladybugs, earthworms, praying mantis, and frogs are garden helpers. Teach children to not harm them.
16. Do not be afraid to try new things, and don't worry about failures. Everything is a learning experience and should be fun!

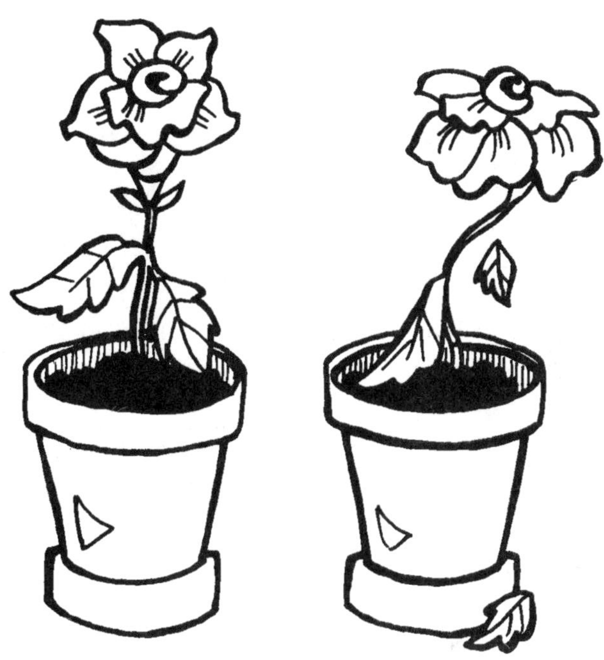

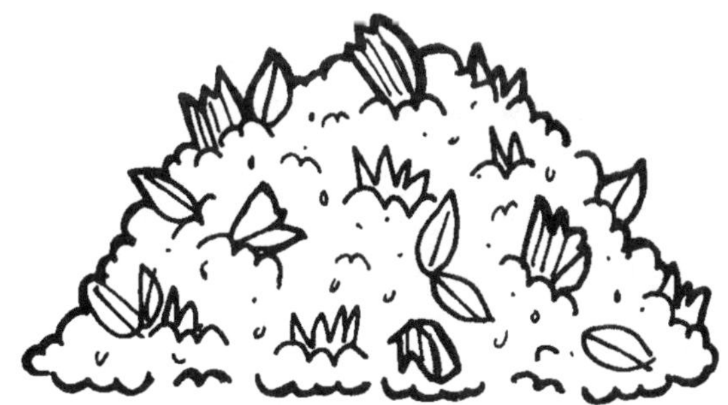

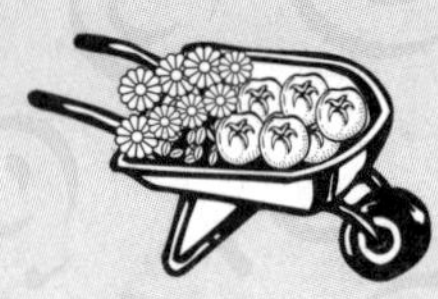

Companion Planting

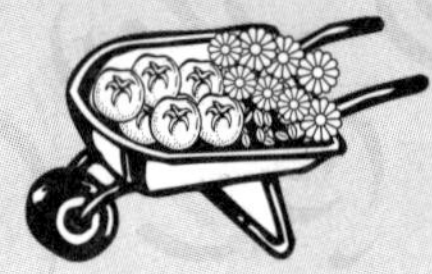

Some plants seem to grow better and resist pests and disease when they are planted near certain neighbor plants. Success may vary with geographic location, soil, and climate. Read about organic gardening to learn more about this concept. Here are some vegetables and their companion plants you may wish to consider as you make choices about what you will plant in your garden.

Vegetables	Companions
Asparagus	Basil, parsley, tomatoes
Beans	Corn, cucumbers, potatoes
Tomatoes	Blue salvia, marigolds
Cabbage, broccoli, cauliflower	Mint, rosemary
Carrots	Peas, leaf lettuce, onions, sage, tomatoes
Corn	Beans, pumpkins, squash, cucumbers
Eggplant	Beans
Lettuce	Carrots, radishes, onions
Parsley	Nasturtiums
Onions, garlic	Beets, lettuce, tomatoes
Peas	Carrots, herbs, radishes, turnips
Peppers	Onions
Potatoes	Cabbage, corn, marigolds
Squash	Corn, nasturtiums
Cucumbers (not near potatoes)	Sunflowers

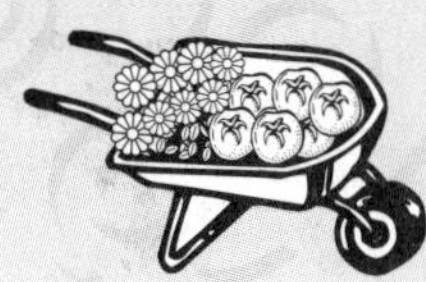

Plants from Cuttings

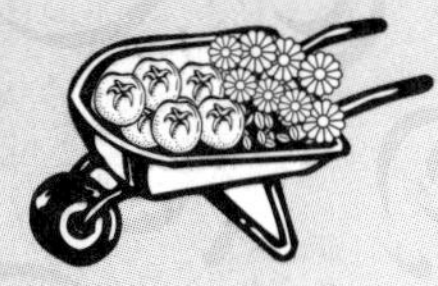

Materials

- plants from which you want to make cuttings (hydrangea, pussy willow, azalea, Christmas cactus, begonia, forsythia, rose of Sharon)
- 4"-diameter clay pots or clean cans
- rooting hormone
- trowel
- sharp knife
- potting soil and sand
- plastic bag

Let's Do It !

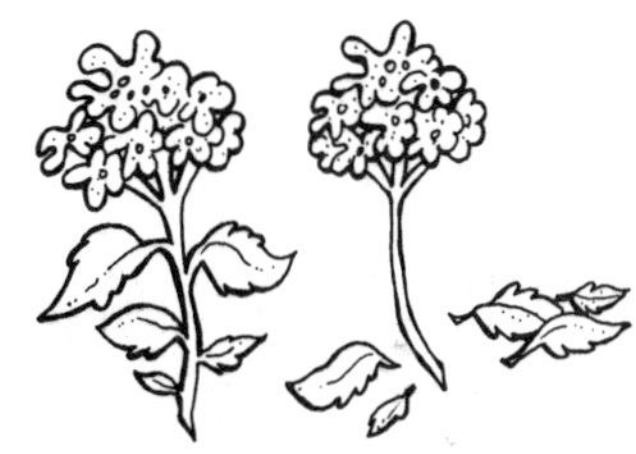

1. Use a clean, sharp knife to cut the plant stems into cuttings 4"–12" long.
2. Remove the lower leaves from the cutting so the part that is submerged in the soil will be free of leaves.
3. Fill 4"-diameter clay pots or clean cans with drain holes punched in the bottom with a mixture of soil and sand. Make a hole in the soil deep enough for the cutting.

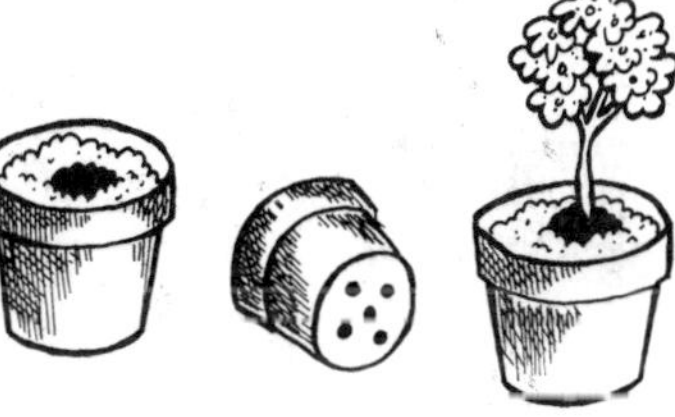

4. Dip the end of the cutting in rooting hormone and shake off the excess. Put the cutting into the hole and firm the soil around it.
5. Water the cutting and keep it damp until its roots develop. You may want to place a plastic bag over the cutting and pot to help retain moisture.

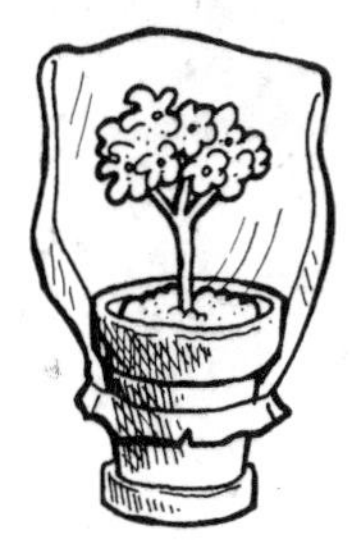

6. When the new plant is well established, transplant it to the yard or to a larger pot filled with potting soil.

Tidbits

✧ Take cuttings in the spring or early summer when there is new growth on plants, but they have not become woody.

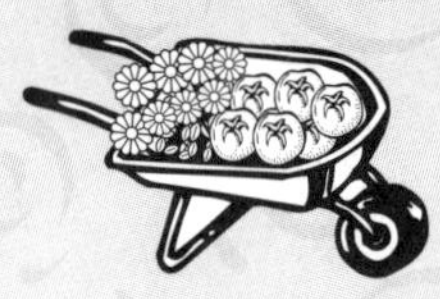

Rooting Plants in Water

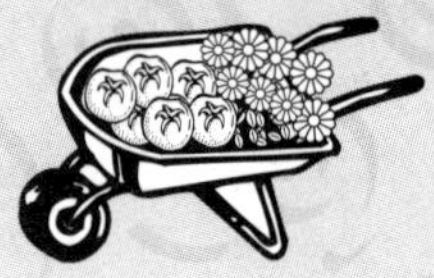

Materials

- cuttings (coleus, Christmas cactus, ivy, impatiens)
- wide-mouthed jars
- water

Let's Do It !

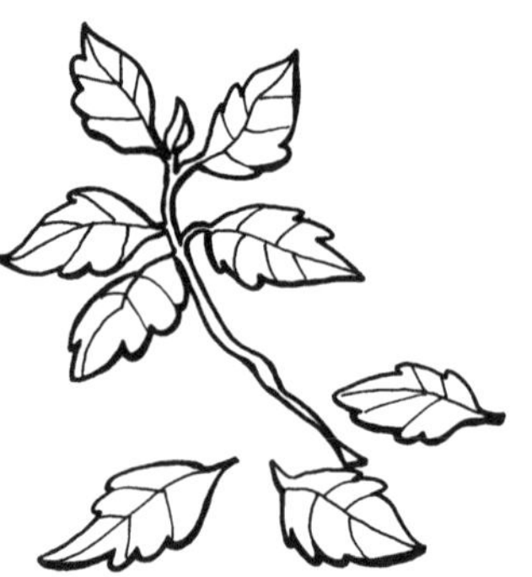

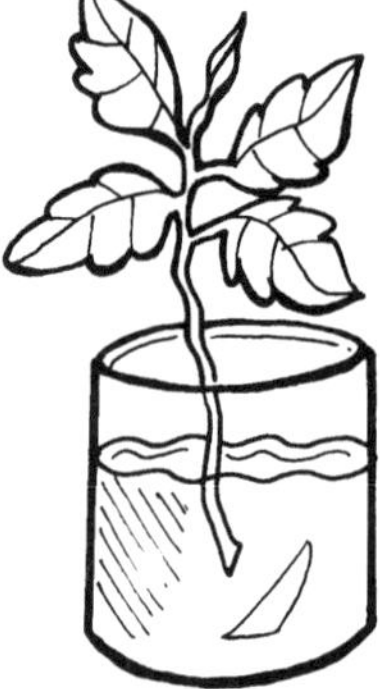

1. Remove lower leaves from cuttings so no leaves will be in the water.
2. Fill the jars with water. Place the cuttings in the jars and put them where they will receive filtered light.
3. Watch the roots sprout. Refill the jars with water as needed.
4. When the plants are rooted, transplant them into the ground or pots.

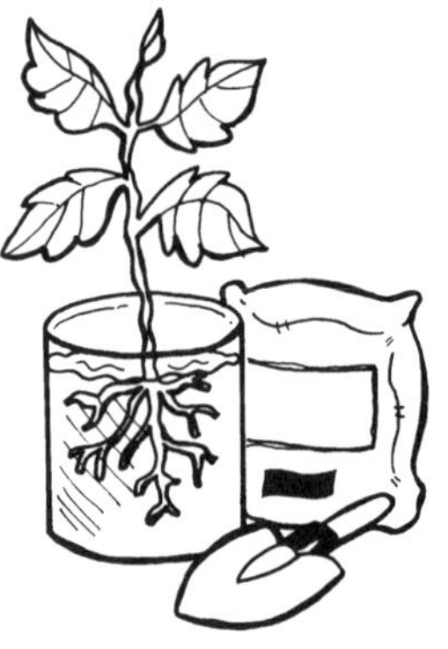

Learn More

Hutchins, Pat. *Titch.* New York: Macmillan/McGraw-Hill School Publishing Co., 1971.

Markmann, Erika. *Grow It! An Indoor/Outdoor Gardening Guide for Children.* New York: Random House, 1991.

Container Gardening. 4th Ed. Menlo Park, CA: Sunset Publishing Corporation, 1984.

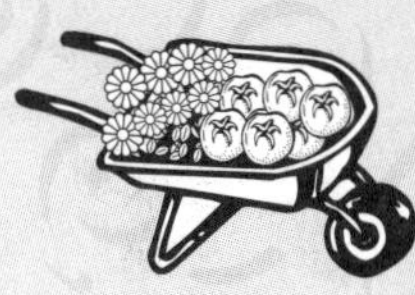

Keep a Gardening Journal

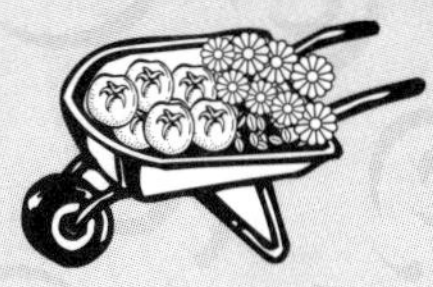

Materials

- notebook
- camera
- seed packets
- film
- plant labels

Let's Do It !

1. Keep a written record of the seeds and sets you plant. Include the names of the varieties planted, the dates you planted them, and the approximate yield or size of your harvest.
2. Attach seed packets and labels to your pages for future reference.
3. Draw pictures or take photographs of your garden during its various stages.
4. List the kinds of fertilizer and soil enrichments used, such as peat, compost, manure, etc.
5. Note your failures and specific problems.
6. Identify harmful insects, pests, or plant diseases and how you treated them.
7. Identify helpful insects and animals that your garden attracted.

More Ideas

- Use your journal to plan your next garden by evaluating your experiences.

  What was successful?

  Which plants did you enjoy the most? Why?

  What will you do in your next garden?

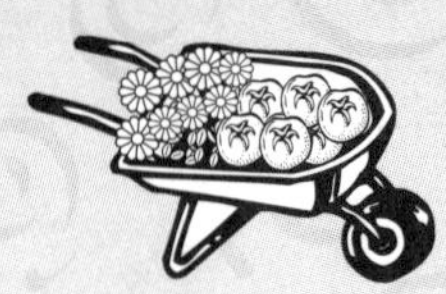

Gardening with Groups of Children

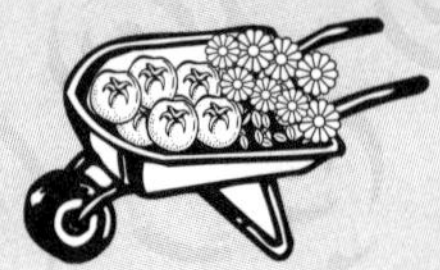

Use the KWL (know/want-to-know/learned) method to teach about plants. Prepare three pieces of poster board by writing on each "What We Know About Plants," "What We Want to Know About Plants," and "What We Learned About Plants."

- When you introduce the gardening idea, have children share what they already know about plants. (Some of it may be incorrect information.) Record it on the "K" (know) chart.
- On the "W" (want to know) chart, list things children say they want to find out and include things you want them to find out.
- After you begin gardening, keep a record of what children discover on the "L" (learned) chart.
- After harvesting or at the end of your gardening project, review and discuss the charts with the children. Were there misconceptions that were corrected? Did they find the answers they wanted?
- Follow up by having each child make an individual book about the gardening experience, or create a class big book, with the children dictating the text and drawing the pictures. Create a display of photos or children's drawings showing the gardening project through its different stages.

K	W	L
What We Know About Plants	**What We Want to Know About Plants**	**What We Learned About Plants**
plants need sun and water to grow	how seeds grow into plants	seeds sprout roots and grow stems and flowers

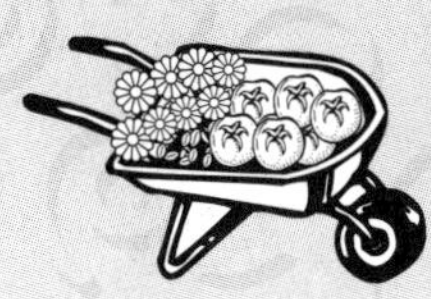

Gardening with Groups of Children

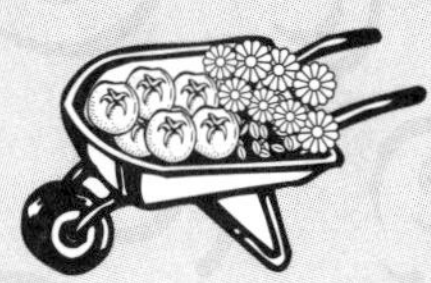

1. Begin gardening at a level you can manage with your group of children, and involve them in the planning process.

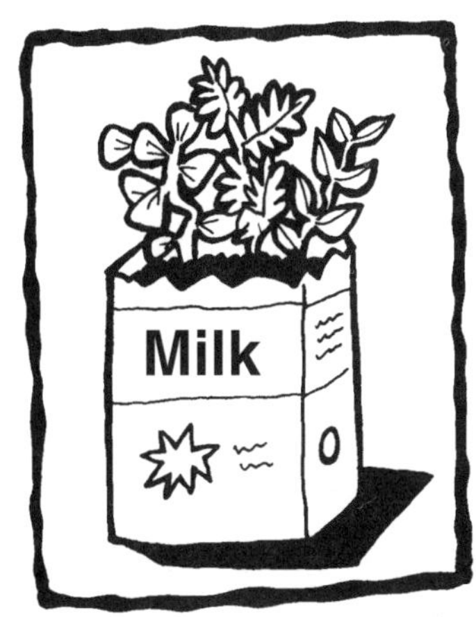

2. If you don't have room for outdoor gardening, use container gardening in the classroom. Even growing seeds in milk cartons is exciting for children.
3. Read related storybooks, and look through seed catalogs and gardening magazines for ideas.
4. Ask parents or resource people in the community to help build raised, easy-to-maintain gardens 3' x 8'.
5. Adjust for children's attention spans. Very young children may only enjoy 15–20 minutes of gardening, while older children may want to work longer.

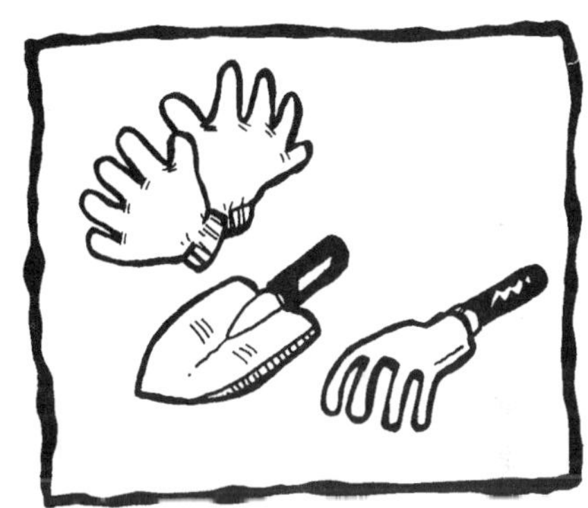

6. Use child-sized tools and gloves, if possible. Assemble all equipment and supplies ahead of time.
7. Demonstrate how to use tools correctly and safely, and supervise for safety. Review and observe the safety rules on page 27.
8. Discuss with children what needs to be done before starting the gardening activity, and plan who will do what jobs, including cleaning up. If they must take turns actually gardening, have children work on gardening journals or draw pictures of their project while they wait their turn.

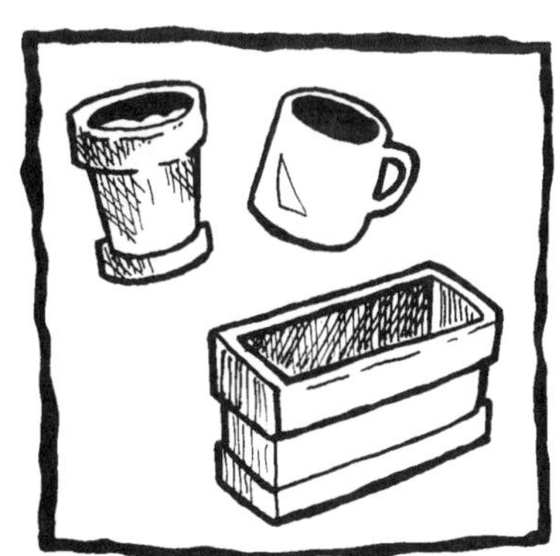

9. Help children develop a sense of ownership and pride in accomplishment by giving each child a plant or plants for which he or she is to be responsible.
10. Incorporate the recycling of different materials and containers for gardening uses.

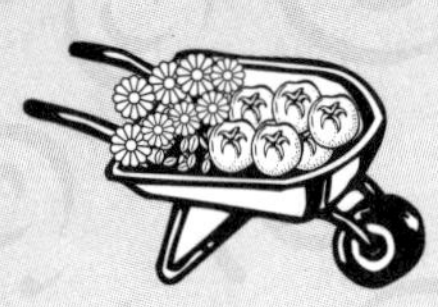

Gardening with Groups of Children

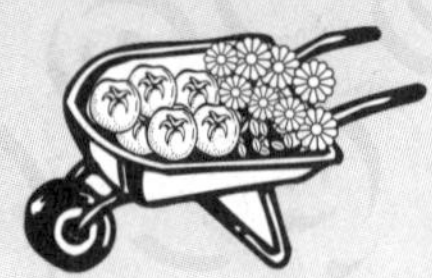

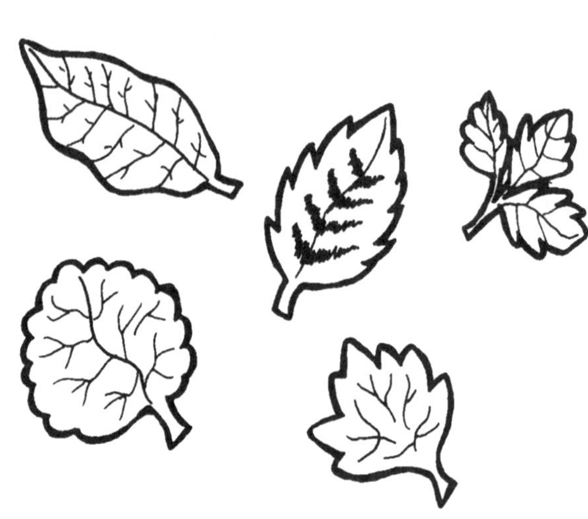

11. Involve children in gathering appropriate materials, such as leaves and grass clippings to use as mulch around plants. Create a compost pile with grass clippings, leaves, and dead plants from the garden.
12. Teach children how to recognize the leaves of flowers and vegetables and to distinguish them from weeds and poisonous plants (page 28).
13. Encourage working with a buddy or in small teams to promote cooperative effort and taking turns.
14. Visit the garden several times a week to weed, water, look for insect pests, harvest, or to simply enjoy seeing what progress the plants have made.
15. Use computers to enhance children's learning experiences, and plan field trips to garden centers or nearby farms.
16. Relate gardening to real life. This book provides many such related activities for children.
17. Use what you grow—and have fun following the recipes, party suggestions, and tips on cooking what you grow.

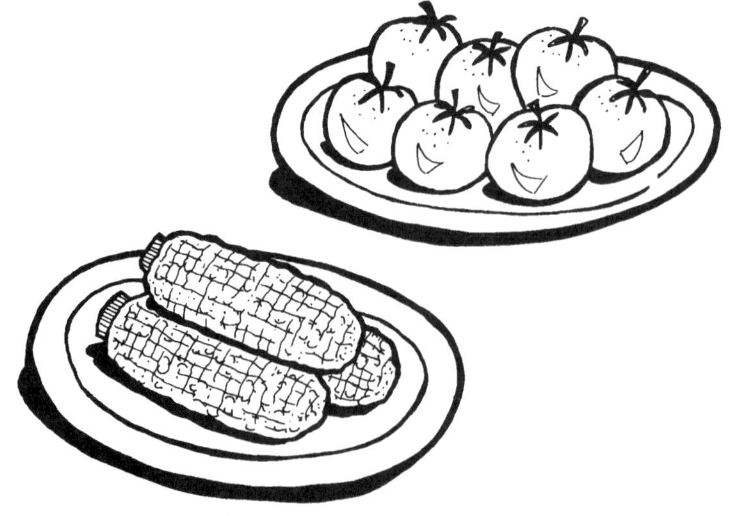

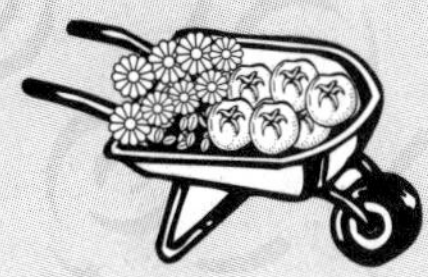

Think About Safety

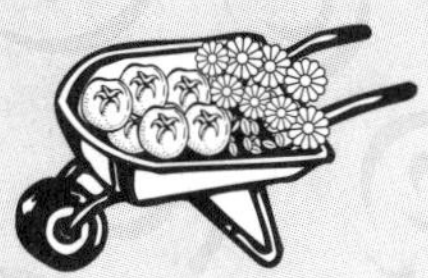

Even though gardening is fun, it also presents some safety hazards you must consider every time you or children work in the garden.

1. Be very careful with chemicals—fertilizer, insecticides, etc.
   - Do not let children apply chemicals or touch them after they have been applied.
   - Follow the container instructions and safety precautions exactly.
   - Cover the skin as much as possible with clothing, safety goggles, and gloves.
   - Do not apply chemicals on a windy day.
   - Be sure you have the appropriate chemical for your plants.
   - Store all chemicals out of the reach of children.
2. Wear thick-soled, closed-toe shoes.
3. Wear gloves to prevent scratches, cuts, blisters, and contact with poisonous plants. Wash gloves frequently. Buy child-sized gloves for children.
4. Walk—don't run or play—in the garden area to prevent damaging plants or hurting yourself or others.
5. Watch where you walk so you don't trample plants.
6. Show children how to use all tools correctly.
7. Point the prongs and blades of tools toward the ground, even when not in use.
8. When using long-handled tools, check behind you to make sure nobody will get hit.
9. Don't throw rocks or dirt.
10. On sunny days, wear sunscreen and a hat.
11. Work in the cooler parts of the day—before ten in the morning and after three in the afternoon.
12. Wear insect repellent, and watch around blooming plants for stinging insects such as bees and wasps.

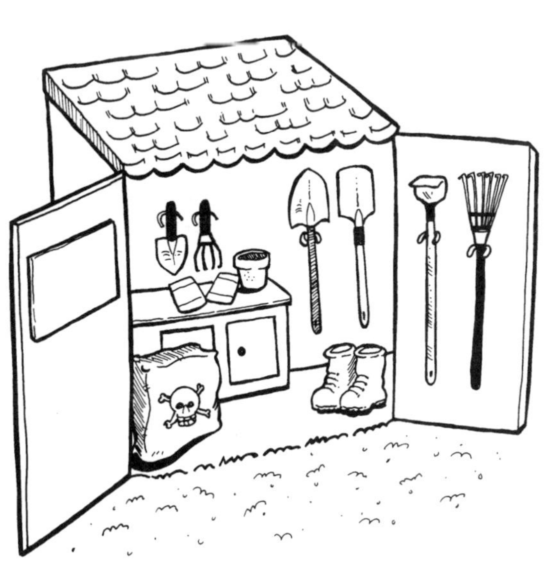

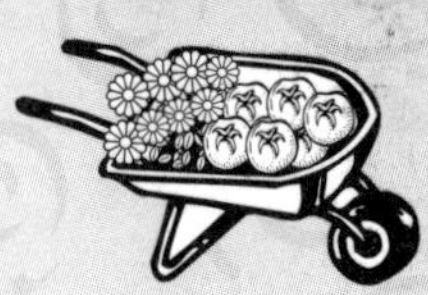

Recognize Some Poisonous Plants

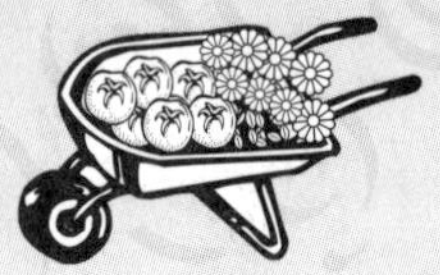

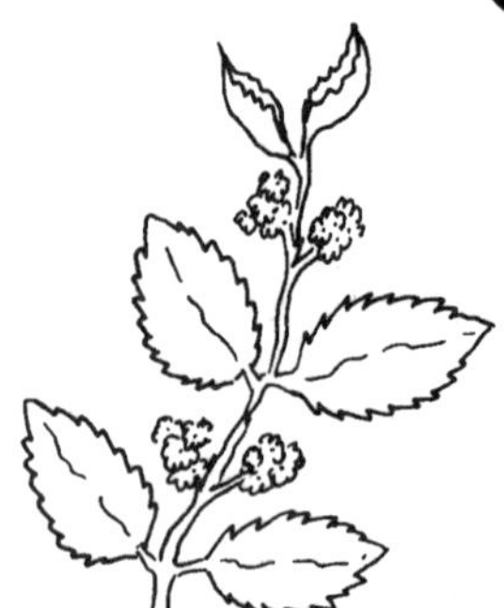

Nettles

Toothed leaves opposite each other

Greenish yellow flowers in clusters

Bristles on stems and leaves

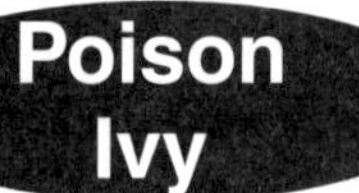

Poison Ivy

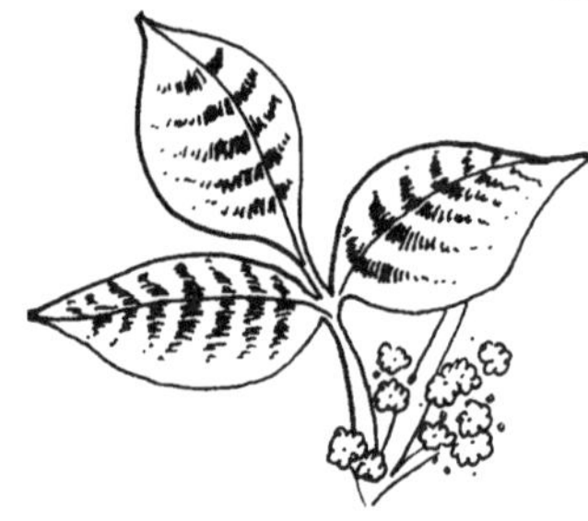

Shrubs or vines with three leaves

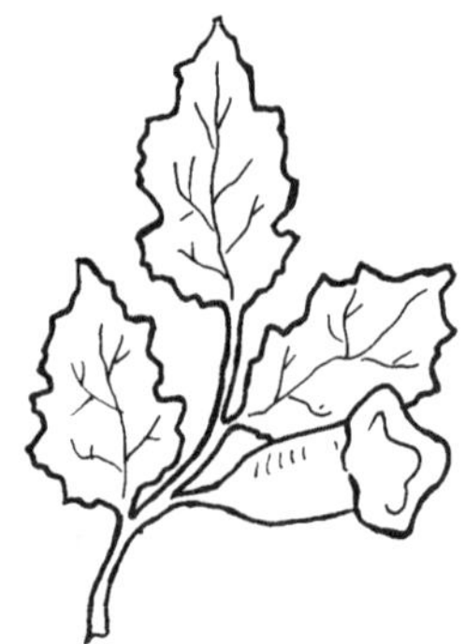

Jimson Weed

Trumpet-shaped white or lavender flower

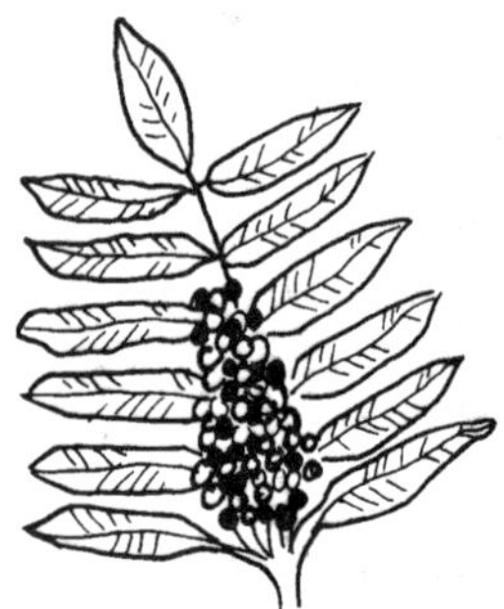

Poisonous Sumac

Shrub with white berries in clusters

Seven to thirteen leaflets

Poison Oak

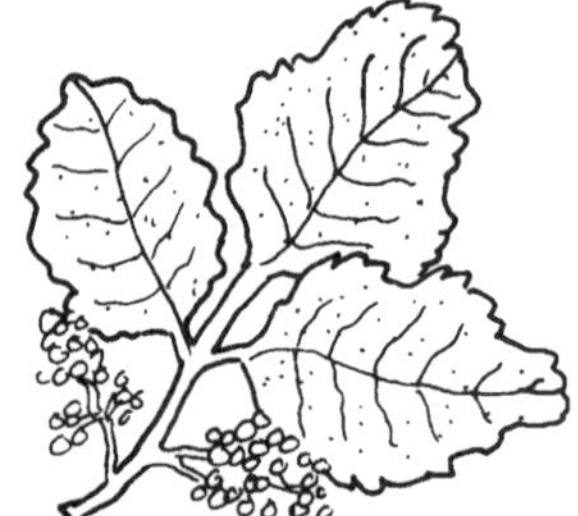

White berries

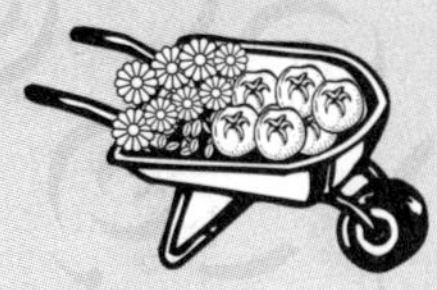

Cooking What You Grow

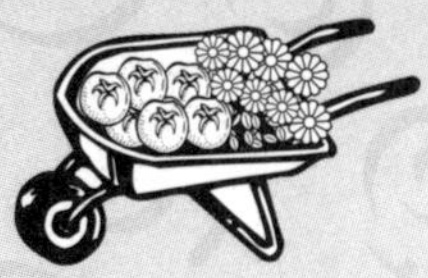

1. Wash your hands before you begin.
2. Read through the recipe and gather together all the items you will need before you start.
3. Use a cutting board when doing cutting, slicing, and chopping.
4. Provide plastic knives with serrated edges for children to use for cutting.
5. Adults should supervise and demonstrate the use of stoves, mixers, blenders, food processors, and sharp knives.
6. Follow recipes step-by-step exactly. Avoid substituting ingredients, which can change the look and taste of the finished food.
7. Use dry-measure utensils for measuring dry ingredients. Level the measures with a spatula.
8. Use liquid-measure utensils for measuring liquids. Check the amount on the specified line.
9. Use hot pads to protect your hands when handling hot pots or pans.
10. Lift lids away from your face so steam will not go into your face.
11. Preheat the oven to the required temperature, if specified in a recipe.
12. Clean up as you cook.

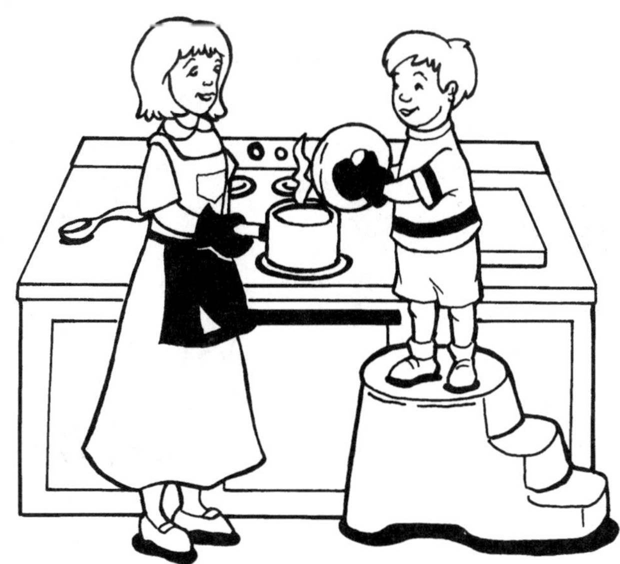

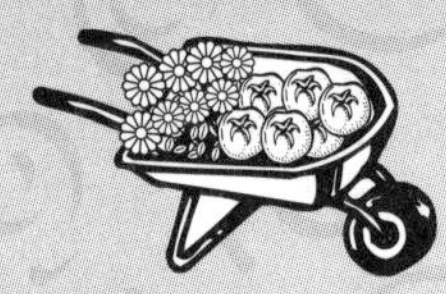

Math in the Kitchen

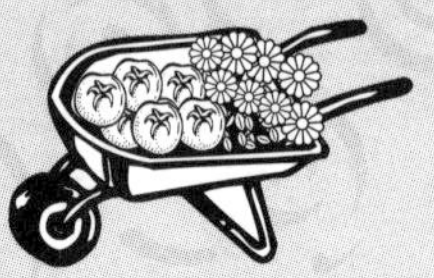

Use the information below as a reference guide.

Equivalent Measures

3 teaspoons = 1 tablespoon
4 tablespoons = 1/4 cup
5 1/3 tablespoons = 1/3 cup
8 tablespoons = 1/2 cup
12 tablespoons = 3/4 cup
16 tablespoons = 1 cup or 1/2 pint or 8 ounces
2 cups = 1 pint or 16 ounces
4 cups = 1 quart, or roughly, 1 liter

4 quarts = 1 gallon
1 fluid ounce = 2 tablespoons
1/2 stick butter or margarine = 1/4 cup
1 stick butter or margarine = 1/2 cup or 1/4 pound
2 sticks butter or margarine = 1 cup or 1/2 pound
4 sticks butter or margarine = 2 cups or 1 pound

Metric Conversions

United States Customary measurement is used throughout this book. For metric conversions, use the information below to find equivalent measurements.

1 teaspoon = 5 milliliters
1 tablespoon = 15 milliliters
1/4 cup = 60 milliliters

1/3 cup = 80 milliliters
1/2 cup = 125 milliliters
3/4 cup = 185 milliliters

1 cup = 250 milliliters

Oven Temperatures

The oven temperature for all recipes in this book is measured in Fahrenheit degrees. To convert Fahrenheit degrees to Celsius, subtract 32 degrees and multiply by 5/9. To convert Celsius degrees to Fahrenheit, multiply by 9/5 and add 32 degrees—or use the handy chart below!

Fahrenheit	Celsius
250°–275°	125°–135°
300°–325°	150°–165°
350°–375°	175°–190°
400°–425°	205°–220°
450°–475°	230°–245°

Linear Measures

Refer to the following measurements for any linear metric conversion information you may need in this book.

1" = 2.54 cm
2" = 5 cm
2 1/2" = 6.4 cm

3" = 8 cm
5" = 25 cm
8" = 20 cm

8 1/2" = 22 cm
9" = 23 cm
11" = 28 cm

12" = 30 cm
14" = 36 cm
17" = 43 cm

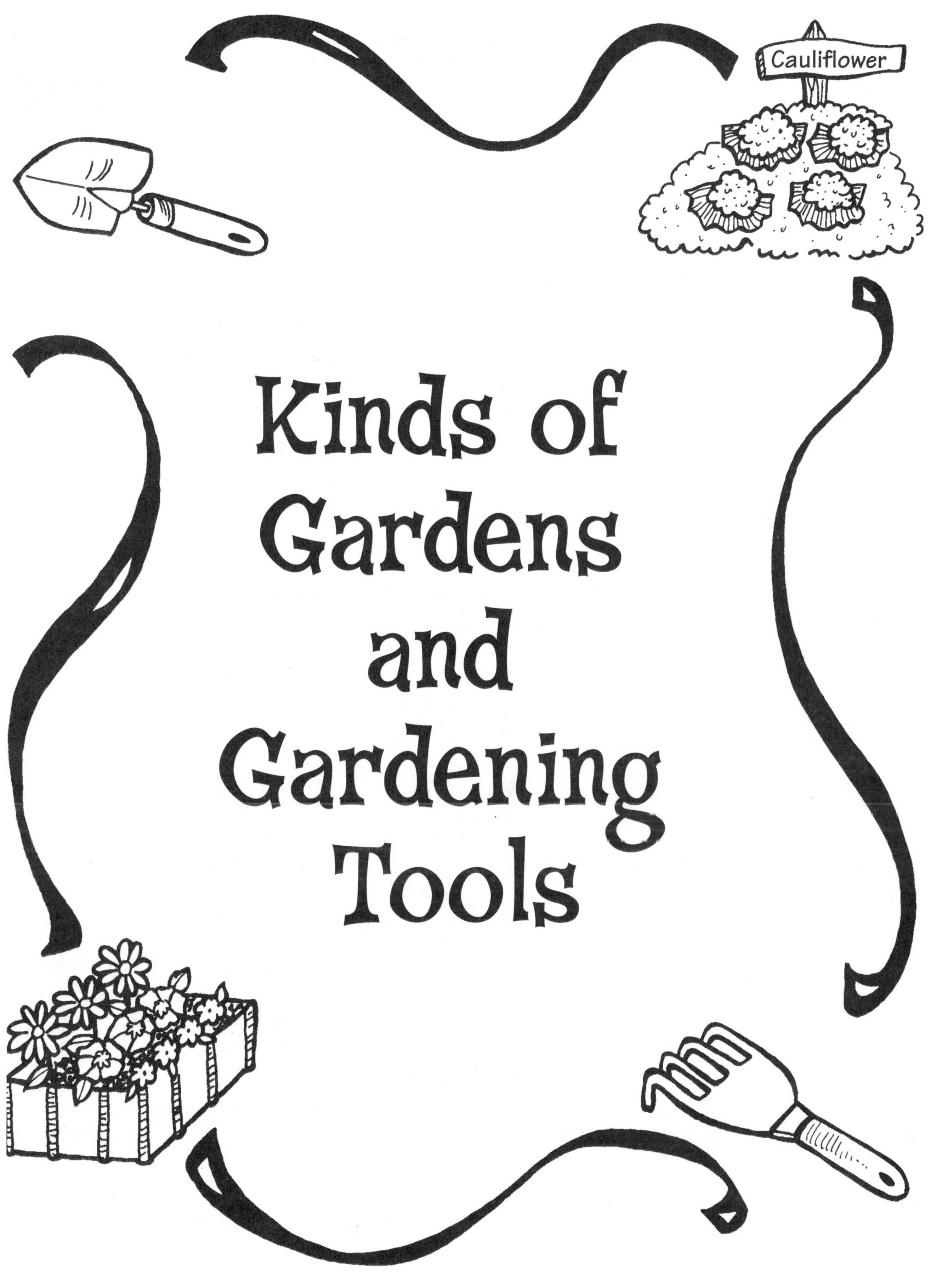

Kinds of Gardens and Gardening Tools

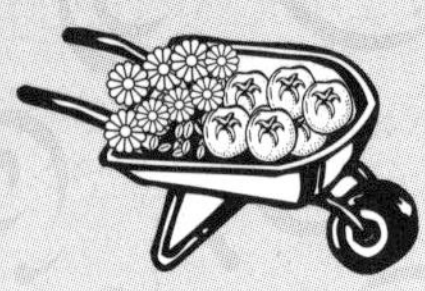

Conventional Gardens

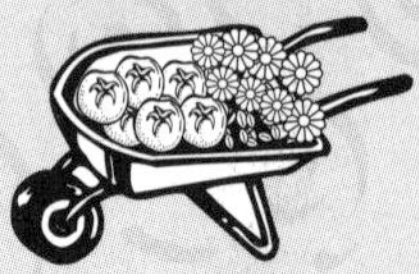

Conventional Gardens

- are as large or as small as your available space and gardening time.
- can be tilled with a plow, garden tiller, or shovel and garden rake.
- accommodate spreading plants, such as watermelons, squash, and peanuts.
- accommodate plants grown in raised rows or mounds.

Tips

- Mulch between rows to preserve moisture and reduce weed growth.
- Work in compost or other organic fertilizers and soil enhancements.
- Weed, water, and check for pests and disease at least once a week.

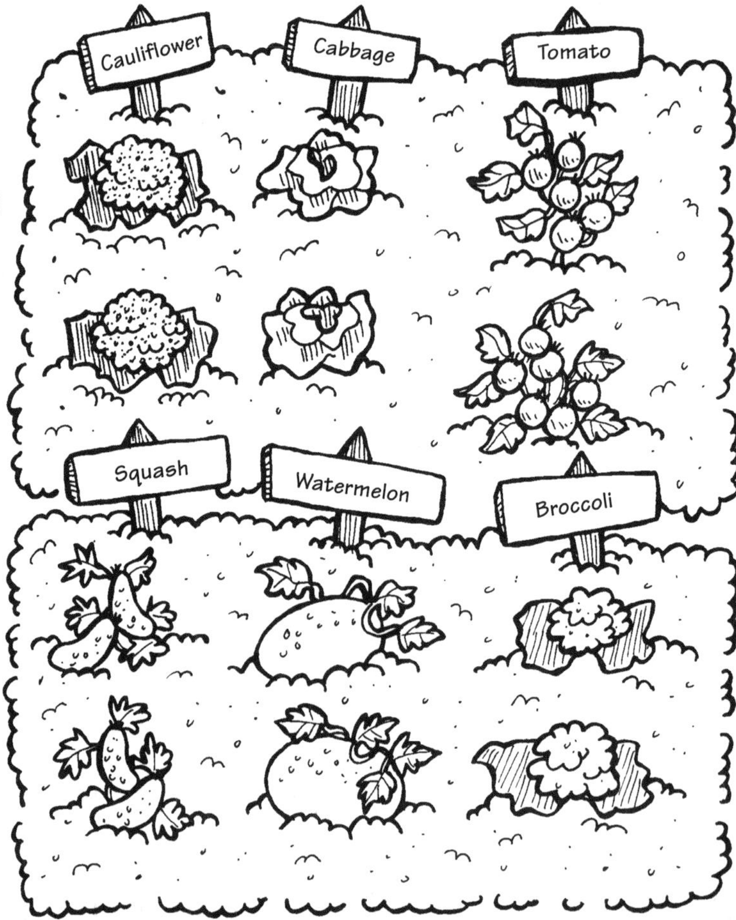

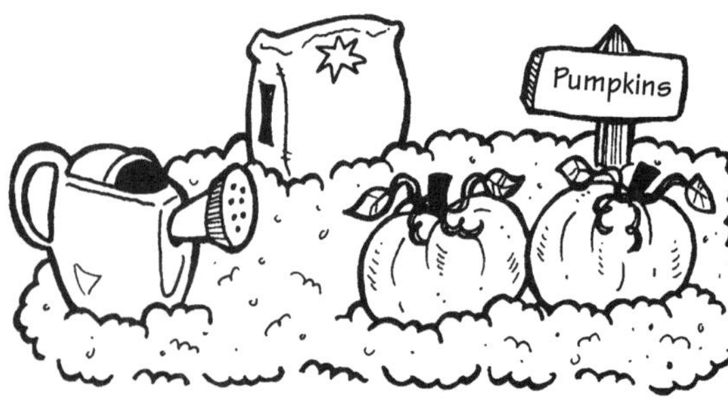

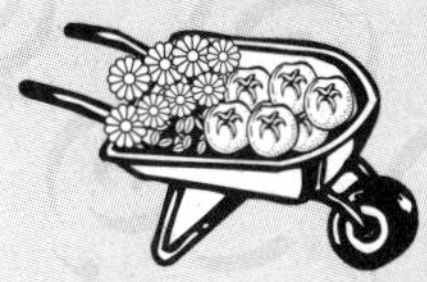

Container Gardens

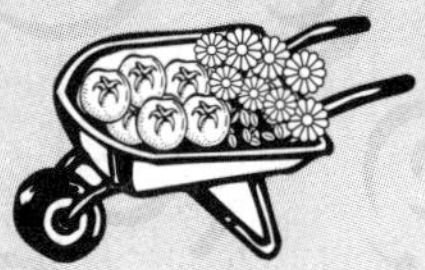

Container Gardens

- can be planted in flower pots, barrels, urns, bottles, bowls, or other containers.
- can be utilized indoors or outdoors and placed in sunny or shady areas.
- provide for easy access, easy maintenance, and easy harvesting.
- need watering more often than conventional gardens.

Tips

- Protect the surface under potted plants and prevent damage by putting pots on trivets or on top of upside-down pots.
- Choose healthy potted plants with no evidence of disease, insects, or yellowing.
- Check the bottom of the pot for protruding roots. Transplant root-bound plants into a larger container.
- Choose flowering plants that are fully shaped and have unopened buds.
- Don't over water, and provide adequate drainage under the container.

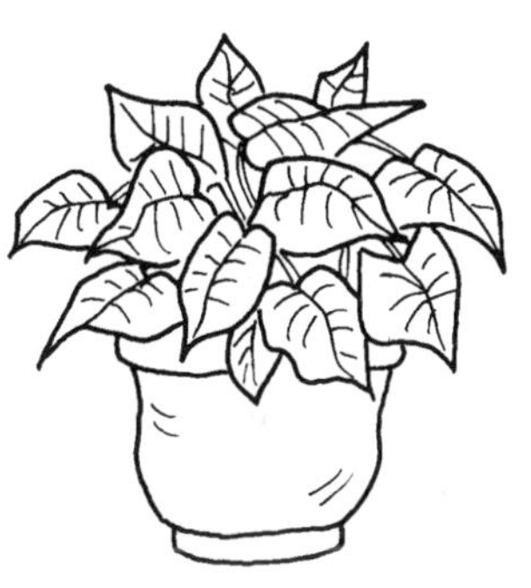

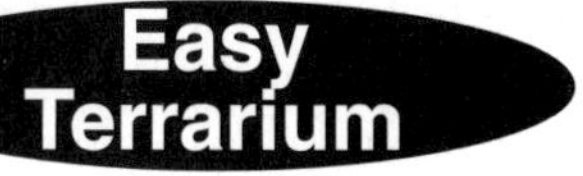

Easy Terrarium

Cut off the top third of two clear, plastic beverage bottles. Put potting soil in the bottom of one, and plant small tropical plants in the soil. Water the plants, being careful not to over water, and put the other bottle on top to form a covered terrarium.

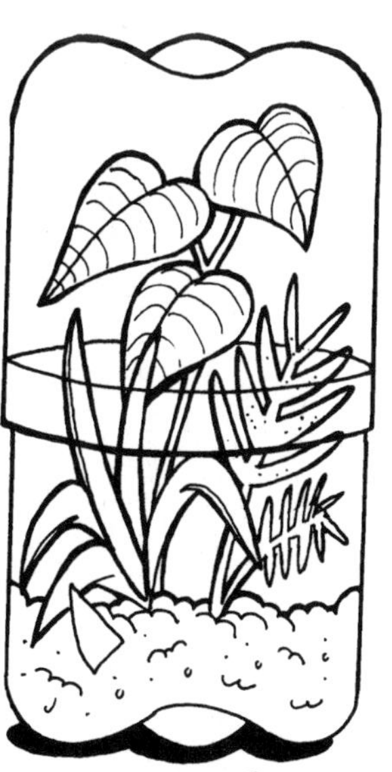

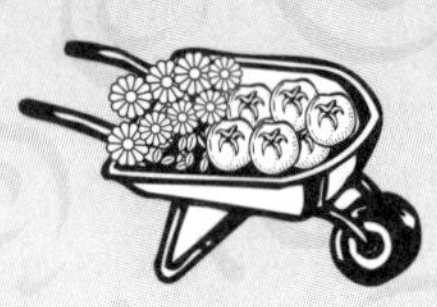

Raised Gardens and Square-Foot Gardens

Raised Gardens

- can be simply soil formed into raised areas on the ground.
- can be formed by framing and filled with soil, compost, and peat.
- allow for easy access, easy maintenance, and easy harvesting, especially if they are 3' wide or less.

Square-foot Gardens

- are formed by framing and filled with soil, compost, and peat.
- provide a delightful way to do intensive gardening with a large variety of plants.
- free a spot for reworking and replanting after one plant has been harvested.

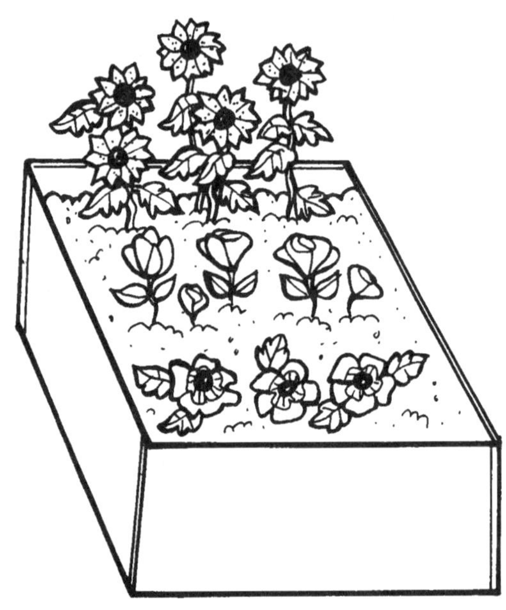

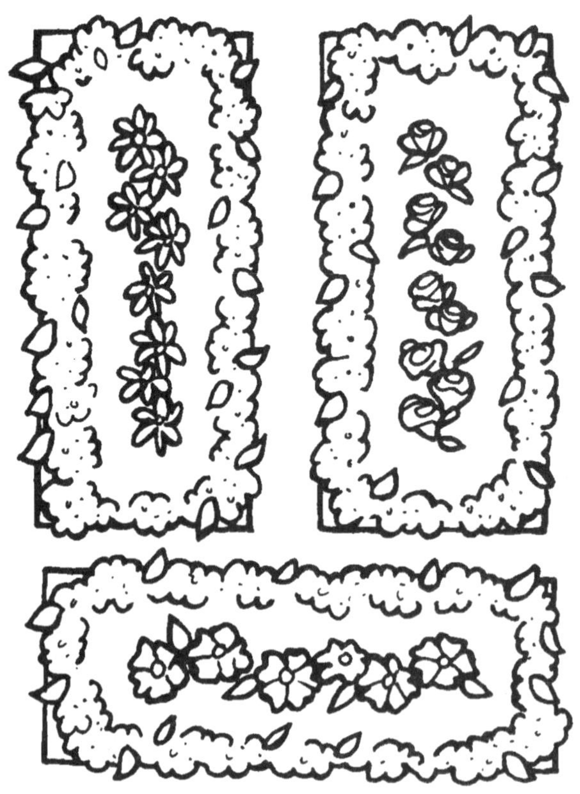

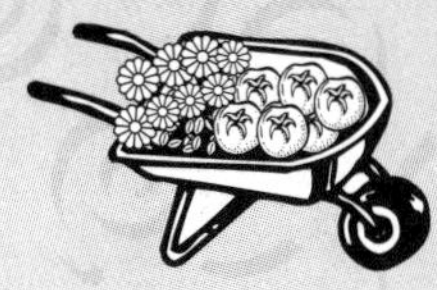

Hydroponic Gardens

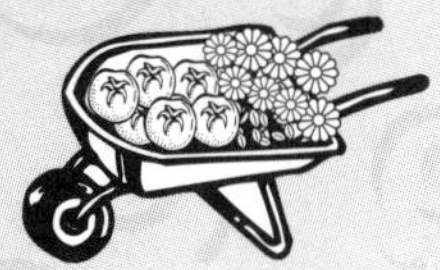

Hydroponics is the technique of gardening without soil. Hydroponics is a combination of two Greek words: "Hydro" which means water, and "ponics" which means working—or working with water. Many countries and regions in the world, including the Middle East, Holland, Russia, Israel, and the United States, grow flowers and vegetables using this technique. Instead of soil, plants are grown in other material such as gravel, sand, sawdust, scoria, perlite, vermiculite, rock wool, and water. The plants are fed with special nutrients or natural minerals dissolved in water. Hydroponic farms which grow large amounts of food are typically found in areas where the soil is poor and the climate is hot and dry, as in deserts.

Hydroponics is not new, but the process is not well known to most people. The floating gardens of China and of the Aztecs of Mexico and the famous hanging gardens of Babylon dating back, thousands of years are examples of hydroponic methods. Modern research shows that compared with soil gardening, hydroponic methods of gardening can produce more nutritious food with less water, in less space.

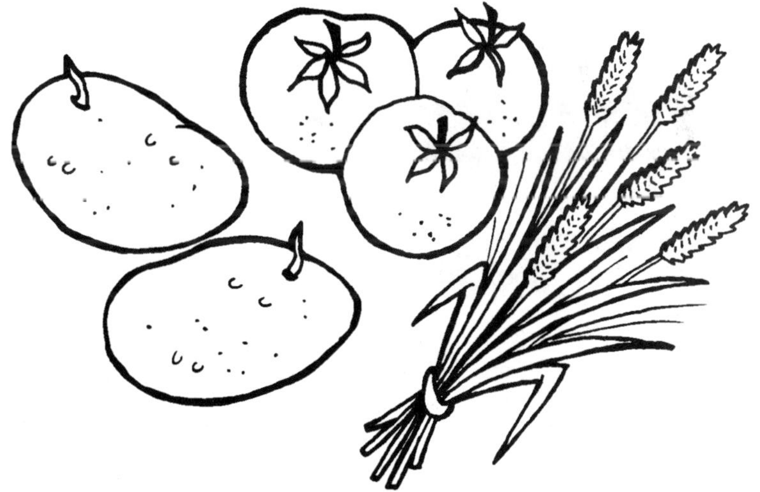

Imagine that you are an astronaut traveling to Mars or some other distant planet. It will take several years to get to your destination in your spacecraft. Since it would not be possible to take all the food you need to survive, you will need a way to grow food on your journey. Hydroponics is the answer to this problem. Scientists at NASA (National Aeronautics Space Administration) are doing experiments to produce food (e.g., wheat, potatoes, lettuce, tomatoes, soybeans) hydroponically for long space missions. The Mir Space Station now circling the earth has a hydroponic system. Hydroponics is truly "space-age" gardening that will help make it possible to explore our universe.

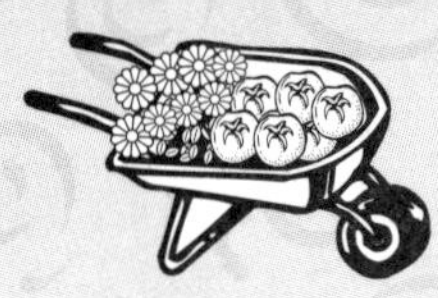

Hydroponic Gardens

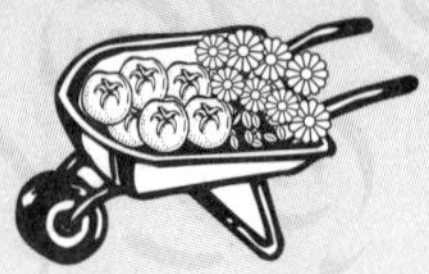

Hydroponic Glossary

Here are some terms that will help you better understand hydroponics.

hydroponics: the technique of growing plants using a non-soil material to which is added a nutrient solution

hydroponic nutrient: the natural mineral elements needed by a plant for its normal growth and development

hydroponic system: the method of delivering nutrient to the plant

Jiffy® Pellet: a small cylindrical disk containing peat moss in a nylon mesh used for starting seeds

germinate: to start developing or growing into a plant from seed

perlite: a soft, white, puffy non-soil material made from volcanic glass

rock wool: a very light fibrous (cotton-candy-like) non-soil material made by heating a mixture of basalt rock, limestone, and silica

scoria: a non-soil material of hard red granules of volcanic origin; loose cinder-like lava

vermiculite: small, lightweight, shiny golden brown non-soil material made from raw mica

Hydroponic Sources

References

Muckle, Edward. *Basic Hydroponics for the Do-It Yourselfer.* Princeton, British Columbia: Growers Press, Inc., 1994.

Sutherland, Struan K. *Hydroponics for Everyone: A Practical Guide to Gardening in the 21st Century.* Melbourne, Australia: Hyland House, 1995.

World Wide Web

http://www.growingedge.com/
http://www.genhydro.com/

Suppliers

Eco Enterprises, Shoreline, WA. Tel: (800) 426-6937
Greentrees Hydroponics, Vista, CA. Tel: (800) 772-1997

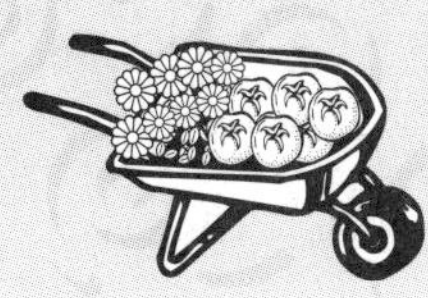

Hydroponic Gardens

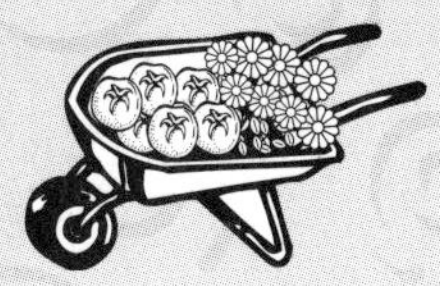

Hydroponically Grown Lettuce

Materials

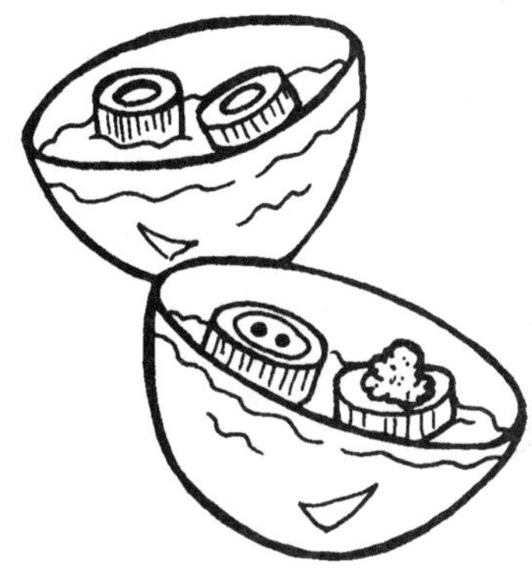

- lettuce seed (e.g., looseleaf, butter, Romaine)
- small plastic or glass dish
- Jiffy® (peat) pellets
- small bag of perlite
- 2 two-liter soda bottles
- 8-oz. or 1-pint bottle of hydroponic liquid nutrient*
- 2-inch square piece of nylon stocking
- rubber band
- scissors

Let's Do It !

Step 1: Place two Jiffy® pellets into a small plastic or glass dish and soak in water for about 10 minutes until the pellets expand to about 1 inch in height.

Step 2: Place two lettuce seeds into the depression in the top of each pellet. Cover the seeds with some of the moist peat.

Step 3: Place the dish with the pellets on a window sill with indirect light.

Step 4: Put a little water in the bottom of the dish once a day to keep the pellets moist, not too wet or too dry.

Step 5: As soon as the seeds germinate (4 to 10 days), put the dish where the plants have at least 2–3 hours of direct sunlight each day. If both seeds germinate in the pellets, cut down the smallest or weakest plant so that only one plant remains.

Step 6: Continue to water until the plant is about 1" high or until roots grow from the bottom of the peat pellet. Now the plant is ready for transplanting into your hydroponic system.

***Suppliers**

Eco Enterprises, Shoreline, WA. Tel: (800) 426-6937
Greentrees Hydroponics, Vista, CA. Tel: (800) 772-1997

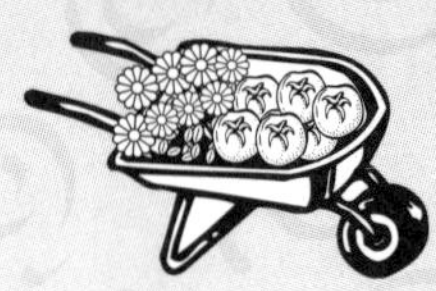

Hydroponic Gardens

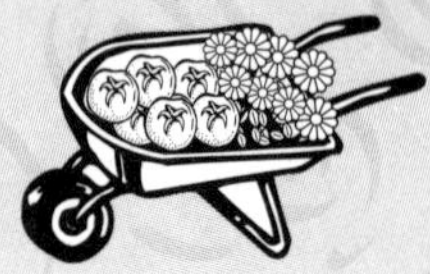

Building Your Hydroponic System

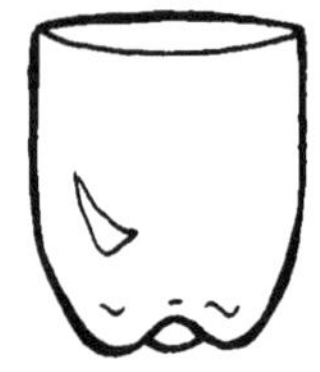

Step 1: Cut each two-liter bottle with scissors as illustrated. You will need one growing container (the top part of the bottle) and two reservoir containers (the bottom part of the bottle). **Caution:** For safety purposes, this step should be done or supervised by an adult.

Step 2: Use the rubber band to attach the piece of nylon stocking over the top of one bottle neck.

Step 3: Turn the bottle top upside down and place it into the bottom portion of one cut-off bottle.

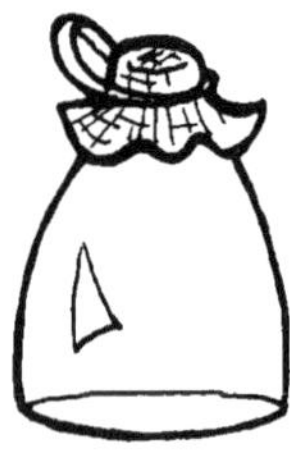

Step 4: Fill the bottle top with perlite to about 2 inches from the top. **Caution:** Avoid breathing perlite dust.

Step 5: Place the peat pellet with the strongest plant into the growing container and fill with more perlite until the pellet is completely covered and the plant extends above the surface.

Maintaining the System

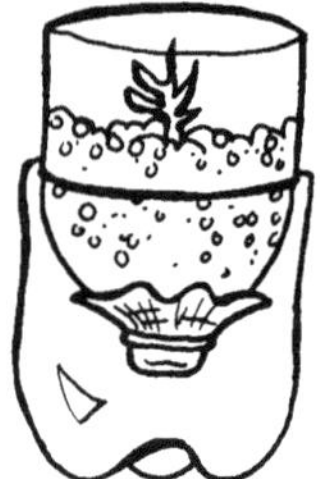

Step 1: Put the plant outdoors if suitable growing conditions exist. (See back of seed package.)

Step 2: Prepare 1/2 gallon of hydroponic nutrient according to instructions. Use only half strength nutrient for the first 2–3 weeks after transplant.

Step 3: Pour about 2 cups of nutrient slowly into the growing container to thoroughly wet the growing material. (Do not pour nutrient directly onto the leaves of the plant.) After the nutrient drains into the reservoir below, remove the growing container and place it into the second reservoir. Cover and store the nutrient in a cool dark place.

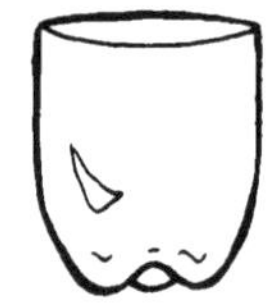

Step 4: Repeat Step 3 two to three times a day with just enough nutrient (about 1/2 cup) to keep the growing material moist.

Step 5: When the plant is about 20 days old, you can begin feeding it with full-strength nutrient.

Harvesting Your Plant

Now you can enjoy eating your hydroponically grown lettuce! You can either pick the lower leaves of the plant as the plant grows or pick the leaves after the plant grows to full maturity in about 40–50 days.

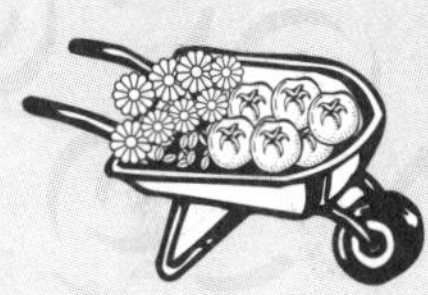

Plant Equipment

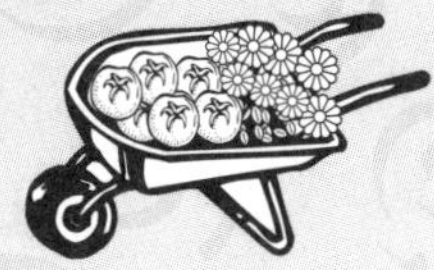

Select gardening tools and equipment that are sturdy and made well. Look for child-sized or short-handled shovels, hoes, and rakes for young children to use. Buckets, watering cans, empty plastic jugs, hammers, string, stakes, wire mesh of different sizes, cans with no sharp edges, and newspaper are also useful to have on hand.

Plant Supports

Vining plants such as pole beans, cucumbers, tomatoes, peas, gourds, and sweet peas need support to keep their produce off the ground and to make harvesting easier. Provide wooden (broom handles) or bamboo stakes for tying up plants with soft materials such as old sheet strips or nylon stockings. Construct trellises out of poles and heavy string or wire fencing. Tie plants loosely so they can grow and not be damaged.

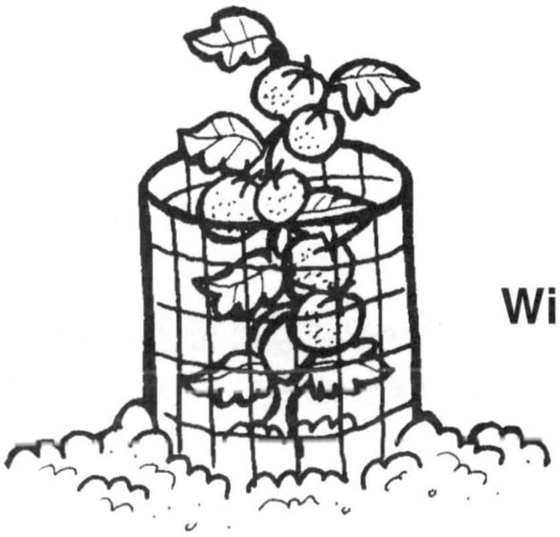

Wire Cage

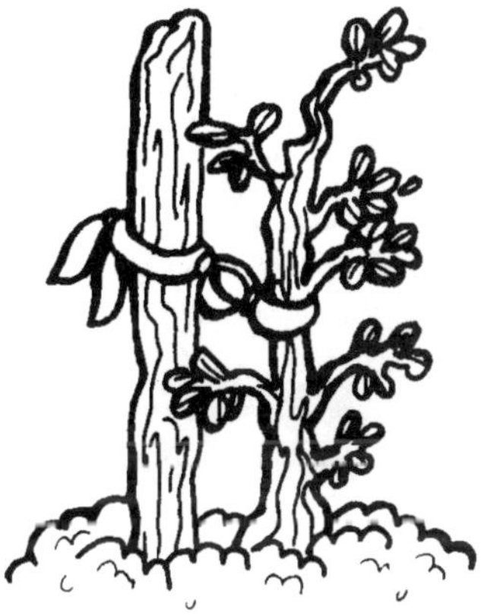

Stakes and Ties

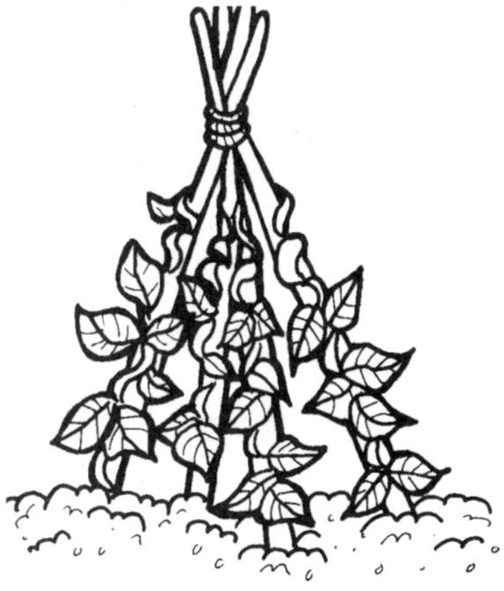

Trellis

Teepee

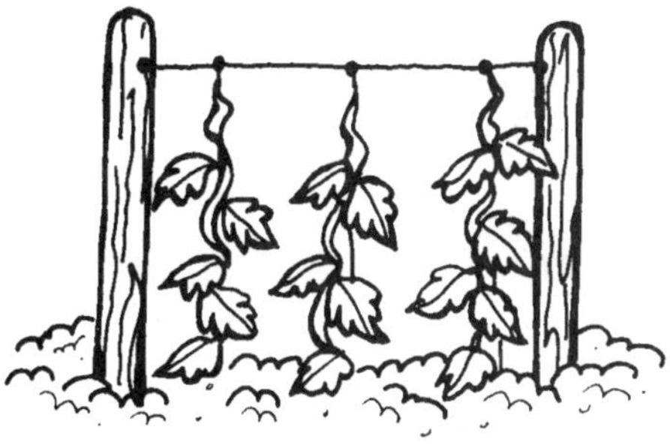

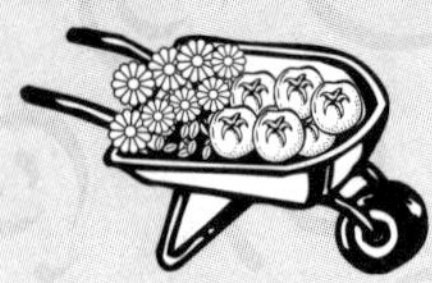

Plant Equipment

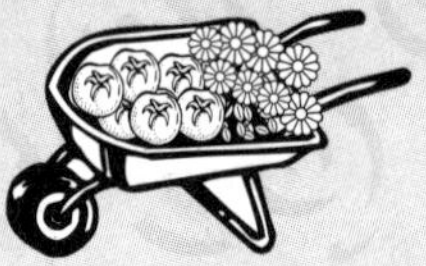

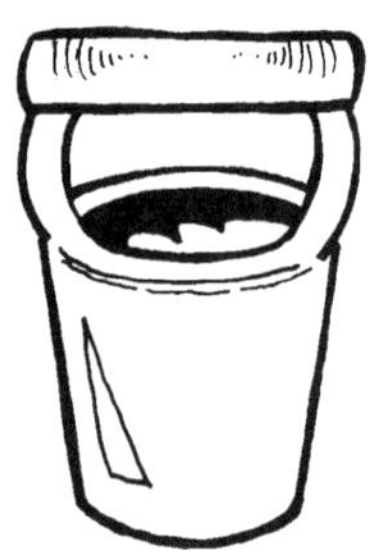

Bulb Planter—cone-shaped hollow tool with a handle; for digging small holes for bulbs or seedlings

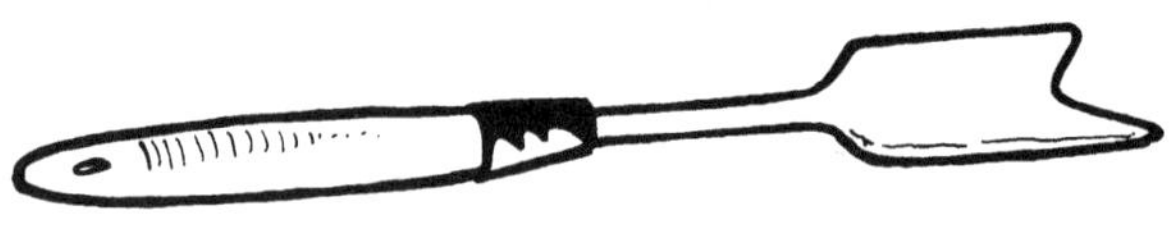

Digger or Weeding Tool—hand-held, forked, and pointed end; for digging weeds

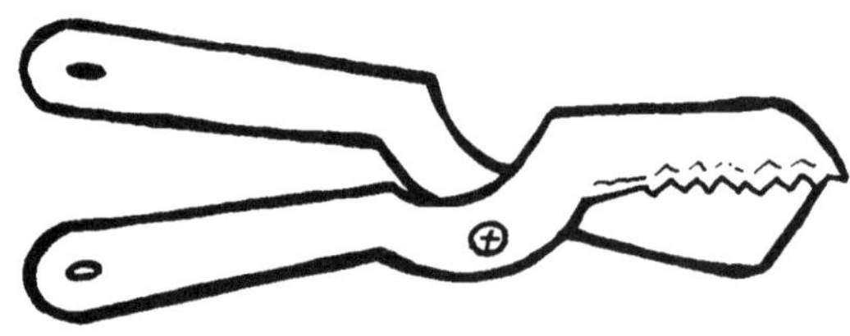

Clippers or By-pass Pruner—for cutting flowers or pruning plants

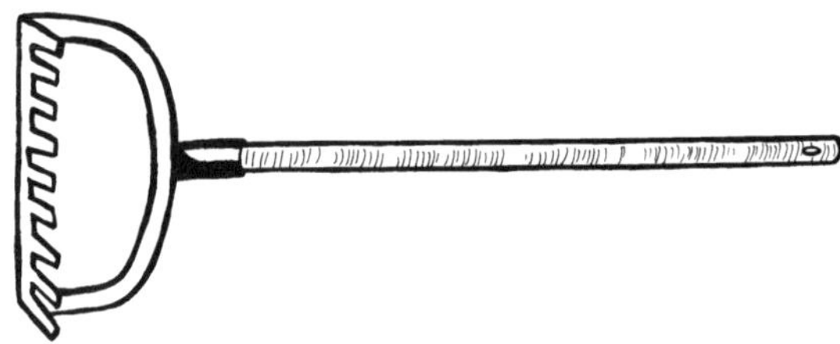

Garden Rake—long handle, stiff tines, for gathering leaves or grass or to loosen or smooth dirt

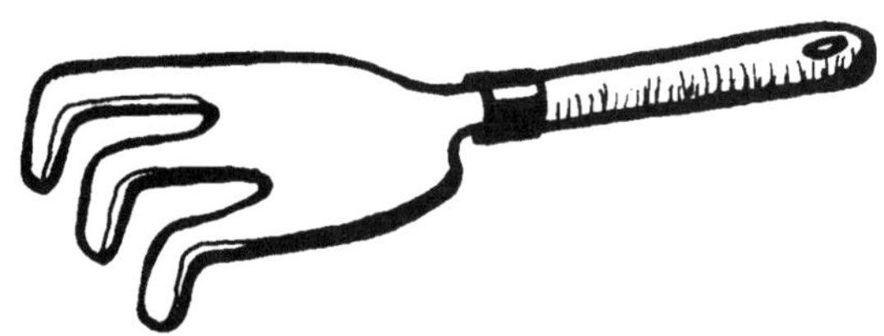

Cultivator—metal claw; for loosening the soil or removing weeds around plants

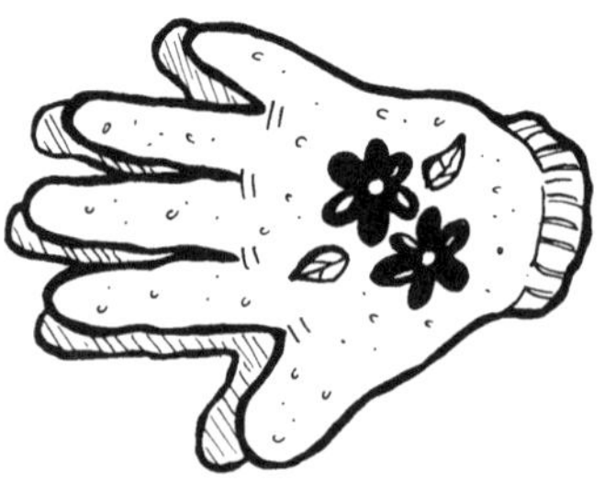

Gardening Gloves—sturdy cloth, vinyl, or leather; for protecting the hands

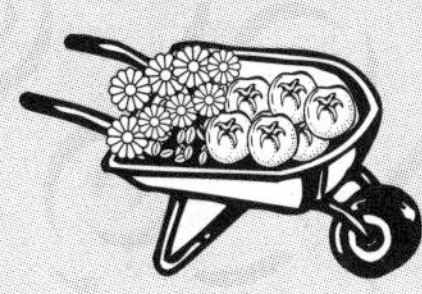

Plant Equipment

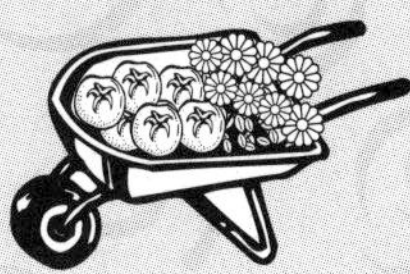

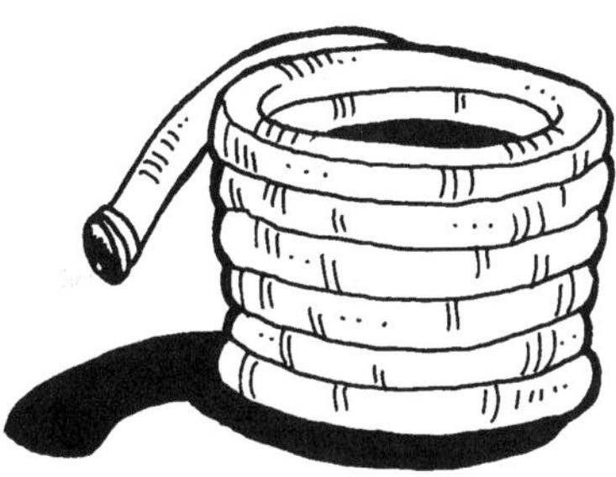

Hose—long, flexible tube; for conveying water or other liquids

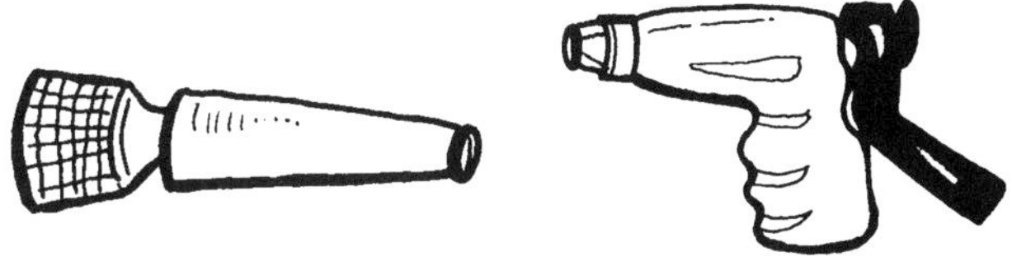

Nozzle—projecting spout used to regulate the flow of water from a hose

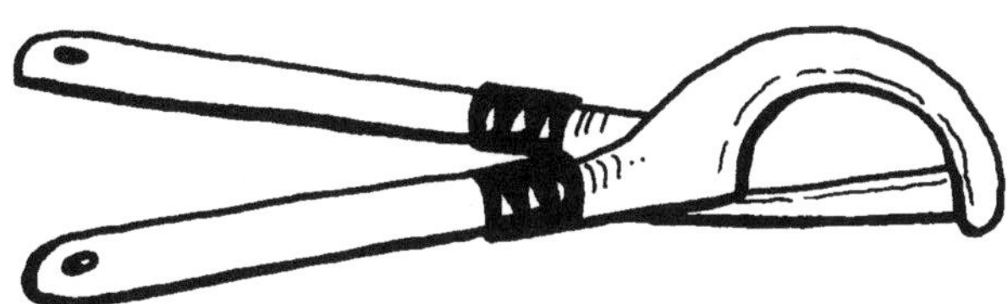

Lopper or Lopping Shears—long handle; for cutting branches or thick stalks

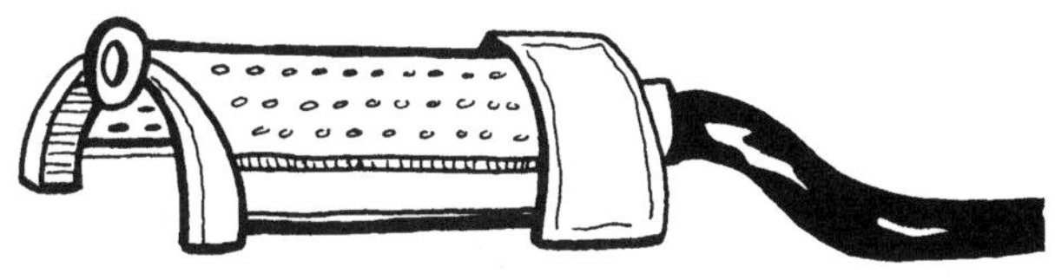

Oscillating Sprinkler—attached to a watering hose; for dispersing water

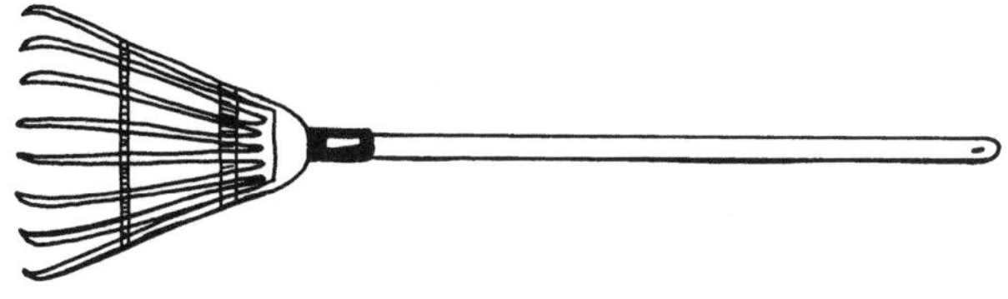

Leaf Rake—long handle, flexible tines; for gathering grass or leaves

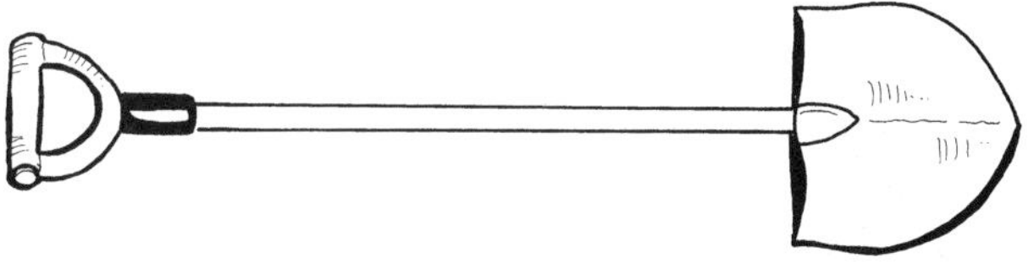

Round-Point Shovel—long handle, somewhat flattened scoop and rounded point; for digging and picking up dirt

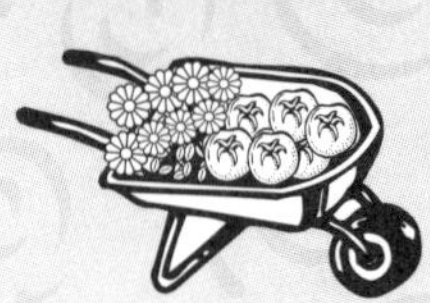

Plant Equipment

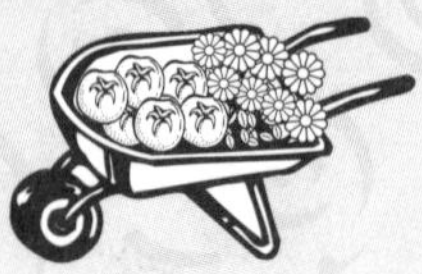

Transplanter—short handle, flattened scoop and sharply pointed end; for digging small holes or lifting seedlings for transplanting; a type of trowel

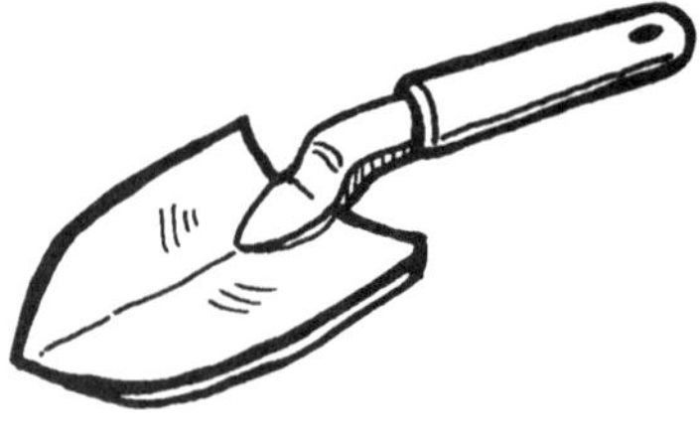

Trowel—short handle, flattened scoop and slightly pointed end; for digging small holes

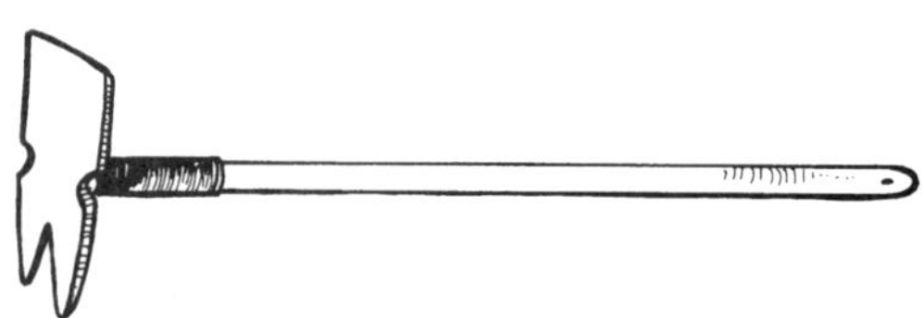

Weeding and Cultivating Hoe—long handle; sharp, flat end for removing weeds or loosening dirt; pronged end for loosening soil around plants

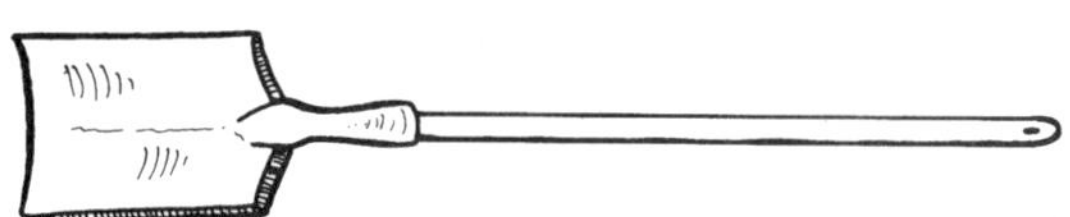

Square-Point Shovel—long handle, flattened scoop and a straight edge; for lifting snow, dirt, or sod

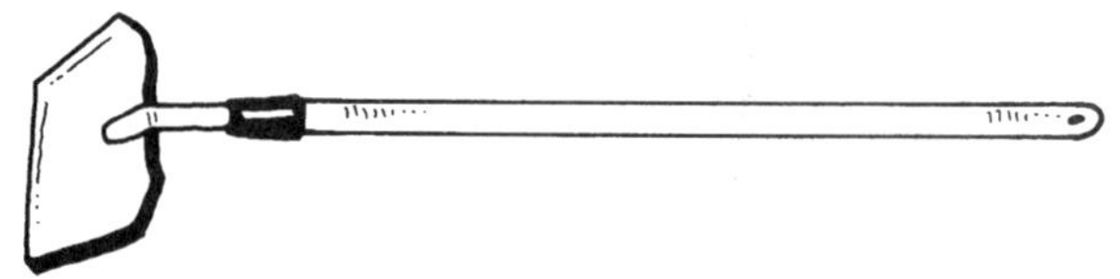

Weeding Hoe—long handle, sharp, flat end; for removing weeds or loosening dirt

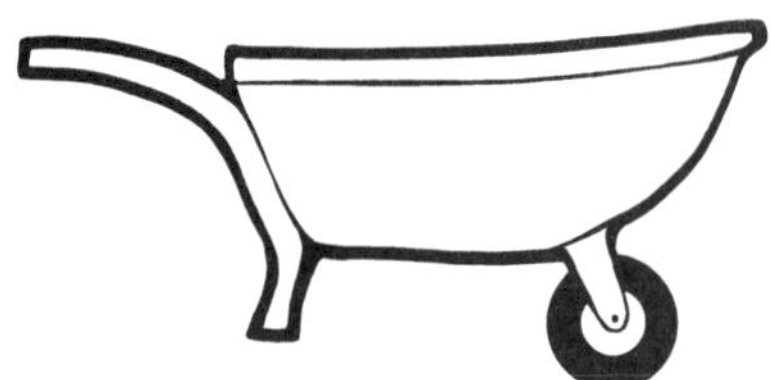

Wheelbarrow—one-wheeled cart with handles; for carrying heavy loads by hand

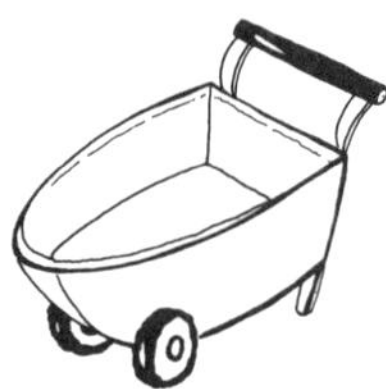

Yard Cart—two-wheeled cart with handles; for carrying heavy loads by hand; more stable-type of wheelbarrow

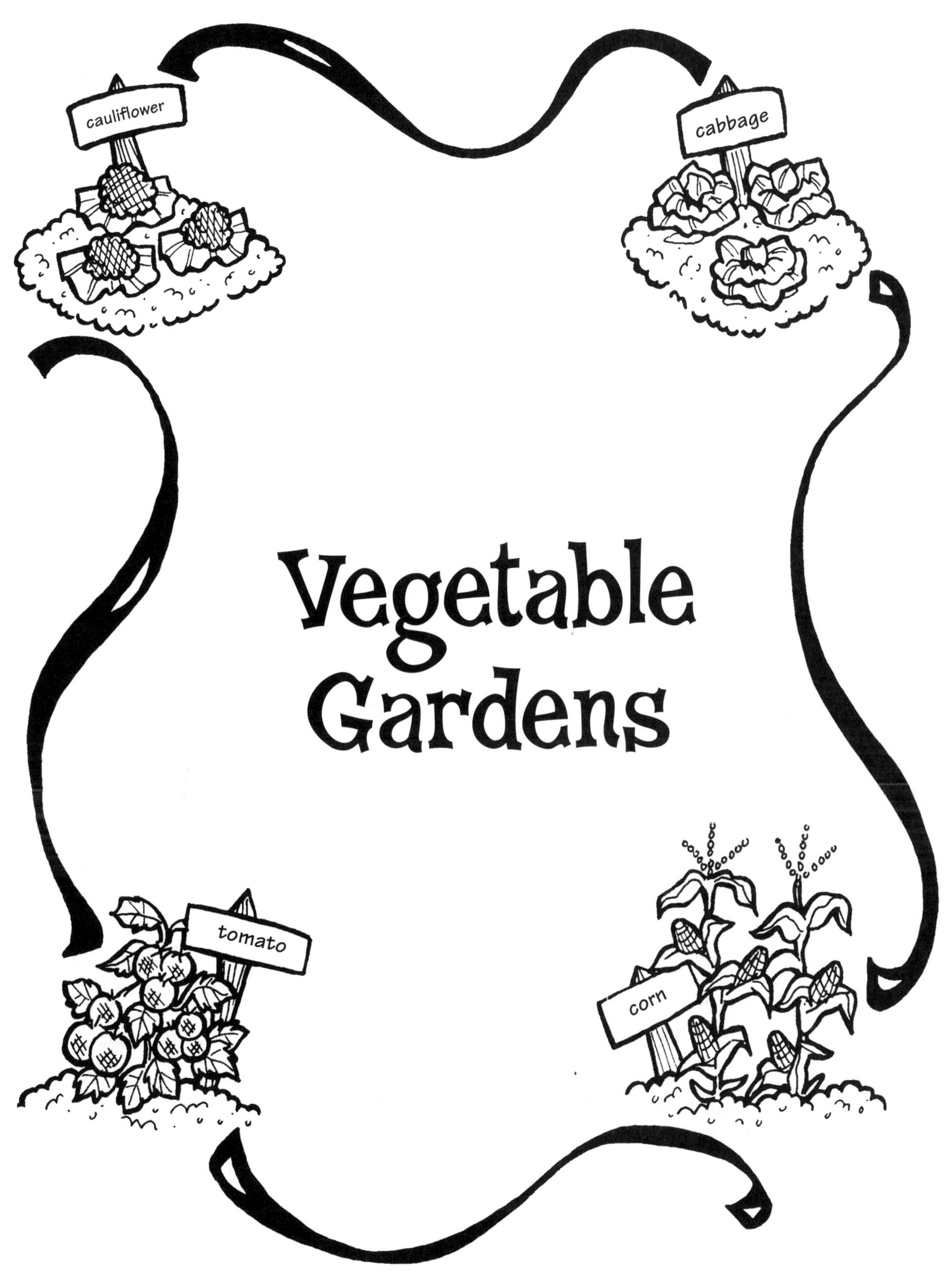
cauliflower
cabbage
Vegetable Gardens
tomato
corn

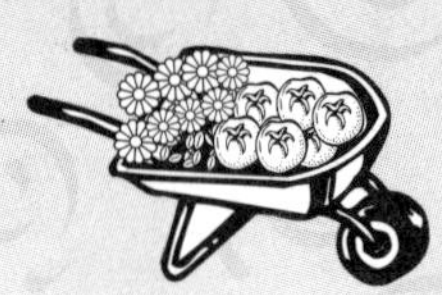

Corn

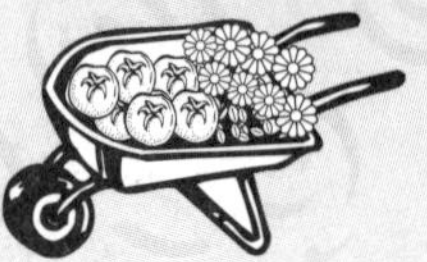

Materials

- corn seeds—sweet silver hybrid, popcorn, or other variety
- hoe
- garden rake
- 8-8-8 fertilizer or organic fertilizer
- mulch

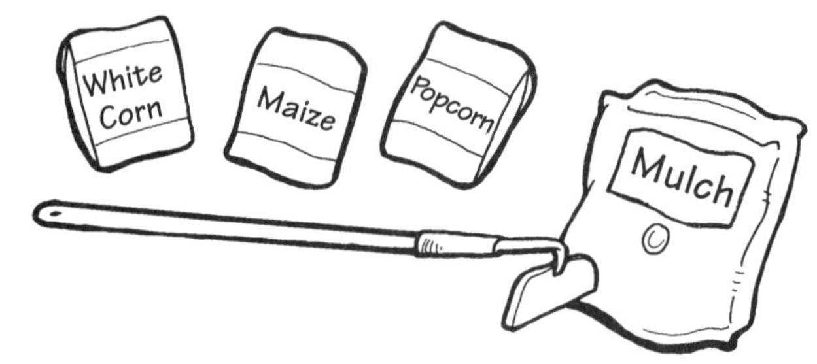

Let's Do It !

1. Work the fertilizer into well-tilled soil.
2. Make at least four parallel rows 12" apart and 1" deep.
3. Drop a corn seed every 4" and cover it lightly with soil. Mulch between the rows.
4. Water every few days until plants are 4"–5" tall.
5. Thin seedlings to about 12" apart.
6. As plants grow taller, use a hoe to pull more dirt up around the stalks to promote more root growth.
7. Apply a side dressing of fertilizer during the growth period. Watch for insect pests.
8. Harvest corn when the ears' silks turn brown and dry. Check the ears for plump, juicy kernels.
9. After harvesting, pull up the old stalks and chop them for the compost pile or turn them under into the soil.

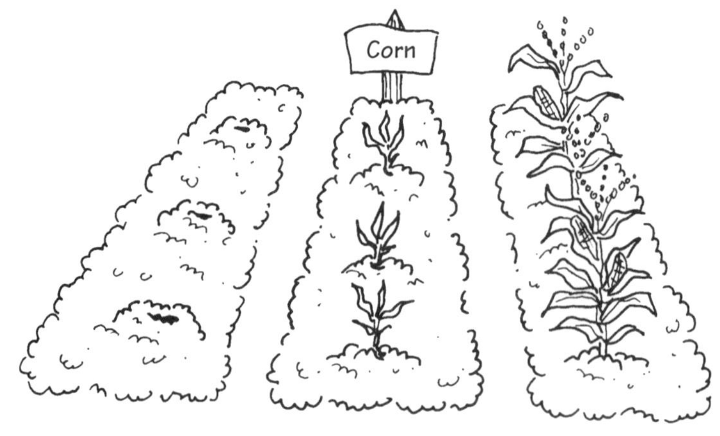

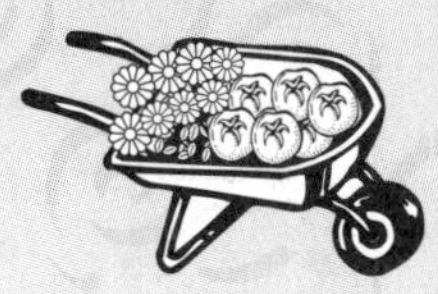

Corn

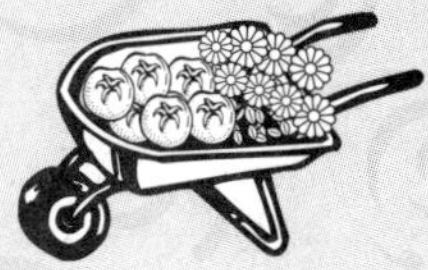

More Ideas

- Plant lima beans, pumpkins, squash, or cucumbers near the corn for companion planting.
- Plant different varieties of corn grown by Native Americans, such as white, blue, or multi-colored corn.
- Plant a popcorn garden. Sell your extra dried corn to earn money, or give it away as gifts.
- Allow some corn to dry on the stalk to use in bird feeders.

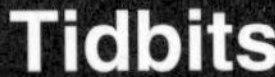

Tidbits

✧ Corn cross-pollinates from plant to plant which should be in rows near each other.

✧ Native Americans introduced corn to American settlers and taught them how to grow it.

✧ Corn is a versatile food that can be eaten in many ways—fresh, parched, or ground—and in many forms—breads, tortillas, tamales, puddings, soups, and others.

Learn More

Aliki. *Corn Is Maize: The Gift of the Indians.* New York: HarperCollins, 1985.

Bial, Raymond. *Corn Belt Harvest.* Boston: Houghton Mifflin, 1991.

Celfe, Albie. *My First Garden Book.* Corte Madera, CA: NK Lawn and Garden Co., 1991.

de Paola, Tomie. *The Popcorn Book.* New York: Holiday, 1978.

Sawyer, Ruth. *Journey Cake, Ho!* New York: Puffin Books, 1978.

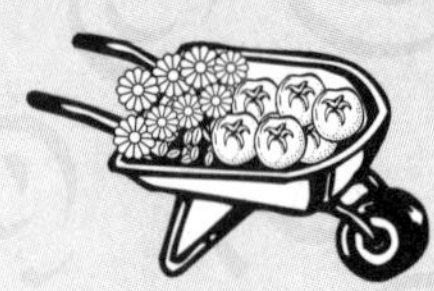

Corn on the Cob

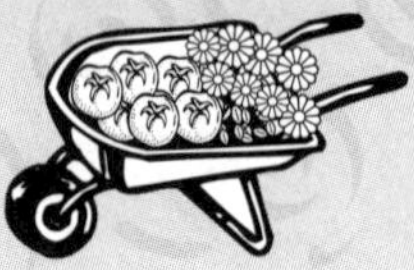

Materials

- fresh ears of corn
- 2 tablespoons sugar
- salt and pepper
- butter
- water to cover corn
- large cook pot with lid
- tongs

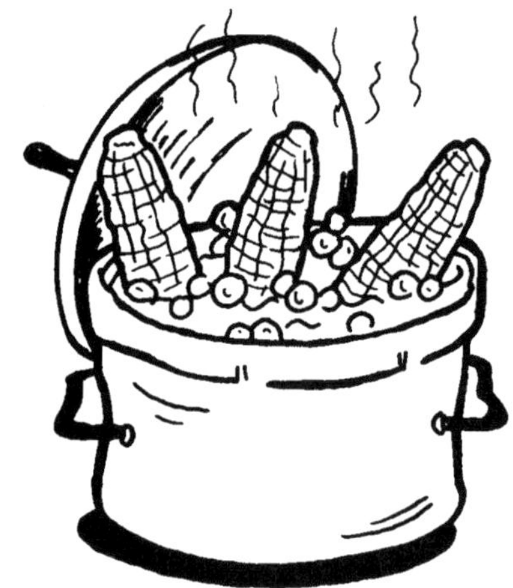

Let's Do It !

1. Remove the husks and silk from the ears of corn, and wash the corn well.
2. Put the water and sugar in a pot and bring it to a boil.
3. Add the corn, and cover the pot. When water returns to a boil, reduce the heat to simmer.
4. Cook the corn until it's tender, about 5–8 minutes.
5. Remove the pot from the heat. Use tongs to lift the corn from the pot and let the ears drain for a short while.
6. Serve the corn while it's still hot. Spread an ear with butter and salt and pepper to taste.

More Ideas

- Cut the kernels off leftover cooked corn and freeze it to use later in soups or casseroles.
- Try different seasonings on the fresh corn. Sprinkle with garlic powder, seasoning salt, or shredded cheese.
- Find your favorite recipe for barbequed corn and follow it.

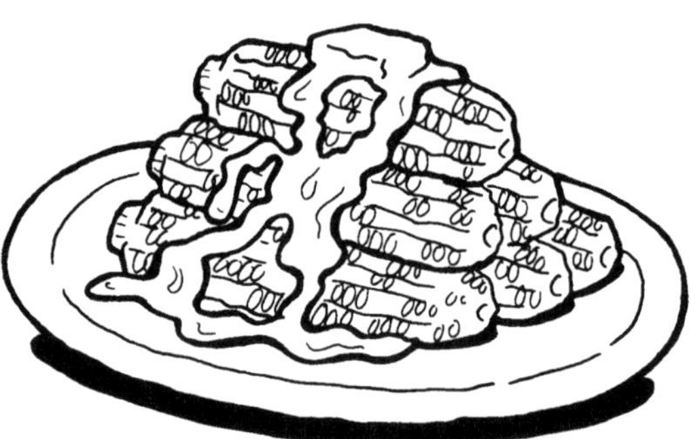

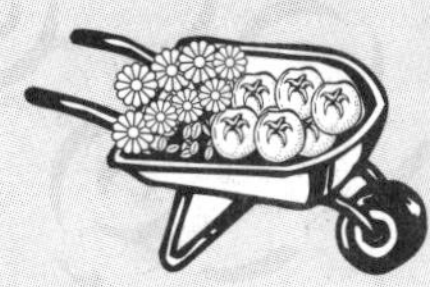

Popcorn

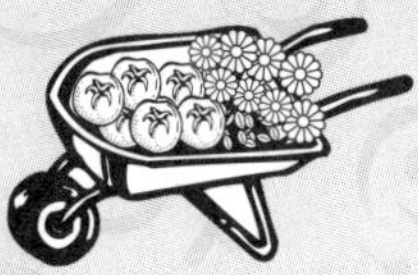

Materials

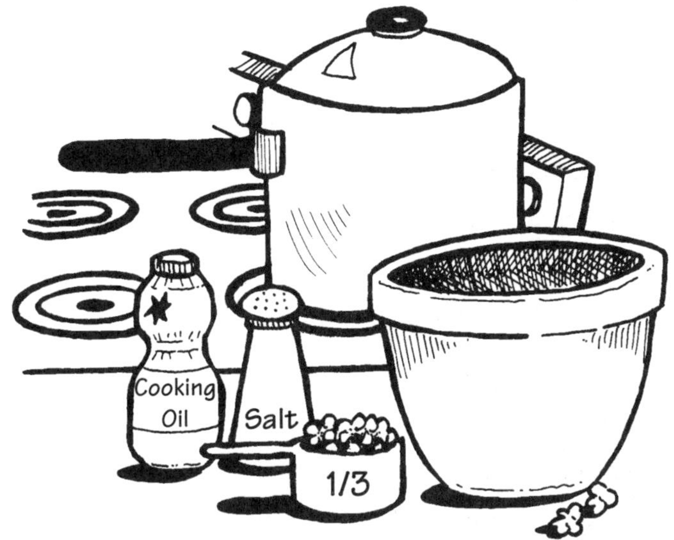

- ⅓ cup popcorn kernels
- salt
- 2 tablespoons cooking oil
- large bowl
- large pot with lid or popcorn popper

Let's Do It !

1. Put the oil and popcorn in a pot or popcorn popper. Cover the pot and put it on high heat. Leave the lid slightly ajar to let the steam escape.
2. When the popping slows, remove the pot from the heat or turn off the popper. Carefully remove the lid.
3. Pour the popcorn into a large bowl and sprinkle the popcorn with salt to taste.

Tidbits

✧ Moisture inside corn kernels causes popcorn to explode when it's heated. Store unpopped popcorn in a sealed container to retain moisture in the corn kernels.

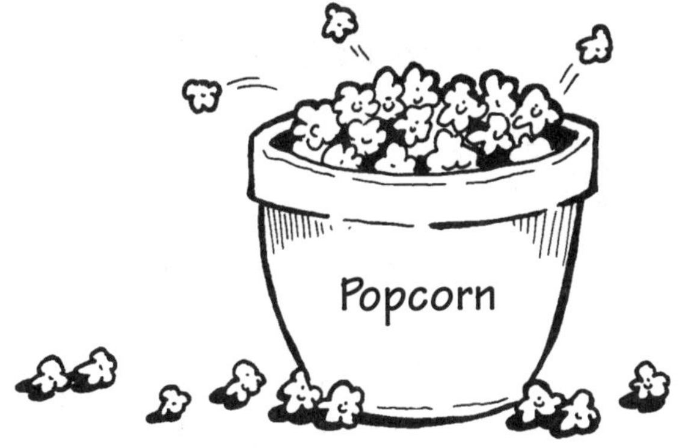

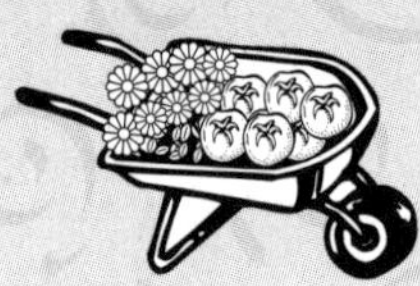

Corn Bread

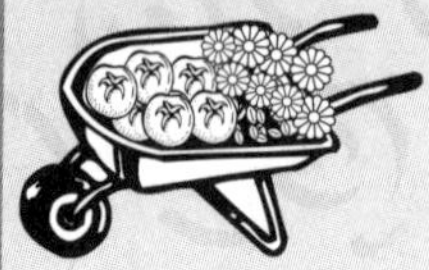

Materials

- 1 cup yellow or white cornmeal
- 1 cup all-purpose flour
- 1/4 cup sugar
- 1 tablespoon baking powder
- 1 teaspoon salt
- 1 egg
- 1 cup milk
- 2 large mixing bowls
- 8" square pan, buttered
- 3 tablespoons vegetable oil

Let's Do It !

1. Mix the dry ingredients together in a bowl.
2. In a separate bowl, combine the oil, egg, and milk and mix well.
3. Add the dry ingredients to the liquid ingredients and stir them until they are just blended.
4. Pour the batter into the buttered pan and bake at 400°F for 25 minutes or until golden brown.

More Ideas

- Serve hot corn bread with butter and jam.
- Use corn bread in place of other dinner breads with such meals as soup, casseroles, and beans.

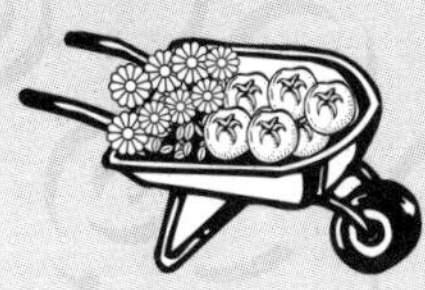

Oh, Shucks!

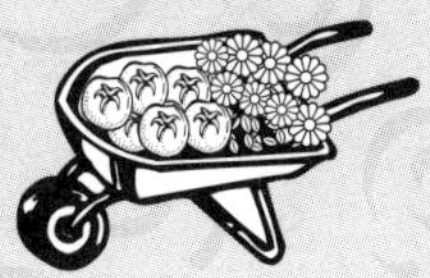

Materials

- dried ears of corn with husks still on (one ear per child)
- newspaper
- small cups (1 per child)
- washable markers
- pencils and small pieces of paper

Let's Do It !

1. Cover the work area with newspaper.
2. Give each child or pair of children an ear of corn, a cup, a pencil and paper, and a marker.
3. Show children how to clean the corn. Remove the husks by pulling them down towards the cob. Pull off the silk.
4. Discuss the possibility of finding dead insects or evidence of insect damage. Name the parts of the ear of corn: husks, silk, kernels, cob.
5. Give children time to clean their corn. Then have them predict how many rows of kernels are on the cob and record their predictions.

   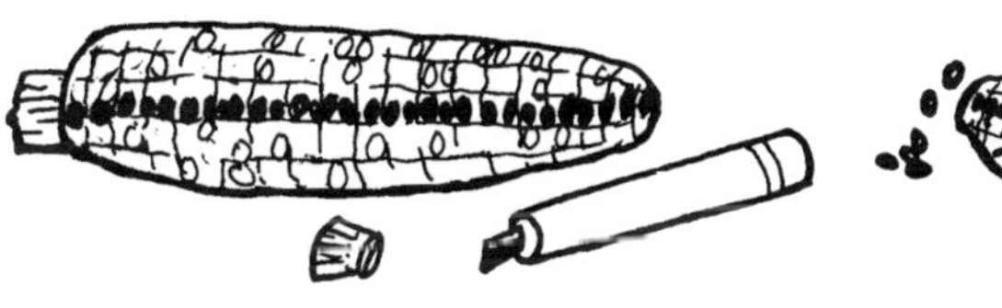

   - Show children how to mark a few kernels on one row to indicate where to start counting.
6. Show children how to remove the corn by pushing the kernels off one end of the cob with your thumb or heel of the hand; work down the rows. Allow time for children to remove their corn kernels.
   - Have children predict how many kernels of corn are on the whole cob and record their predictions.
   - Then have children count the number of kernels in one row and again predict how many kernels are on the whole ear of corn. Record the second predictions.
   - Have children put their kernels in a cup and then count them to see whether their predictions were correct. Which way of predicting was more accurate?
7. Save the cobs, kernels, and husks for other activities.

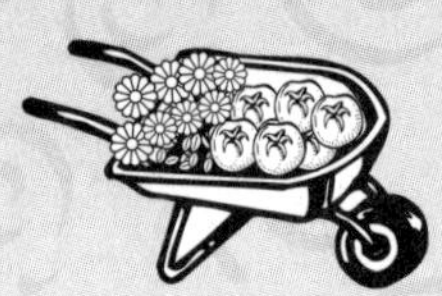

Cornhusk Dolls

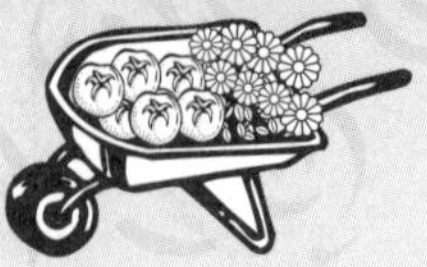

Materials

- dried cornhusks and silks
- string
- scissors
- paint and paintbrushes
- white glue or hot glue gun and glue sticks
- container

Let's Do It !

1. In the container, soak the cornhusks in water until they are soft and pliable.
2. Select 3 husks about the same length, fold them together, and tie a string 1" below the fold to form the head.
3. Cut 2 husks into 3" lengths to make arms. Tie strings about ½" from each end to form the hands. Trim the husks at the hands' ends.
4. Put the arms through the body husks and secure them with a string tied around the body underneath the arms. Trim the husks at the body's end.
5. Slit the body husks to form the legs, and tie the legs ½" from the ends. Trim the husks at the legs' ends.
6. Paint facial features on the head, and glue corn silks on the head for hair.

Tidbits

✧ Dried husks are from ears of corn dried in the field. Check at a farmer's market to find dried corn with the husks on.

✧ Remove the soiled and damaged outer husks and use the finer-textured husks from the inside.

✧ Mildew spots can be removed by soaking the husks for a few minutes in a solution of bleach and water.

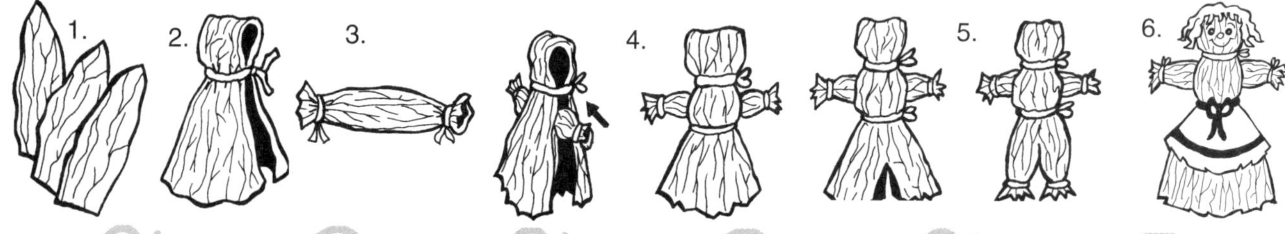

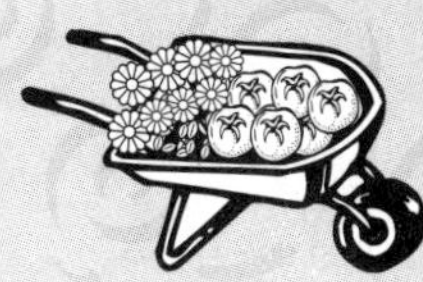

Corncob Dolls

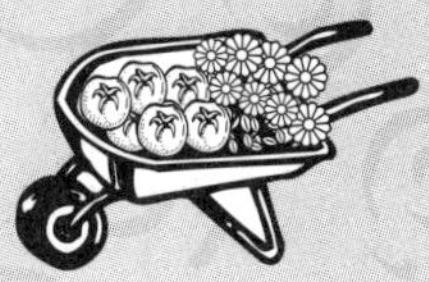

Materials

- clean, dried corncobs
- knife
- craft paints and small brushes
- dried corn silks
- small, dried black-eyed peas
- pipe cleaners
- white glue

Let's Do It !

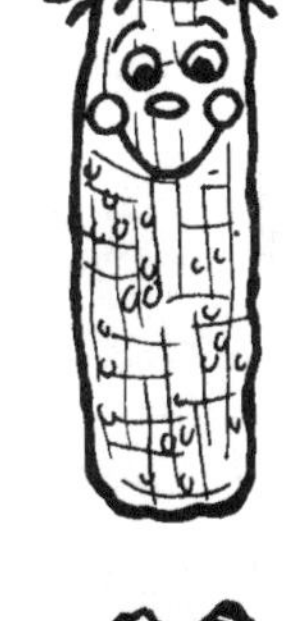

1. Cut the cob 5"–6" long.
2. Allow about 1½" for the head, and paint a face on it. You may wish to use the peas for the eyes and nose.
3. Glue dried corn silks on the head for hair.
4. Cut two pipe cleaners about 4" long for arms. Insert the arms into sides of the corncob about ¼" below the head, and glue them in place. Make a loop in each end for hands.
5. Cut two pipe cleaners 6" long for legs. Insert them into the bottom of the cob, and glue them in place. Make a loop in each end for feet.

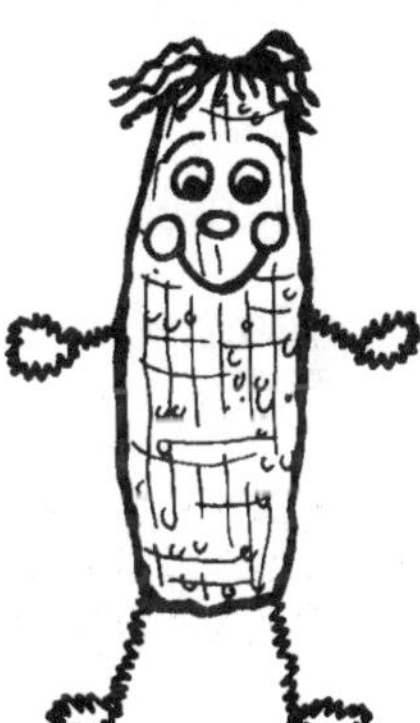

More Ideas

- Make clothes for your dolls. Glue a 3" length of cotton or synthetic batting or three layers of cornhusks around the body of the doll to give it shape and softness. Use fabric scraps to make clothes for the dolls. Decorate them with buttons, sequins, and rickrack.

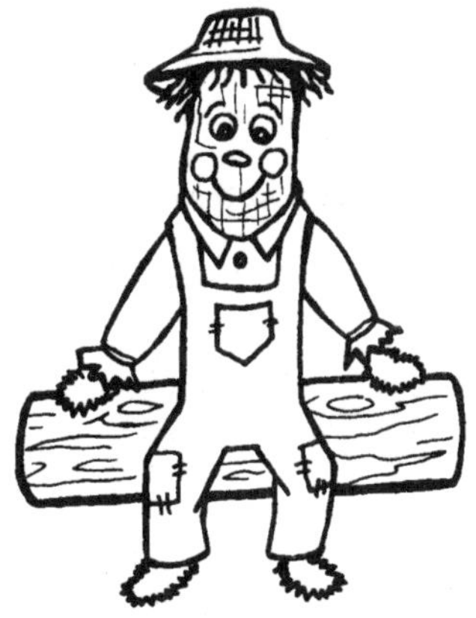

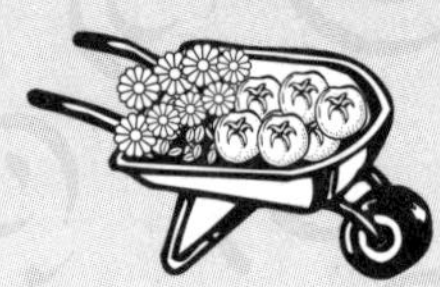

Scarecrow

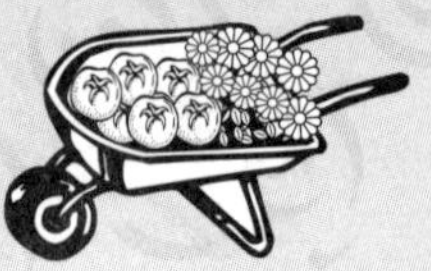

Materials

- dried cornstalks
- twine
- scissors
- permanent markers
- old clothes, shoes, hat, gloves
- cornhusks or straw
- old pillowcase
- pole or old lawn chair
- yarn
- hot glue gun and white glue

Let's Do It !

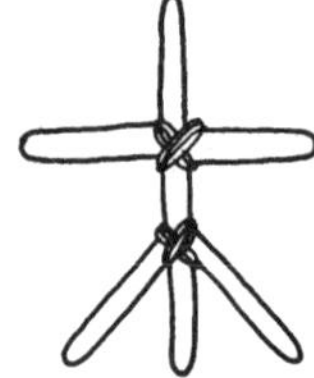

1. Make the skeleton of the scarecrow by tying corn-stalks (or old mop/broom handles) together where the arms and legs meet the body.
2. Stuff the pillowcase with dried cornhusks or straw and tie the bottom with twine to form the head.

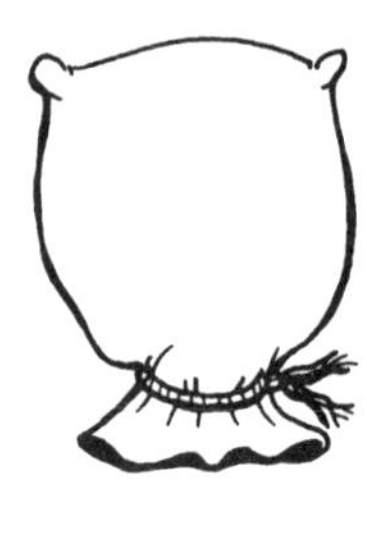

3. Draw on facial features and freckles.
4. Glue pieces of yarn on the head for hair.
5. Place the stuffed head on the neck part of the frame and tie it securely.
6. Dress the scarecrow in old clothes and stuff the body with straw. Tie up the ends of the shirt sleeves and pants to prevent the stuffing from coming out.
7. Tie the scarecrow to a pole stuck in the ground, or place it in an old lawn chair.

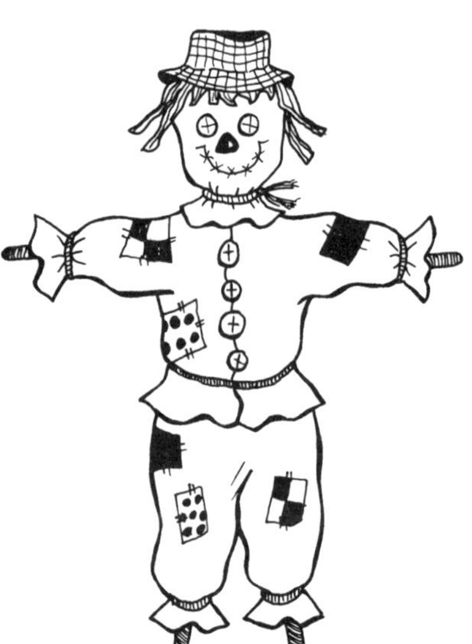

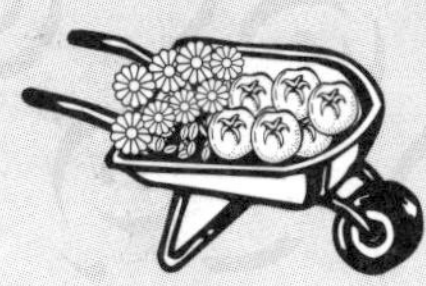

Corn Art

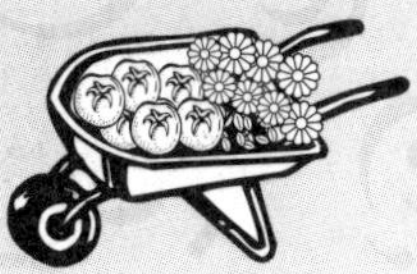

Materials

- corncobs
- dried corn kernels
- dried husks
- corn silk
- assorted beans and seeds
- tempera paints and small brushes
- tagboard, poster board, or paper plates
- art paper
- hot glue gun and white glue
- shallow trays
- juice cans
- markers

Let's Do It !

✧ Corncob Printers—Make corncob printers by rolling the cobs first in shallow trays of tempera paint and then on art paper. Use different cobs for different colors.

✧ Corncob Totem Poles—Use markers or tempera paint to add features and designs. Glue on beaks, wings, or other shapes made with cornhusks or art paper.

✧ Corn Collage—Create a collage or picture by gluing corn parts, along with other beans and seeds, onto poster board, tagboard, or paper plates. Decorate with tempera paints or markers.

✧ Corn Containers—Decorate juice cans by gluing on corn designs.

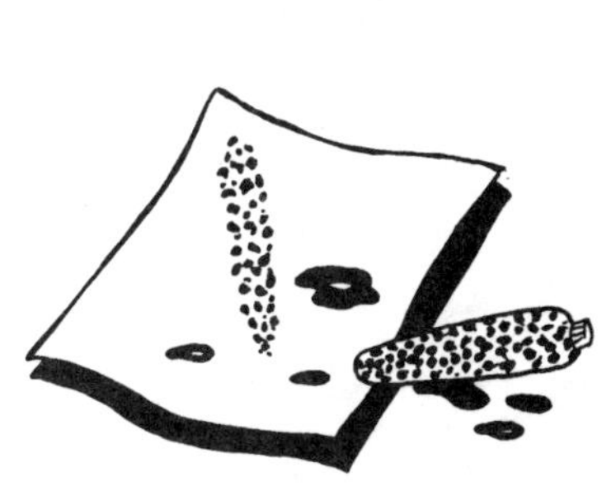

Corncob Printer

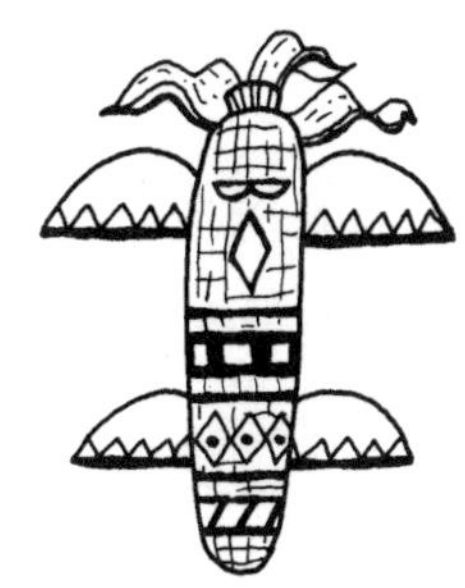

Corncob Totem Pole

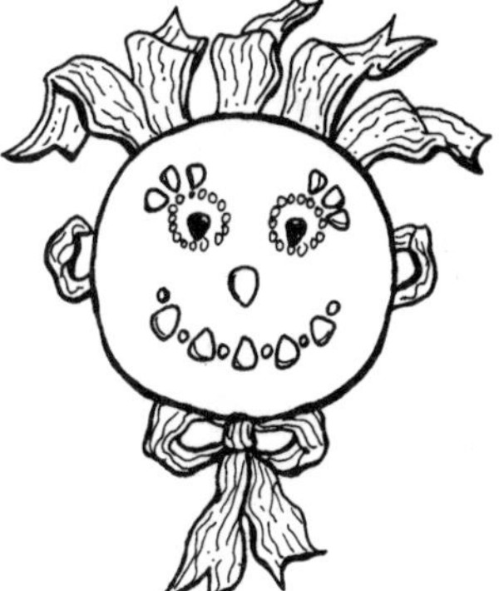

Corncob Collage

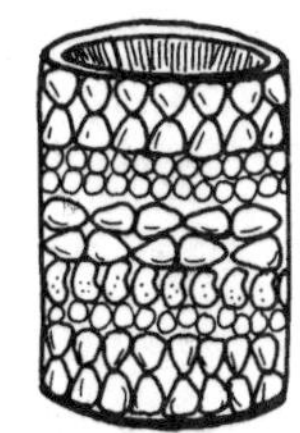

Corn Container

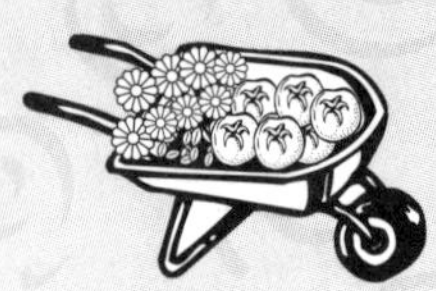

Tomatoes

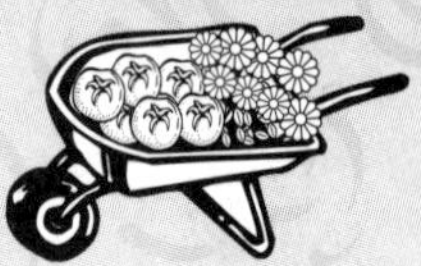

Materials

- tomato plants
- trowel
- peat or compost
- 10-10-10 fertilizer
- wire cages or stakes
- cloth strips or old nylon stockings

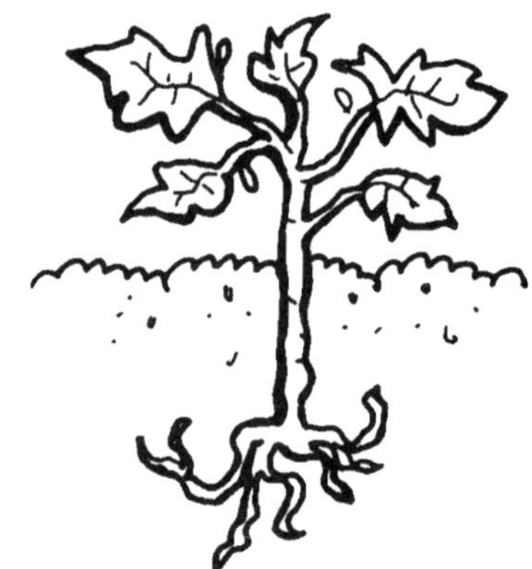

Let's Do It !

1. Work the peat or compost and fertilizer into well-tilled soil.
2. Remove the lower leaves from the seedlings and plant them about 4" deep to develop a strong root system.
3. Space plants 2' apart.
4. Place a wire cage around each plant, or pound a tall, sturdy stake into the ground near each one. When plants are about 12" tall, tie them loosely to the stake.

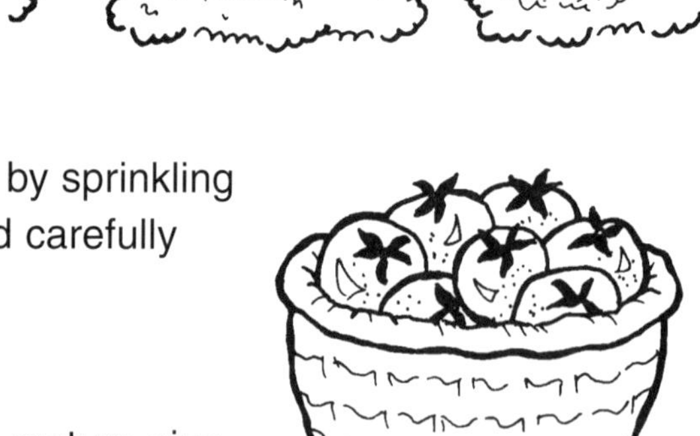

5. Mulch around the plants to discourage weeds and retain moisture.
6. Every two or three weeks, apply a side dressing by sprinkling a small amount of fertilizer around the plants and carefully working it into the soil and thoroughly watering.
7. Remove any insects that appear.
8. Pick tomatoes, green or ripe, when they are at a mature size.

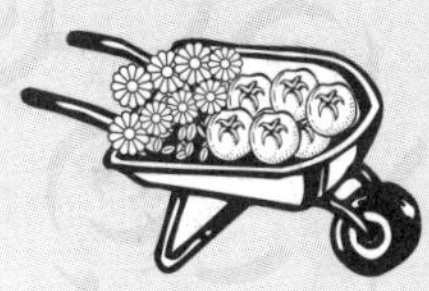

Tomatoes

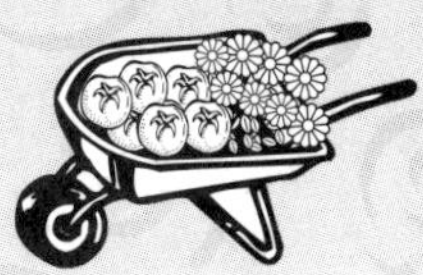

More Ideas

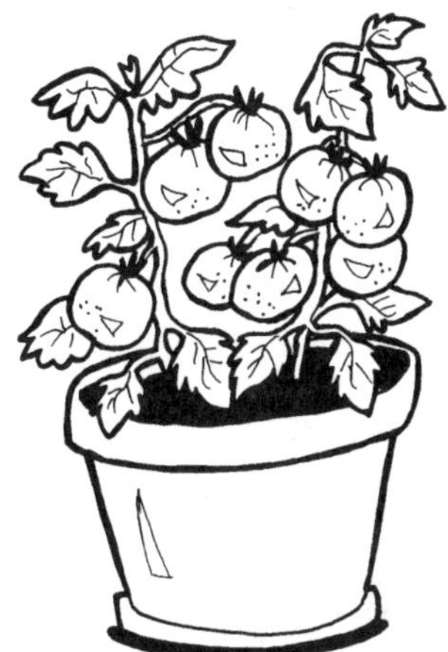

- If you are limited on space, plant tomatoes in large containers placed in a sunny spot. Two or three plants will probably produce enough to feed a family through the growing season.
- Plant cherry tomatoes as well as other varieties to provide crops over a longer period of time. Look for early producing varieties.

Tidbits

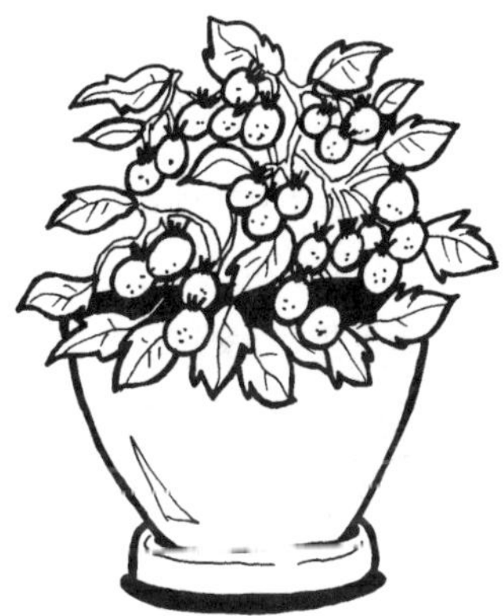

✧ Wait to plant until after the last frost. Tomatoes produce best when night temperatures are between 55°F and 75°F.

✧ Tomatoes are a good sources of vitamin C.

✧ Bushy varieties require little support, and all fruit matures about the same time. Indeterminate varieties produce fruit over a longer period of time and need support.

Learn More

Ehlert, Lois. *Eating the Alphabet: Fruits & Vegetables from A to Z.* New York: Harcourt Children's Books, 1989.

Thacher Hurd, Edith. *Tomato Soup.* New York: Crown Publishers, Inc., 1992.

Pulleyn, Micah and Sarah Bracken. *Kids in the Kitchen.* New York: Sterling Publishing Co., 1995.

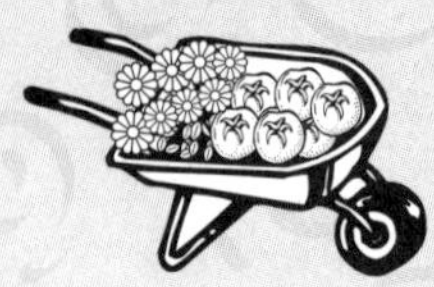

Tomato Soup

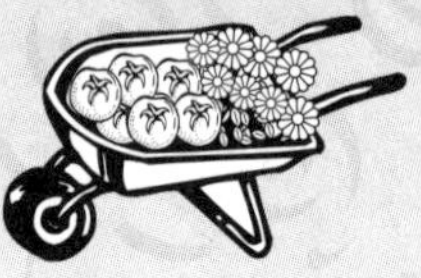

Materials

- 6 tomatoes
- 1/4 cup onion, chopped
- 1/2 cup celery, chopped
- 2 teaspoons sugar
- paring knife
- wire whisk
- croutons
- cutting board
- 1/2 cup butter
- 4 cups milk
- salt and pepper
- 6 tablespoons flour
- 1 bay leaf
- saucepans
- large pot

Let's Do It !

1. Put the tomatoes into a pot with enough water to cover them.
2. Bring the water to a boil, and cook the tomatoes about 5 minutes or until the skins loosen.
3. Drain the tomatoes and let them cool. Then remove their cores and skin and chop them up.
4. Put 2 cups of tomato chunks in a saucepan, cover them with water, and simmer them with the onion, celery, and sugar for 15 minutes.
5. Make 4 cups of cream sauce.
   - Melt the butter in a saucepan.
   - Stir in the flour and cook 1 minute.
   - Gradually blend in the milk and add the seasonings.
   - Simmer the mixture until it is smooth and creamy, stirring often with a whisk.
   - Remove the bay leaf.
6. Stir the cream sauce into the tomato mixture.
7. Serve the soup hot and garnish it with croutons.

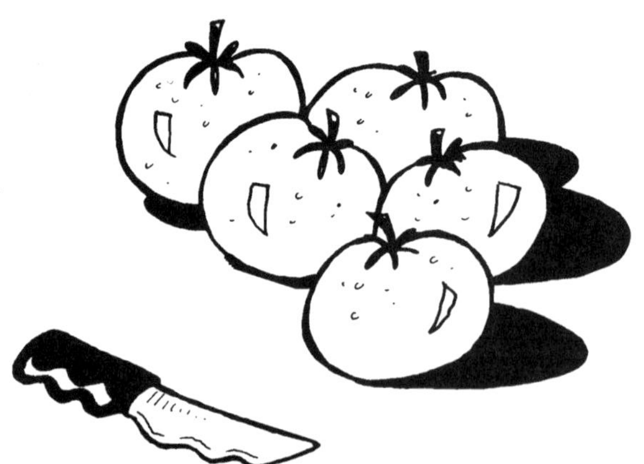

More Ideas

- Add leftover corn and rice to tomato soup and serve it with cornbread.

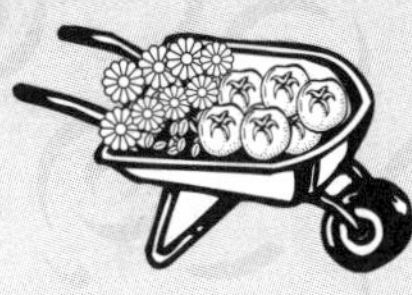

Fried Green Tomatoes

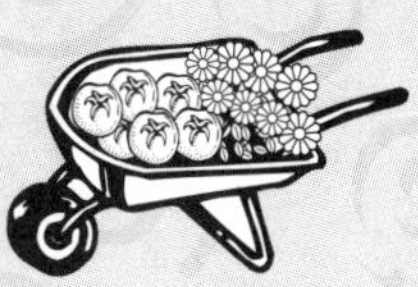

Materials

- 6 firm, mature, green tomatoes
- 1 cup flour
- 1 teaspoon salt
- 1/4 teaspoon black pepper
- cooking oil
- 2 pie pans
- large frying pan
- wide metal spatula
- paring knife

Let's Do It !

1. Wash and core the tomatoes. Slice them 1/4" thick and set them aside in a pie pan.
2. Mix the flour, salt, and pepper in the other pie pan.
3. Dredge the slices of tomato in the seasoned flour mixture.
4. Heat 3 tablespoons of oil in a frying pan. Fry the coated tomato slices until they are golden brown, turning them once.
5. Serve the fried tomatoes hot.

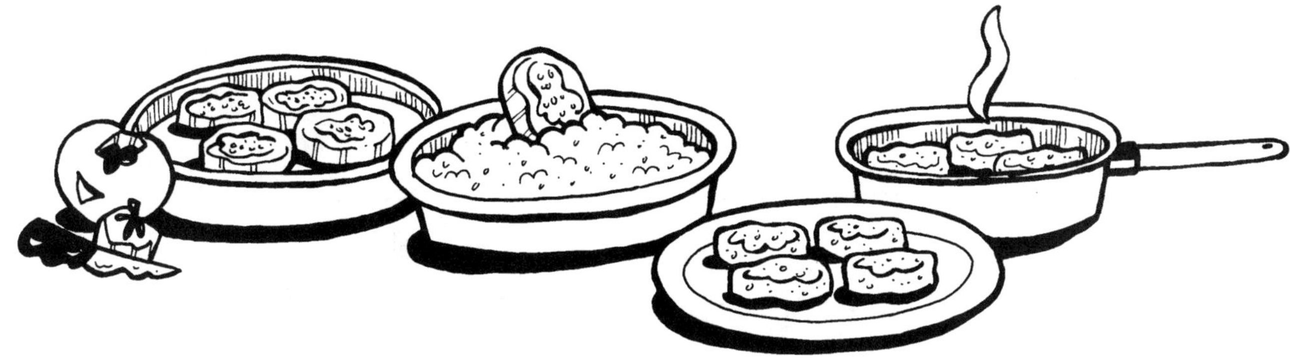

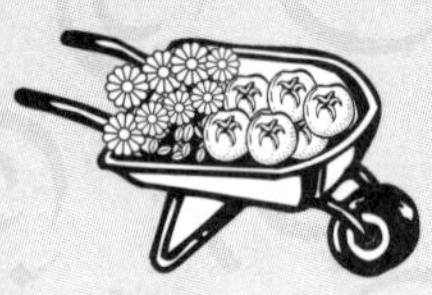

Italian Marinated Tomato Salad

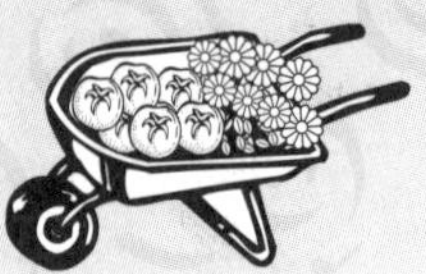

Materials

- 4 large, firm, ripe tomatoes
- 1 clove garlic, minced
- 1 medium onion, sliced
- 1 teaspoon dried oregano or fresh chopped basil
- 1/4 teaspoon pepper
- 6 tablespoons olive oil
- 3 tablespoons wine vinegar
- paring knife
- medium bowl
- cutting board

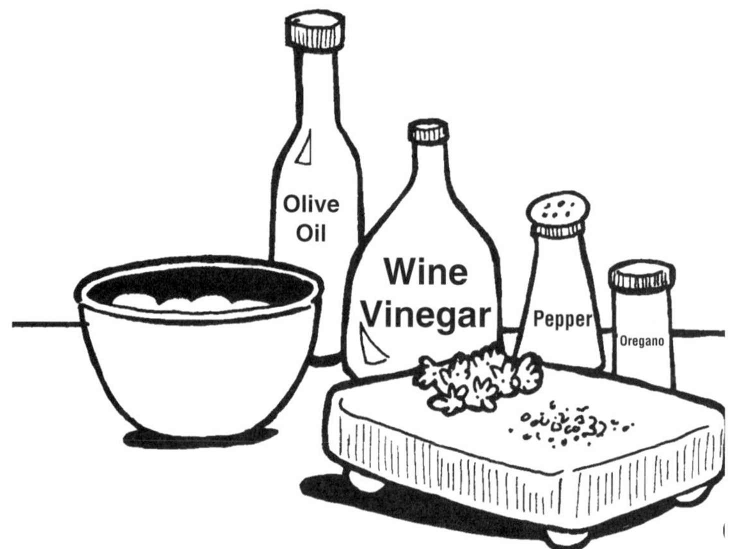

Let's Do It !

1. Wash and core the tomatoes, and cut them into bite-sized pieces.
2. Combine all the tomatoes and the onion in a bowl. Sprinkle them with garlic, oregano or basil, olive oil, wine vinegar, and pepper and gently stir to mix the tomatoes and the onion with the marinade.
3. Cover the bowl, place it in the refrigerator, and allow it to sit for several hours. Stir the mixture occasionally.
4. Serve the salad chilled.

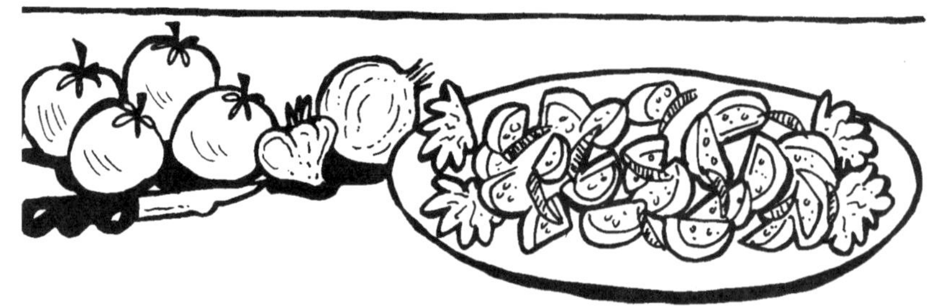

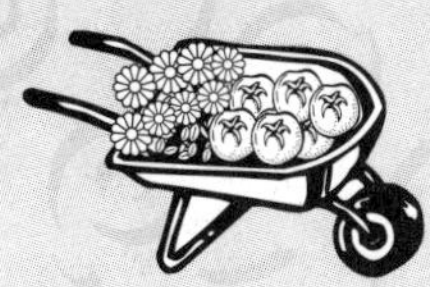

Book Fun

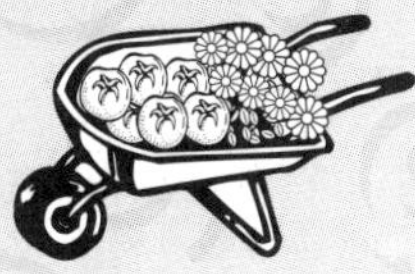

Materials

- *Tomato Soup* by Edith Thacher Hurd. New York: Crown Publishers, 1992.
- 1 can tomato soup
- 1 can (soup can) of water
- medium bowl
- several small bowls
- 5" squares of cloth
- assorted items with strong odors such as vinegar, onion, cologne
- scissors
- pencil
- paper

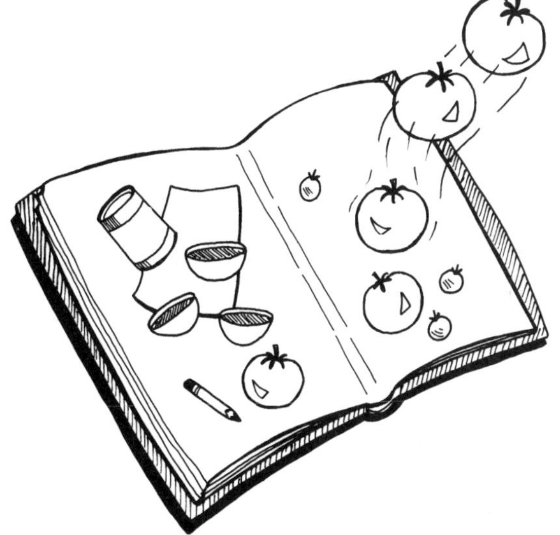

Let's Do It !

1. Read the story aloud and discuss it. Do you think tomato soup will really take out odors? Test to find out.
2. Blend the tomato soup and water in the medium bowl, and pour it into four or five small bowls.
3. Label each bowl with one of the odor-producing substances you have.
4. On each cloth square, put one odorous substance. Smell the cloths and then immerse each cloth in its corresponding bowl.
5. After five minutes, remove the cloths from the soup, squeeze out excess soup, and rinse thoroughly in water.
6. Smell each cloth.
   - Did the soup remove the odors?
   - Did it work on all the substances you tested? If not, which ones failed the test?
   - Summarize what you learned.

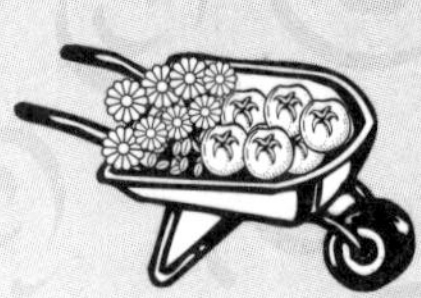

Peppers

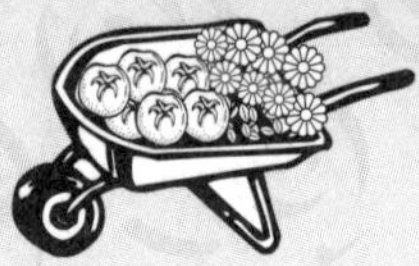

Materials

- trowel
- fertilizer
- pepper plant seedlings

Let's Do It !

1. Use a trowel to dig a hole deep enough for the root ball of the plant. Plant the seedlings the same depth as in their container.
2. Space plants 2' apart.
3. Press the soil firmly around the plants and water them well.
4. During the growing season, provide a side dressing of fertilizer a few times. Water plants regularly.
5. Peppers may be picked when full size and green, or you can wait until they turn red. They produce until there's a hard freeze.

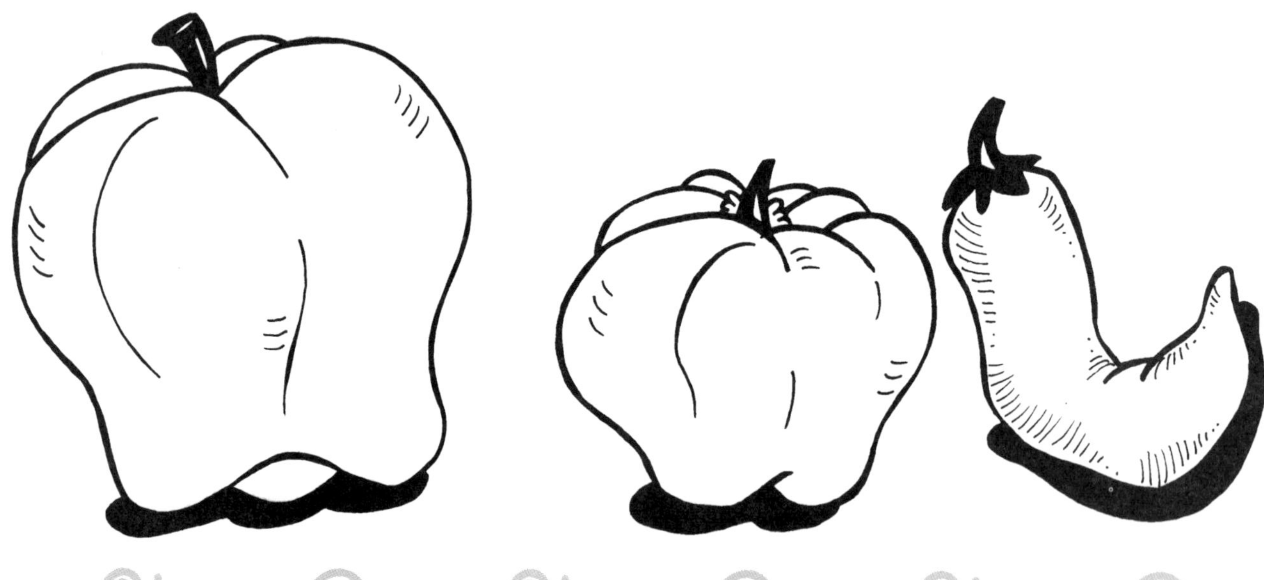

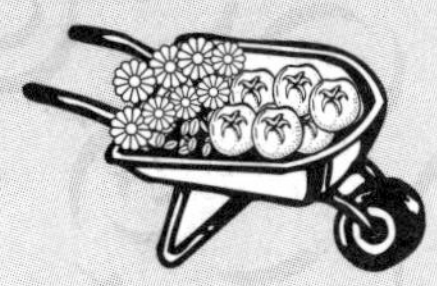

Peppers

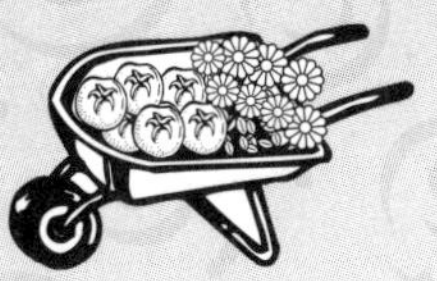

More Ideas

- Plant several varieties of peppers such as bell peppers, banana peppers, chili peppers, and yellow peppers.
- Dry chili peppers and tie them together by their stems for a useful and decorative display.
- Do the Peter Piper tongue twister.

  Peter Piper picked a peck of pickled peppers.
  A peck of pickled peppers Peter Piper picked.
  If Peter Piper picked a peck of pickled peppers,
  How many pickled peppers did Peter Piper pick?

Tidbits

✧ Wait to plant peppers until after the last frost.

✧ Peppers are a good source of vitamin C.

✧ Cayenne and chili peppers add a hot, spicy flavor to foods.

Learn More

Florian, Douglas. *Vegetable Garden.* San Diego, CA: Harcourt Brace Jovanovich, 1991.

Pallotta, Jerry and Bob Thompson. *The Victory Garden Vegetable Alphabet Book.* Watertown, MA: Charlesbridge Publishing, 1992.

Stewart, Martha. *Martha Stewart's Gardening Month by Month.* New York: Clarkson Potter Publishers, 1991.

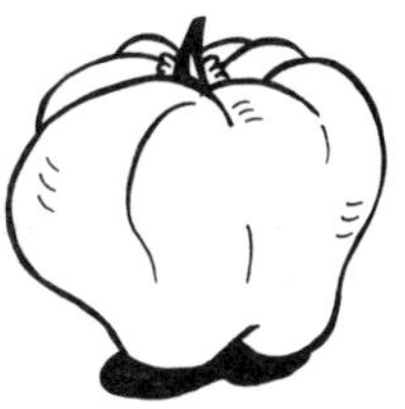

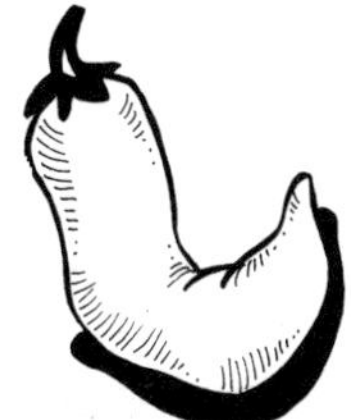

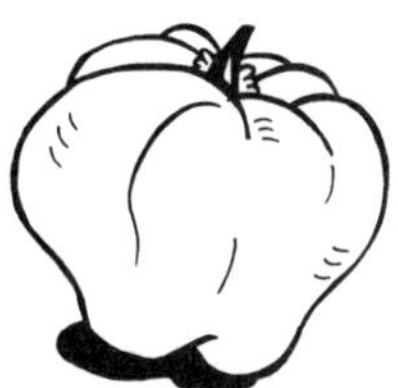

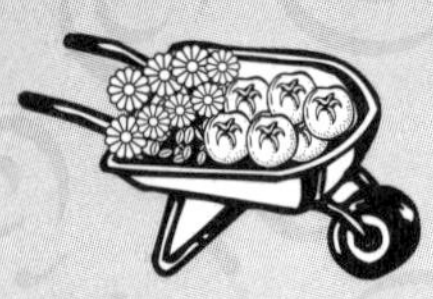

Stuffed Peppers

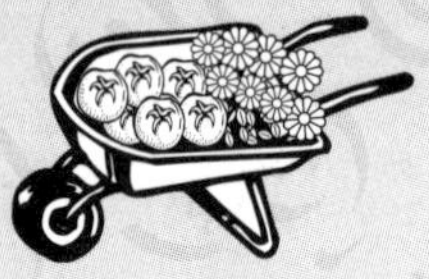

Materials

- 4 whole, large green peppers
- ½ pound lean ground beef
- 1 small onion, chopped
- ½ teaspoon pepper
- ½ cup quick-cooking rice
- water
- 1 can condensed cream of tomato soup
- ½ teaspoon garlic salt
- knife
- 1½ quart covered casserole dish
- frying pan
- large saucepan with lid
- spoon
- liquid measuring cup

Let's Do It !

1. Preheat the oven to 375°F.
2. Remove the stems from the peppers and cut a thin slice off the top of each. With the spoon, remove the seeds and interior membranes, and wash the peppers thoroughly.
3. Put 5 cups of water in a large saucepan, and bring it to a boil.
4. Carefully place the peppers into the boiling water. Cover the pan, cook 5 minutes, and then drain the peppers and put them aside to cool.
5. Put 1½ cups of water and the rice in a saucepan. When it comes to a boil, cover the pan.
6. Reduce heat to low and simmer the rice for 20 minutes or until tender.
7. Add the ground beef and chopped onion to a frying pan and cook them until the onions are transparent and the beef is brown. Drain the beef but leave it in the pan.
8. Add the garlic salt, pepper, cooked rice, and 1 cup of tomato soup to the frying pan. Simmer for a few minutes.
9. Spoon beef mixture into each pepper. Stand the peppers upright in a baking dish. Add a few tablespoons of water to the remaining soup and pour it over the peppers.
10. Cover the baking dish and bake for 30 minutes.

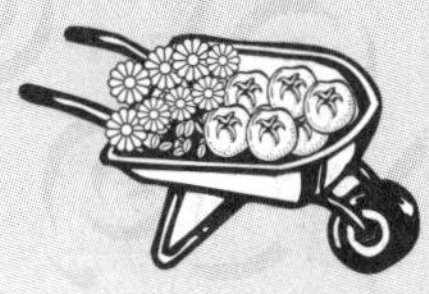

Tasting Party

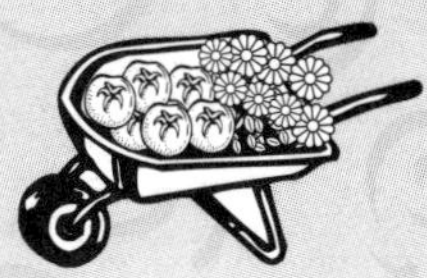

Materials

- peppers, washed and sliced
- radishes, scrubbed and small roots removed
- cucumbers, washed and sliced
- carrots, cleaned and cut into strips
- cherry tomatoes
- salad dressings and dips
- serving fork
- sturdy paper platters
- napkins
- small bowls
- spoons
- vegetable platter or tray
- lemonade and pitcher
- paper cups

Let's Do It !

1. Ahead of time, clean and prepare the vegetables, and chill them.
2. Put the salad dressings and assorted dips into small bowls, and add a spoon to each. Ask guests to put the dips on their plates rather than dunk vegetables into the bowls.
3. Serve buffet style so guests may help themselves.

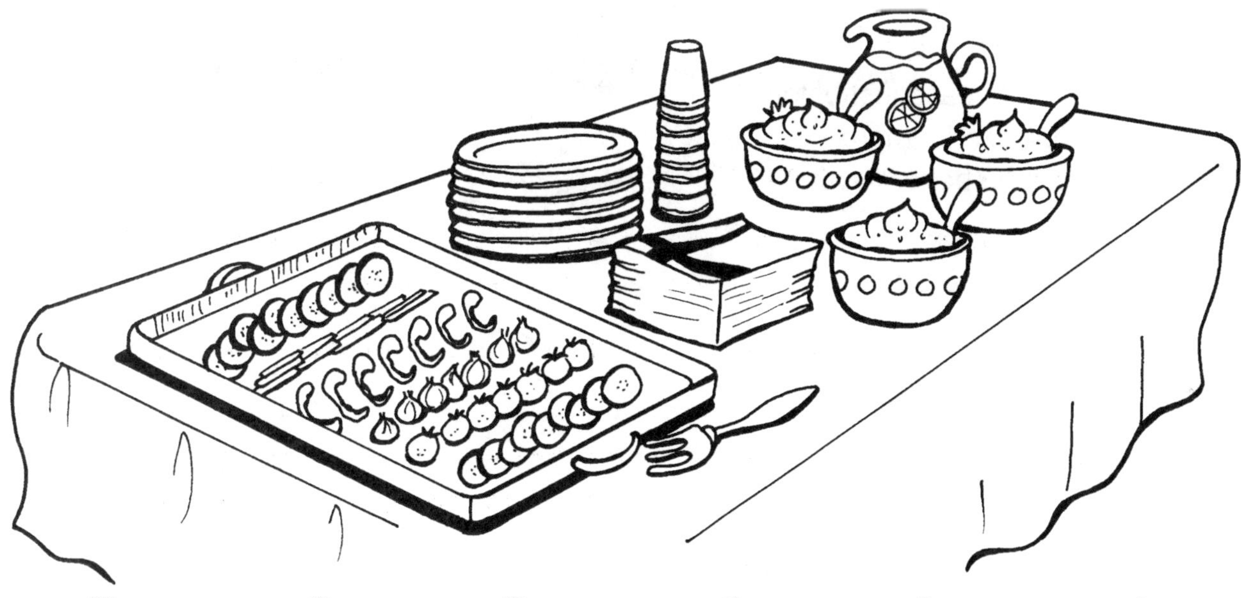

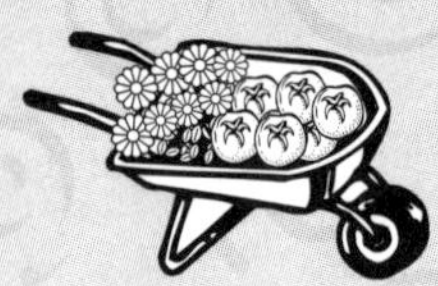

Beans and Peas

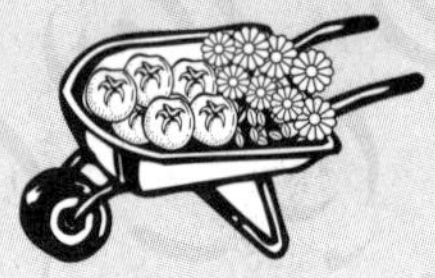

Materials

- bean and pea seeds
- hoe
- fertilizer
- craft sticks
- fine-tip permanent marker

Let's Do It !

1. Work the fertilizer into well-tilled soil.
2. Make rows 1"–2" deep and 2' apart. Label the rows with craft sticks.
3. Plant the seeds 4" apart, cover them lightly with soil, and water them thoroughly.
4. During the growing season, weed and water as needed.
5. Pick peas and beans just before reaching full size for more tenderness and better flavor.
6. To dry peas or beans, allow them to dry on the plants.
7. Turn the old plants into the soil to add nutrients to the soil.

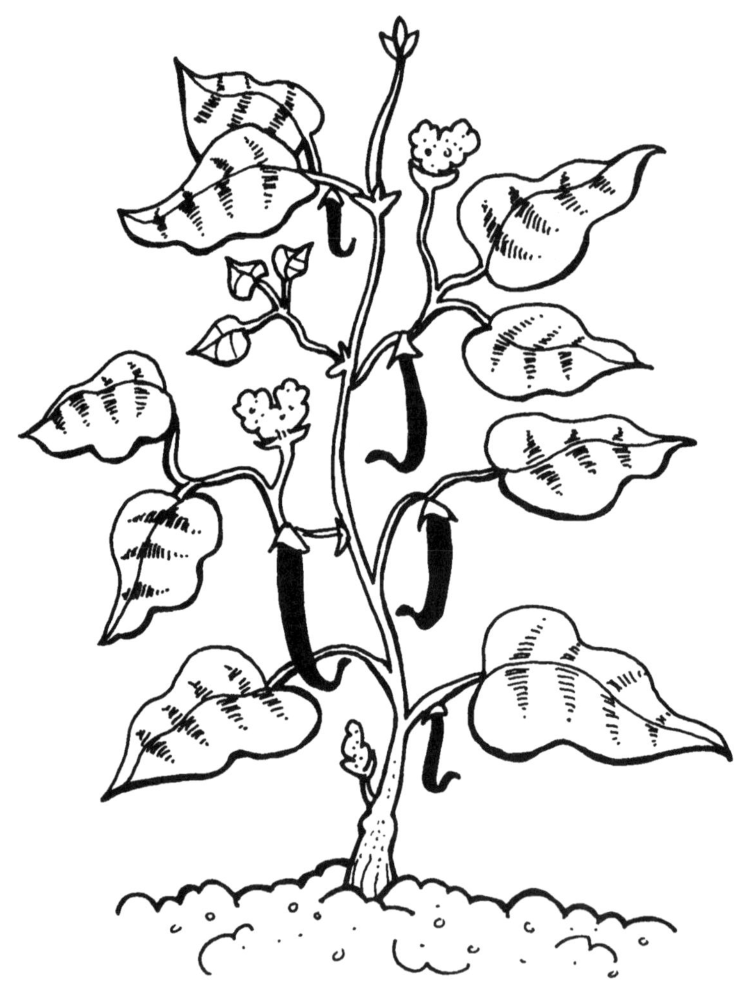

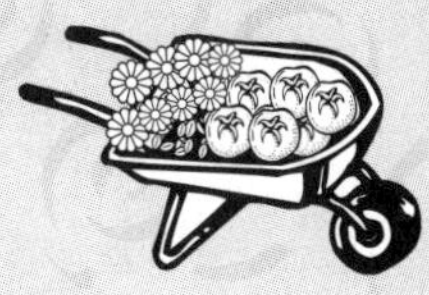

Beans and Peas

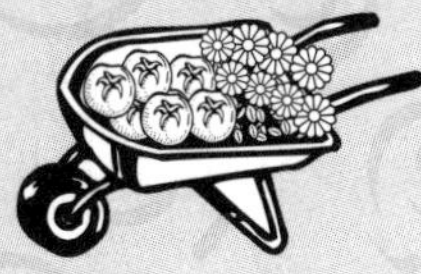

More Ideas

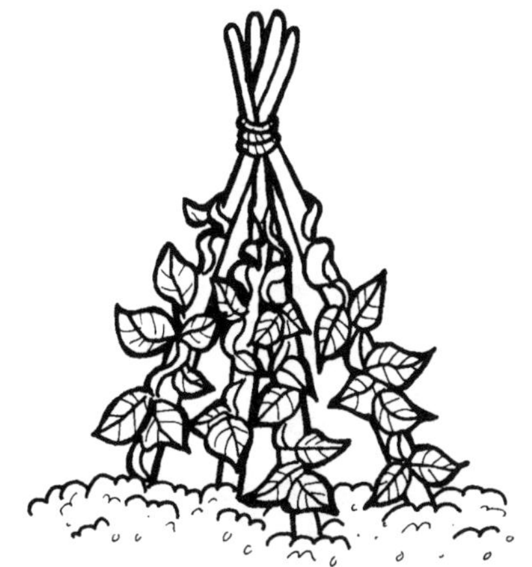

- Plant beans and peas near their companion friends.
- Plant seeds three weeks apart for a succession of crops.
- Build a teepee for pole beans or vining peas.

Tidbits

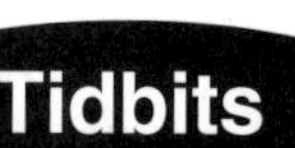

✧ Peas like cool weather and can be planted three weeks before the last frost is expected.

✧ Beans like warm weather, so plant them after the last frost.

✧ The pods and seeds of beans and peas are edible.

✧ Some varieties are climbing vines while others are short and bushy.

✧ Some varieties of peas have fragrant blossoms and are grown for the flower.

Learn More

Berger, Melvin. *All About Seeds (Do-It-Yourself Science).* New York: Scholastic, Inc., 1992.

Gillis, Jennifer Storey. *Green Beans and Tambourines.* Pownal, VT: Story Communications, Inc., 1995.

Thaler, Mike. *The Princess and the Pea-ano.* New York: Scholastic, Inc., 1997.

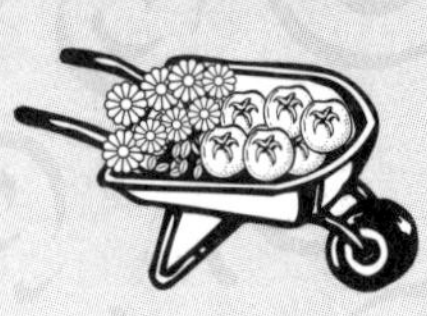

Sugar Peas—Pennsylvania Dutch Style

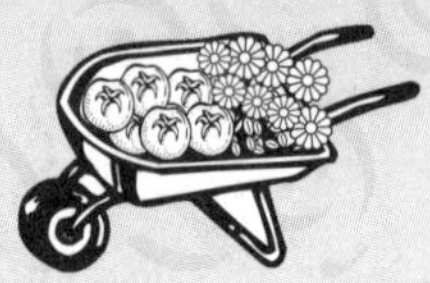

Materials

- 4 cups fresh sugar peas
- $^{1}/_{2}$ cup water
- 1 teaspoon salt
- 1 teaspoon sugar
- 1 tablespoon butter
- 1 cup milk
- saucepan with lid
- salt and pepper
- colander

Let's Do It !

1. Wash the peas and remove the strings.
2. In a saucepan, combine the peas, water, salt, and sugar. Cover the pan and bring the water to a boil.
3. Reduce the heat, cook 2–3 minutes, and drain the peas well.

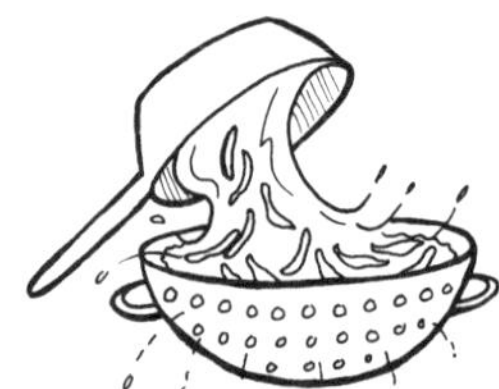

4. Add the butter and stir it until it's melted and then add the milk.

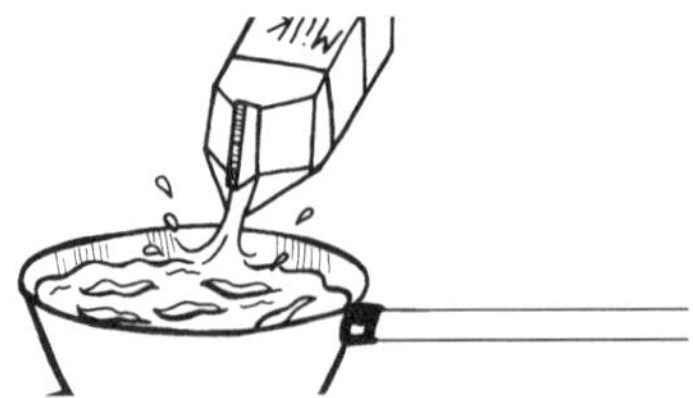

5. Season the peas to taste with salt and pepper. Heat them at medium temperature until the milk is hot.

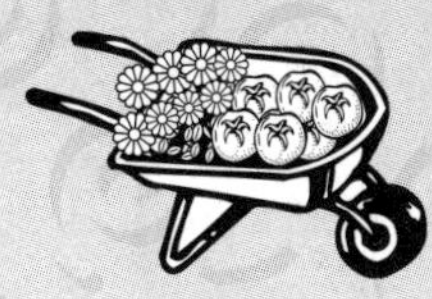

Cooked Green Beans

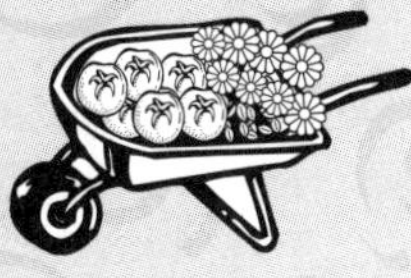

Materials

- 1 pound fresh green beans
- 2 tablespoons butter
- salt and pepper
- saucepan with lid
- 1/2 cup water
- colander

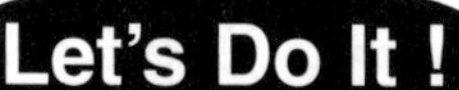

Let's Do It !

1. Remove the strings from the beans. Wash the beans and snap them in half.
2. Place the beans and water in the saucepan, cover it, and bring it to boil.
3. Reduce the heat and cook the beans until crisply tender (about 10 minutes).
4. Drain the beans in the colander, and add butter and seasonings. Serve hot.

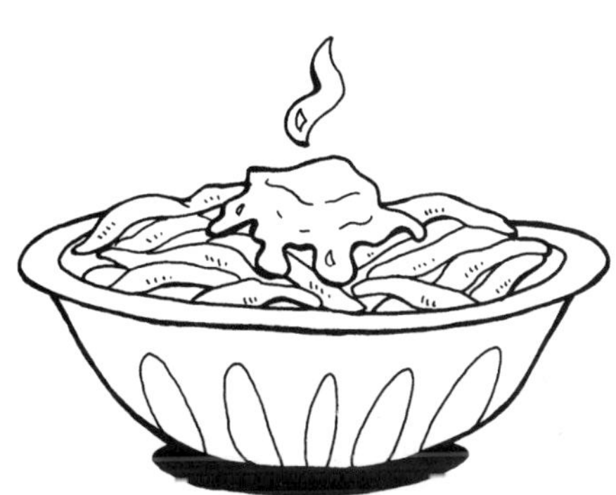

More Ideas

- Green Beans Almondine: Sauté 1/2 cup of slivered almonds in 2 tablespoons of butter and add them to cooked green beans.
- Country Green Beans: Sauté 1/3 cup of chopped smoked ham and 3 tablespoons of minced onion in 1 tablespoon of butter until the onion is transparent. Add the mixture to cooked green beans. Add 1/4 cup chopped parsley and 3 tablespoons of toasted almonds. Heat and serve hot.

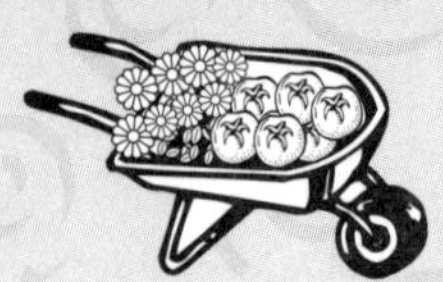

Green Bean Salad

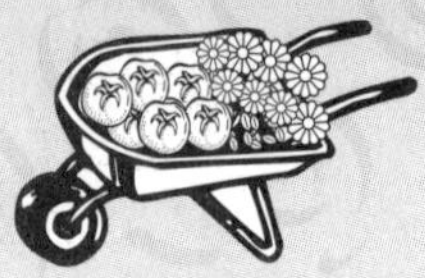

Materials

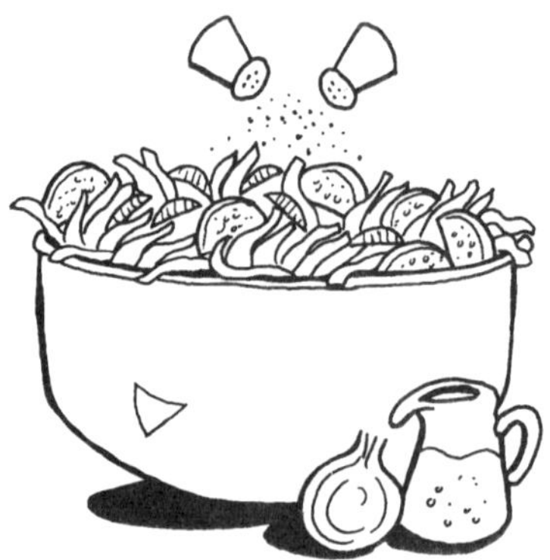

- 2 cups green beans (use drained canned cut green beans or fresh green beans cooked until crisply tender)
- 1 medium onion, sliced
- 1 large ripe tomato
- 6 tablespoons olive oil
- 3 tablespoons wine vinegar
- ½ teaspoon garlic salt
- ¼ teaspoon black pepper
- saucepan with lid
- bowl
- knife
- cutting board
- colander
- mixing spoon

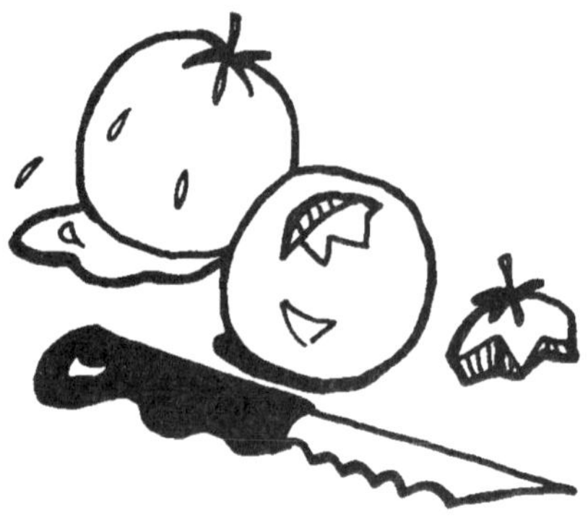

Let's Do It !

1. Wash and core the tomato and then cut it into bite-sized pieces.
2. Wash the green beans and remove the strings, if necessary.
3. Cook the beans in ½ cup of water in a covered saucepan until crisply tender. Drain the beans in the colander and allow them to cool.
4. Combine the tomato, beans, onion, olive oil, vinegar, garlic salt, and pepper in a bowl and mix them thoroughly.
5. Chill at least one hour before serving.

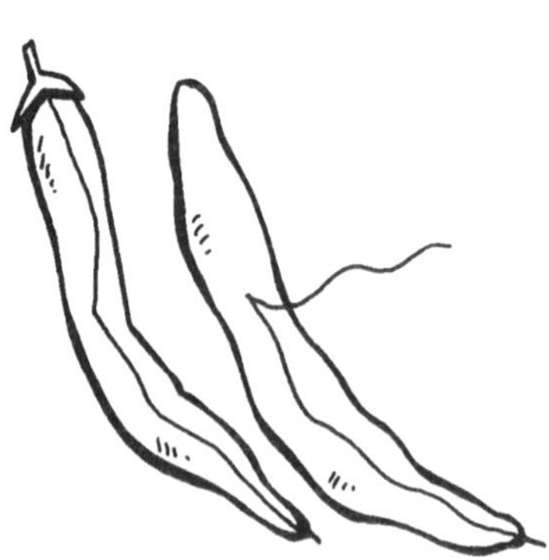

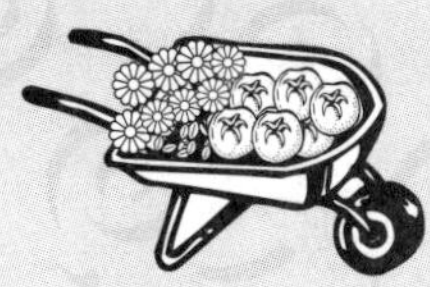

Three-Bean Salad

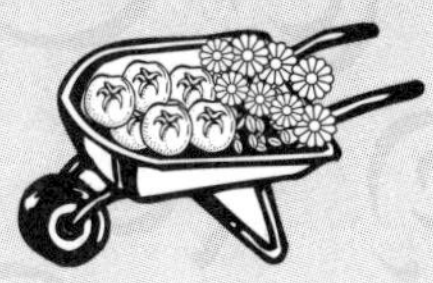

Materials

- 1 can wax beans, cut
- 1 can green beans, cut
- 1 can kidney beans
- $^{1}/_{2}$ cup celery, sliced thin
- 1 green pepper, sliced thin
- 1 small jar chopped pimiento
- 1 small onion, chopped
- 1 clove garlic, minced
- $^{2}/_{3}$ cup sugar
- $^{1}/_{2}$ cup wine vinegar
- 1 teaspoon salt
- $^{1}/_{2}$ teaspoon pepper
- small saucepan
- $1^{1}/_{2}$ quart casserole dish with lid
- colander
- cooking spoon

Let's Do It !

1. Drain the liquid from the beans and the pimiento. (If you use fresh green beans, remove the strings, wash them, and snap them in half. Cook covered in $^{1}/_{2}$ cup of water until crisply tender. Drain and cool.)
2. Combine all of the ingredients in the first column in a casserole dish.
3. Prepare the marinade.
   - Combine the sugar, vinegar, salt, and pepper in a saucepan.
   - Heat and stir until the sugar is dissolved.
   - Remove the pan from the heat and cool five minutes.
   - Pour the marinade over the bean mixture.

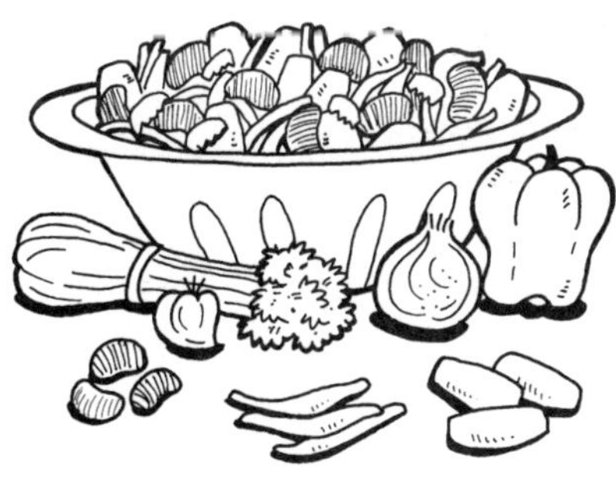

4. Cover the dish and chill the salad in the refrigerator overnight. Stir a few times.
5. Serve chilled.

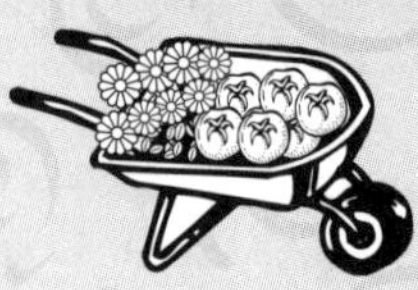

Kid-Sized Bean Teepee

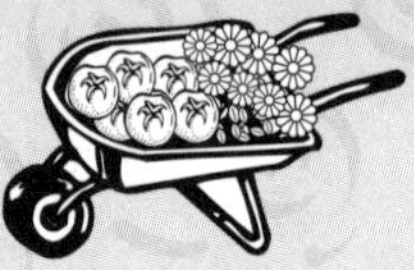

Materials

- 6 poles or stakes 6'–8' long
- heavy twine
- mulch
- straw
- hoe
- bean seeds

Let's Do It !

1. Use the hoe to make a raised hill about 4' in diameter.
2. Arrange the poles in a large circle just inside the perimeter of the hill and tie them together at the top with twine.
3. Leave the space between two of the stakes open enough for a child to crawl through.
4. Mulch inside the teepee.
5. Plant bean seeds in holes 2" deep by the poles.

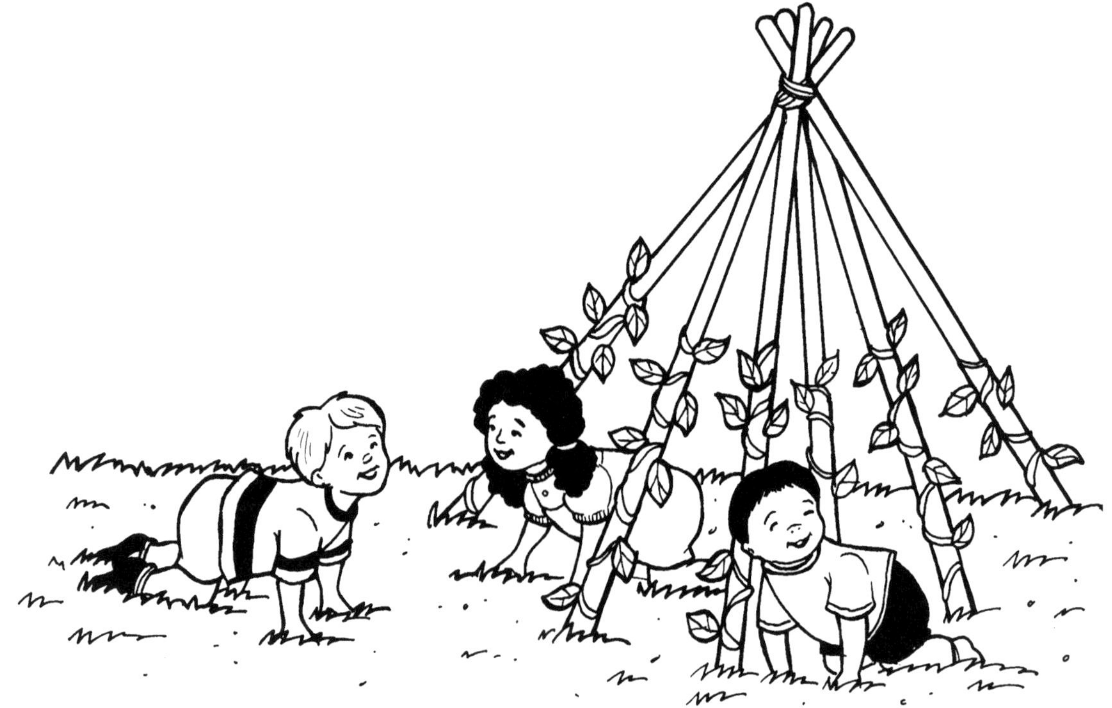

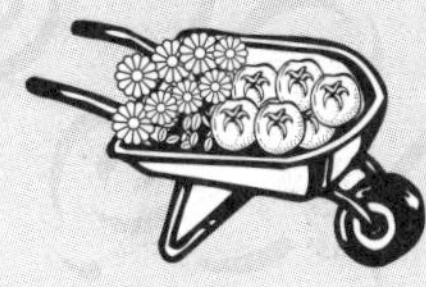

Seed Jewelry

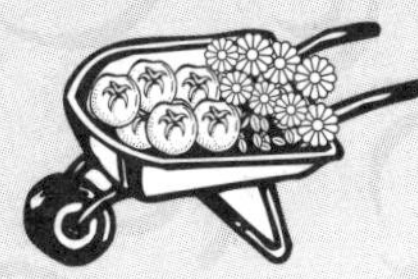

Materials

- assorted seeds (dried peas and beans, sunflower, watermelon, black-eyed peas, squash, pumpkin, cantaloupe)
- heavy thread
- blunt-tip needle
- thimble
- scissors

Let's Do It !

1. Cut a piece of thread long enough to go around your neck or wrist. Leave about three inches to tie the ends.
2. Lay out seeds in a pattern to string onto your bracelet or necklace.
3. Use the needle and thimble to string the seeds onto the thread. Tie a knot in the thread after you string each seed to hold it securely.

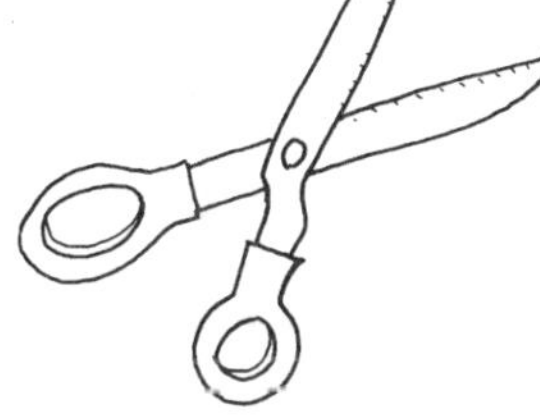

More Ideas

- Make a headband out of poster board. Glue seeds to the headband.
- Make a seed mosaic by cutting out a shape from poster board. Glue seeds onto the shape. Turn your mosaic into a wall hanging by gluing thick rug yarn around the edge of the shape to make a frame.
- Decorate juice cans by gluing on seed designs.
- Draw a picture on poster board or construction paper and glue seeds onto the drawing. Decorate with markers or crayons.

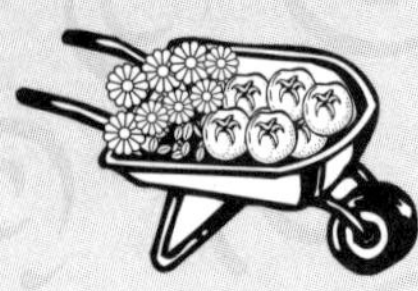

Hot Weather Theme Garden

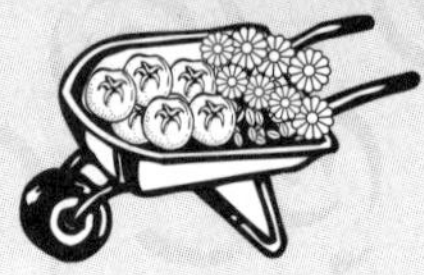

Materials

- hoe
- garden rake
- trowel
- craft sticks
- seeds or seedlings of summer vegetables
- fine-tip permanent marker
- fertilizer
- supports for plants

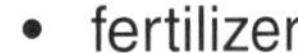

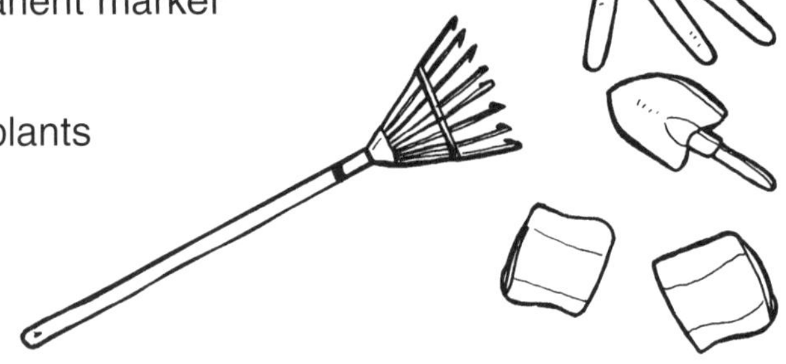

Let's Do It !

1. Plan where you will plant each vegetable and the space you need for each.
2. Work the fertilizer into well-tilled soil.
3. Make rows or hills for your vegetables and label them with the craft sticks. Check this book and the backs of seed packets for planting information. See page 20 for "companion planting" information.
4. Provide support for tomatoes, beans, and cucumbers.
5. Plant the seeds and seedlings and water them thoroughly.
6. Remove weeds and regularly watch for insects or pests.
7. Water the garden and thin plants, as needed.
8. Harvest each crop as it matures.

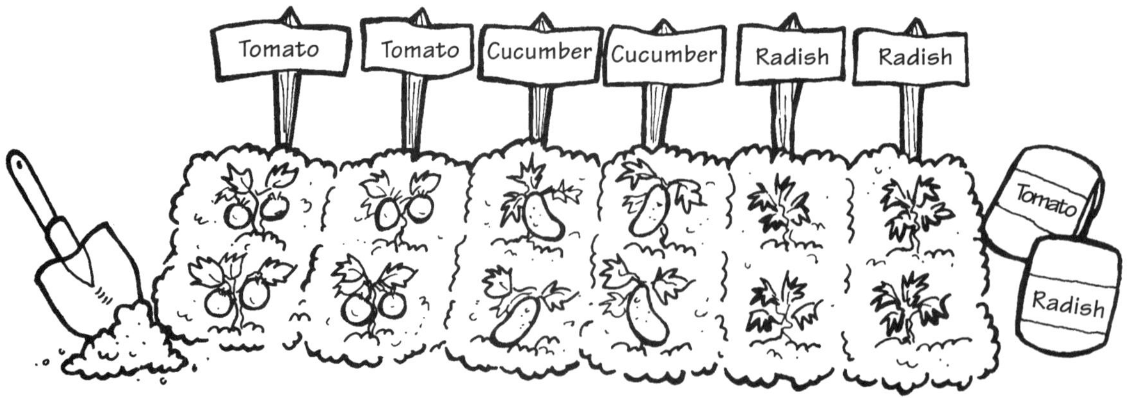

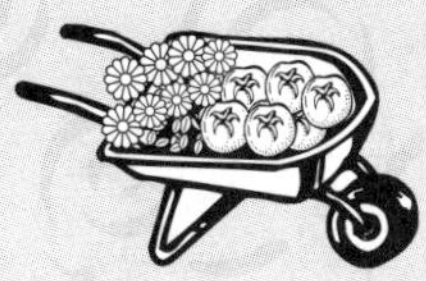

Hot Weather Theme Garden

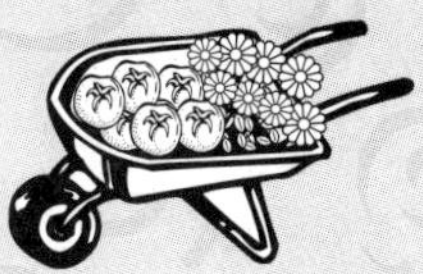

More Ideas

- Plant different varieties of lettuce and spinach.
- Plant successive crops to enjoy over a longer time.
- Plant a fruit salad garden with strawberries, watermelon, and cantaloupe.

Tidbits

✧ Plant summer gardens after the last frost.

✧ Theme gardens are interesting and creative to plan and grow.

✧ It's fun to make salads from vegetables and fruit you grow yourself.

Learn More

Draznin, Sharon. *Simple Cooking Fun.* Huntington Beach, CA: Teacher Created Resources, Inc., 1997.

Ehlert, Lois. *Eating the Alphabet: Fruits & Vegetables from A to Z.* New York: Harcourt Children's Books, Publishers, 1989.

Potter, Beatrix. *The Tale of Peter Rabbit and Other Stories.* New York: Knopf, 1982.

Stewart, Martha. *Martha Stewart's Gardening Month by Month.* New York: Clarkson Potter Publishers, 1991.

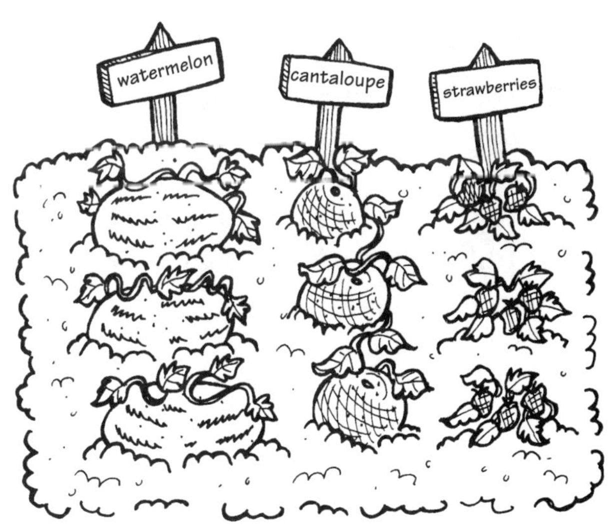

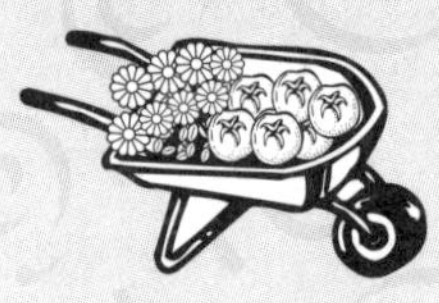

Crunchy Salad with Dressing

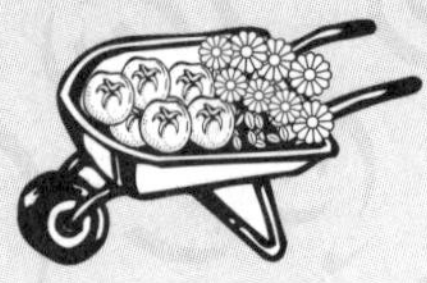

Materials

- $^1/_2$ pound fresh spinach, washed and torn
- 2 tablespoons slivered almonds
- $^3/_4$ cup shredded red cabbage
- $^1/_4$ cup raisins
- $^1/_2$ cup celery, sliced
- $^1/_4$ cup sugar
- $^3/_4$ teaspoon dry mustard
- $^3/_4$ teaspoon salt
- $1^1/_2$ tablespoon onion, minced
- $^1/_4$ cup vinegar
- $^1/_2$ cup vegetable oil
- jar with lid
- pie pan

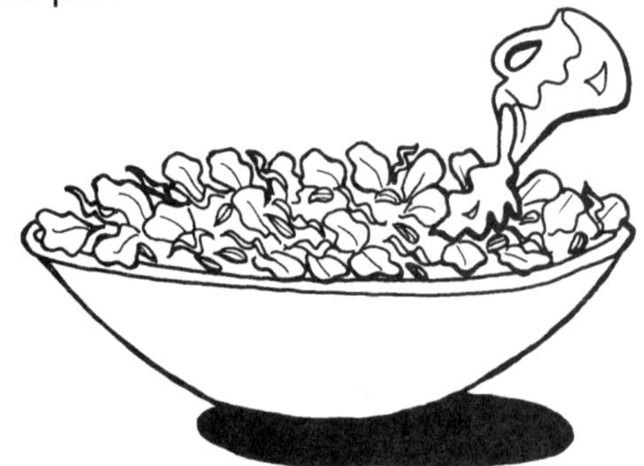

Let's Do It !

1. Put the slivered almonds in a pie pan and toast them in the oven at 400°F.
2. Combine the vegetables, toasted almonds, and raisins in a salad bowl and chill overnight.
3. Prepare the dressing.
   - Put minced onion, sugar, dry mustard, salt, vinegar, and oil in a jar.
   - Put the jar lid on tightly and shake the jar vigorously.
   - Chill the dressing for several hours.
4. Shake the dressing well, pour it on the salad, and toss together.

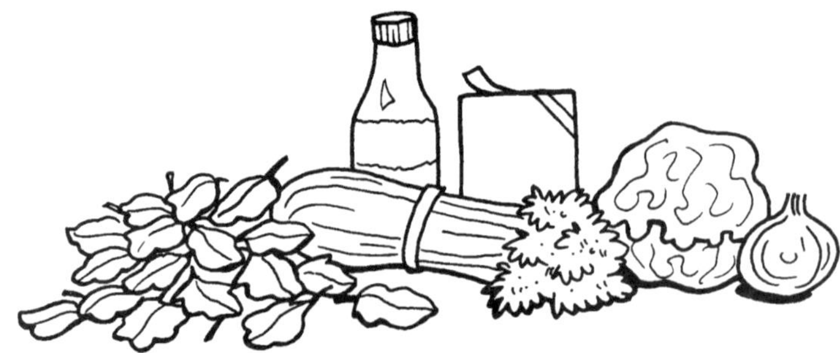

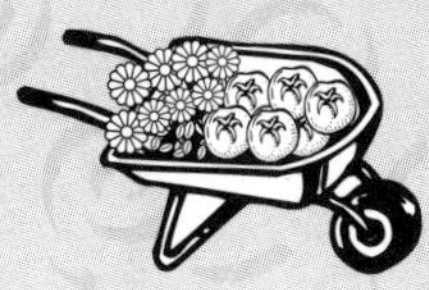

Salad Party

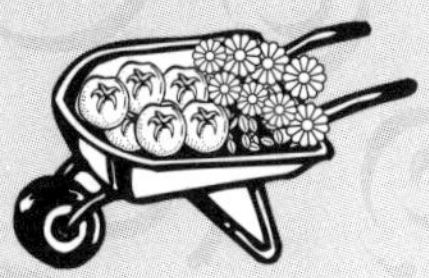

Materials

- lettuce
- spinach, stems removed
- assorted other vegetables, sliced
- assorted crackers
- assorted salad dressings
- plastic forks
- paper plates
- napkins
- paper cups
- serving plates or bowls
- beverages
- large resealable plastic bags

Let's Do It !

1. Wash and prepare vegetables ahead of time. Chill in large resealable plastic bags.
2. Set a table buffet style.
3. Let everyone make his or her own salad.

More Ideas

- Provide unsalted sunflower seeds, nuts, whole-grain croutons, and other healthy additions for guests to sample on their salads.
- Make herb salad dressing (page 120) to serve with your salad fixings.

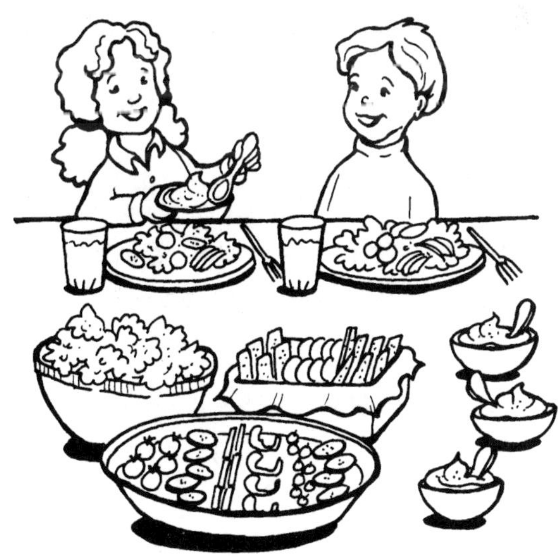

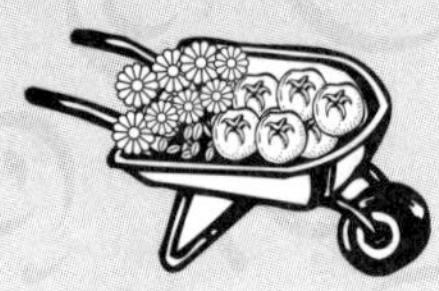

Squash and Cucumbers

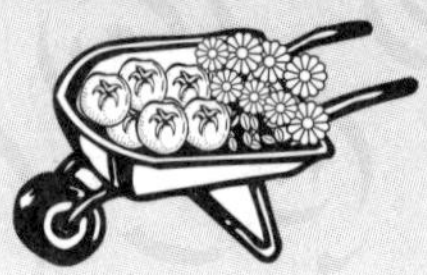

Materials

- seeds for a variety of squash and cucumbers
- fertilizer
- trowel
- hoe
- hose or watering can
- craft sticks
- fine-tip permanent marker
- garden rake
- sharp knife
- trellis

Let's Do It !

1. Work the fertilizer into well-tilled soil.
2. Plant seeds in raised hills about 3' in diameter across and 6" high or in raised rows 2'–3' wide. Plant 3–4 seeds in each hill according to package directions. Label with the craft sticks.
3. Cover the seeds and water them thoroughly.
4. Water and weed the plants regularly. Watch for squash borers, stink bugs, and mildew. Bugs can be handpicked off the plants.
5. Pick summer squash and cucumbers before they get too big and tough. Use a knife to cut through thick stems.

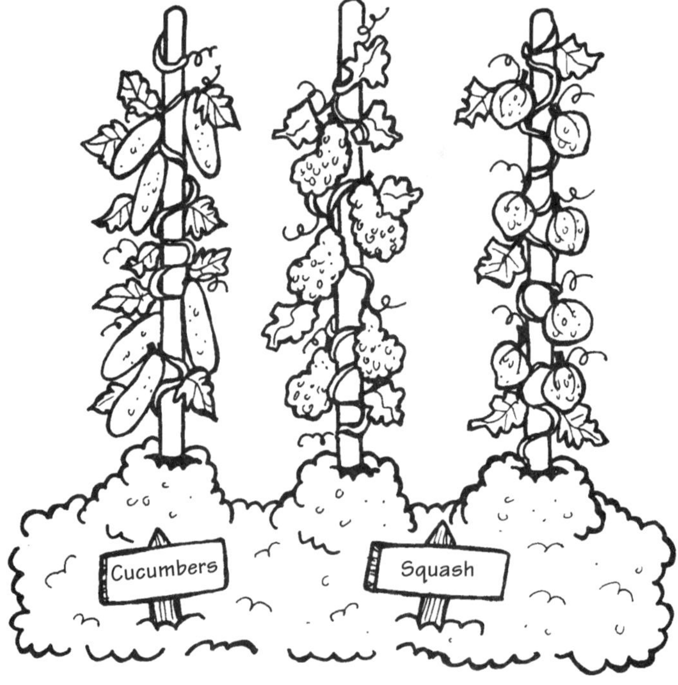

6. After harvesting, remove any diseased plants from the garden. Turn into the soil the remaining healthy plants.

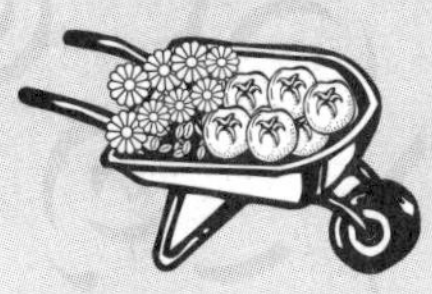

Squash and Cucumbers

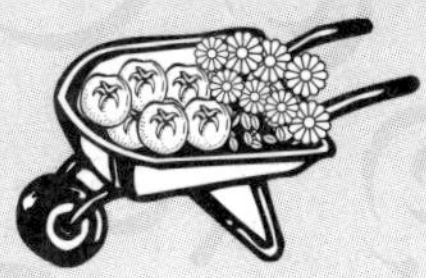

More Ideas

- Plant nonvining cucumbers or squash in large containers.
- Plant summer squash (yellow crookneck or zucchini), fall squash (acorn or butternut), and winter squash (Hubbard).
- Use wire fencing with 4" mesh to make a vertical or tunnel trellis.

Tidbits

✧ Seeds may be planted a week or two before the last frost is expected.

✧ Squash and cucumbers are members of the same vining-vegetable family as pumpkins and gourds.

✧ Summer and fall squash and cucumbers are picked when immature and tender; winter squash are picked when they are mature.

Learn More

Carle, Eric. *The Very Hungry Caterpillar.* New York: Philomel Books, 1969.

Ehlert, Lois. *Growing Vegetable Soup.* New York: Scholastic, Inc.,1987.

Thacher Hurd, Edith. *Tomato Soup.* New York: Crown Publisher, Inc., 1992.

Penner, Lucille R. *A Native American Feast.* New York: Macmillan Publishing Co., 1994.

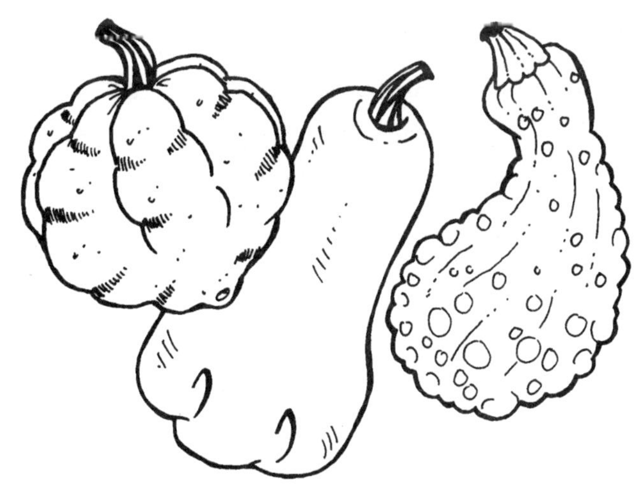

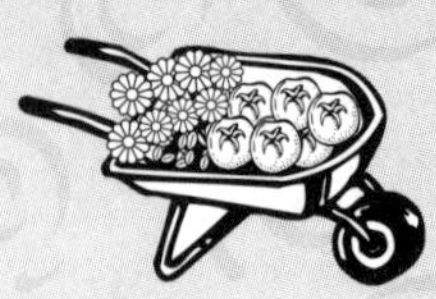

Stir-Fry Squash Medley

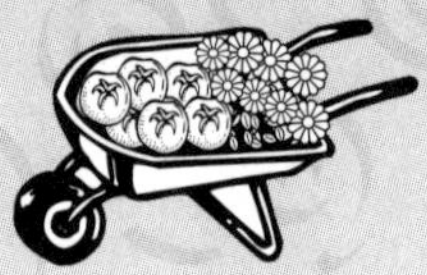

Materials

- 2 or 3 yellow crookneck squash
- 1 zucchini squash
- 1 or 2 carrots
- 1–2 tablespoons vegetable oil
- frying pan
- salt and pepper
- other vegetables (green beans, peas, broccoli)

Let's Do It !

1. Wash the vegetables, and cut off the stems and ends.
2. Slice the squash 1/4" thick and carrots at an angle, 1/8"–1/4" thick.
3. Put the vegetable oil into a frying pan and sauté the vegetables over a medium heat until crisply tender. Stir gently and add seasonings.
4. Serve hot.

Tidbits

✧ Summer squashes include zucchini, straight neck, crook neck, patty pan, and cocozelle and should be picked when they are firm and heavy.

✧ Winter squashes include acorn, banana, butternut, pumpkin, and Hubbard and should be picked when their rinds are hard.

✧ Some squash flowers can be fried and eaten.

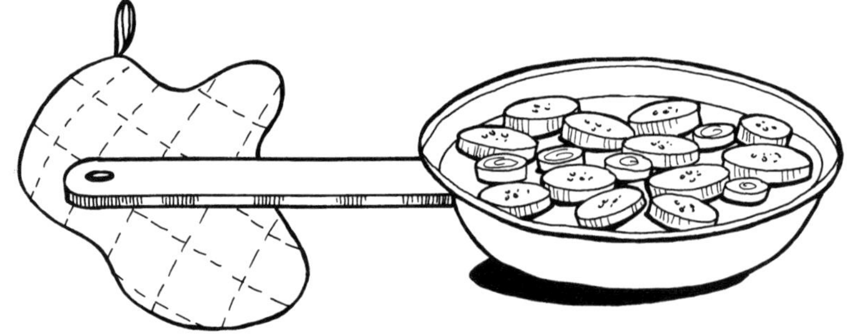

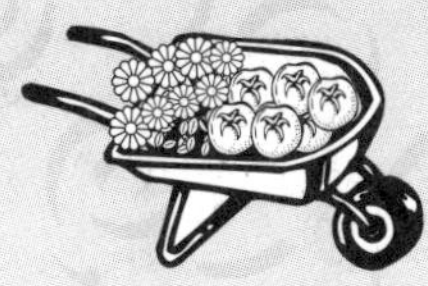

Butternut Squash with Nutmeg

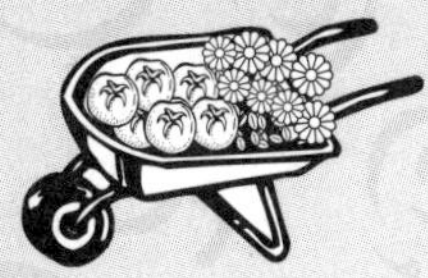

Materials

- 1 butternut squash
- 2 tablespoons butter
- 1/2 teaspoon nutmeg
- 1/4 teaspoon pepper
- knife
- cutting board
- 1/2 cup of water
- saucepan with lid

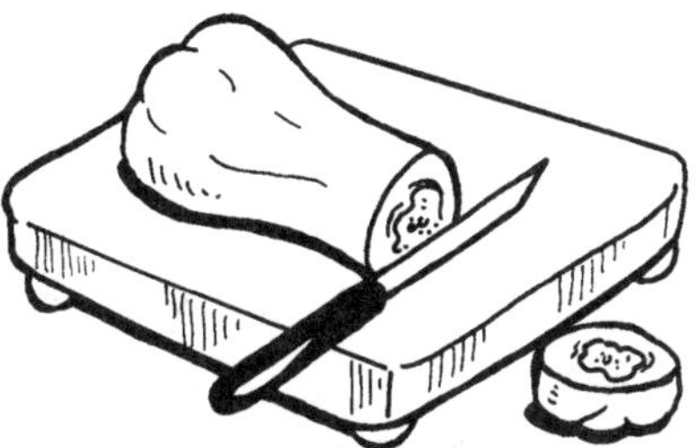

Let's Do It !

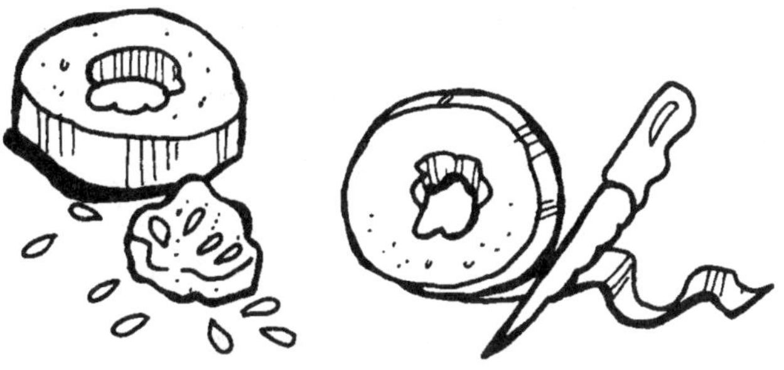

1. Cut off the stem and bottom of the squash.
2. Cut the squash into 1" slices and remove the seeds and membrane.
3. Pare off the outer skin and then cut the squash into bite-size chunks.
4. Put the chunks in a saucepan with 1/2 cup of water and cook until tender—about 20 minutes. Drain the squash.
5. Add butter, nutmeg, and pepper, and stir until the butter is melted and the seasonings are well blended. You may wish to mash the squash.
6. Separate the seeds from the membrane, wash and dry them, and save them for seed-related art activities.

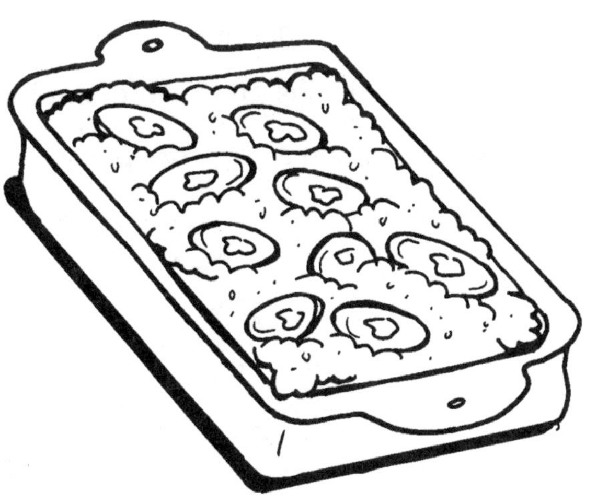

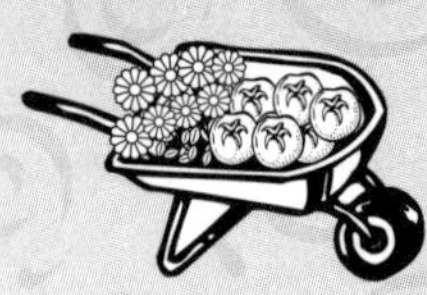

Pumpkins

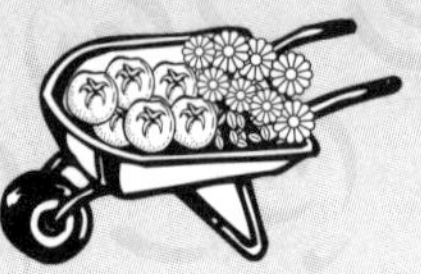

Materials

- pumpkin seeds
- fertilizer
- hoe
- garden rake
- hose or watering can

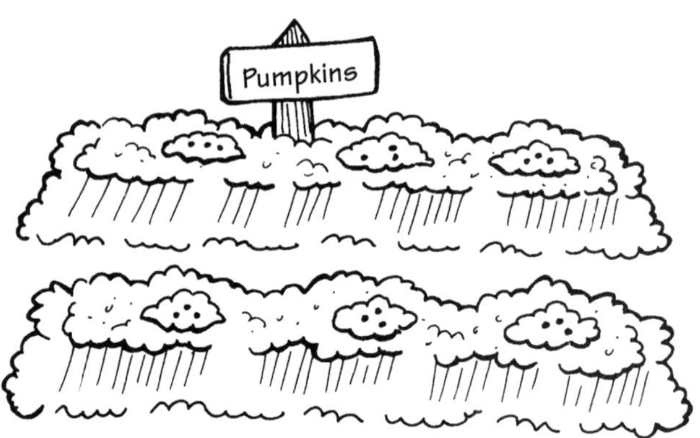

Let's Do It !

1. Work the fertilizer into well-tilled soil. To reduce leaf growth, avoid giving plants fertilizer high in nitrogen.
2. Use the hoe to build raised hills or raised rows at least 2' apart.
3. Plant 3–4 seeds in each hill or in rows according to package directions.
4. Cover the seeds and water them thoroughly. Weed and water the plants regularly.
5. Pinch off the tops of vines after the plants bloom and baby pumpkins begin to develop. This diverts more nutrients to the pumpkins.
6. Watch for insects that need to be removed.
7. When the pumpkins are mature, cut them off the vines, leaving a stem on each pumpkin.
8. Store pumpkins in a cool, dry place.

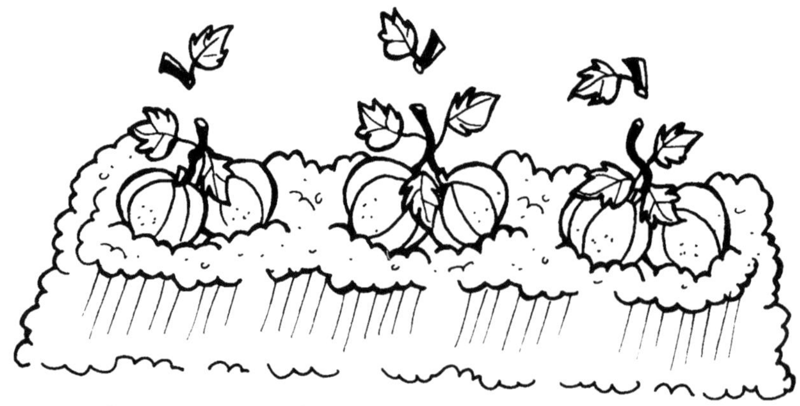

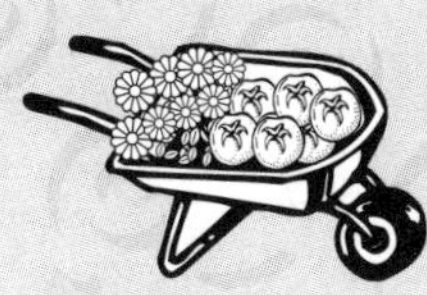

Pumpkins

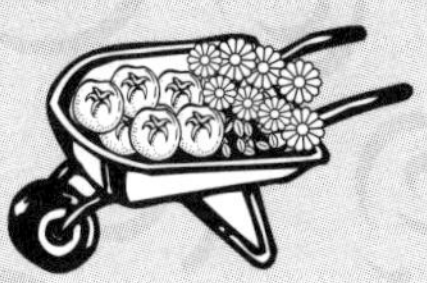

More Ideas

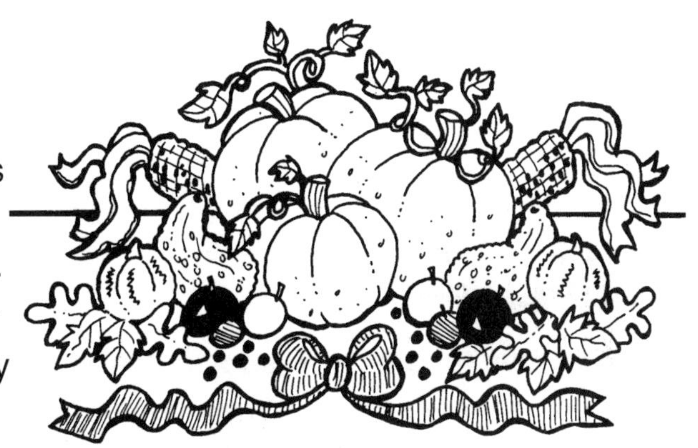

- Plant Jack-Be-Little pumpkins to stuff and bake or to use for fall decorations.
- Plant gourds along a fence line or trellis.
- Make a centerpiece decoration with pumpkins of various sizes.
- Make a pumpkin man by stacking three different sized pumpkins (from large to small) after removing the stems of each one. Decorate by drawing a face, gluing on stick arms, and adding a scarf and hat.
- Place a flower pot in a hollowed out pumpkin to make a decorative centerpiece.

Tidbits

✧ Pumpkins are in the same family of vegetables as cucumbers and squash.

✧ There are different varieties of pumpkins. Some are better for cooking, while others make good jack-o'-lanterns.

Learn More

Berenstain, S. and J. Berenstain. *The Berenstain Bears and the Prize Pumpkin.* New York: Random House, 1990.

Hall, Zoe. *It's Pumpkin Time.* New York: Scholastic Paperbacks, 1999.

King, Elizabeth. *The Pumpkin Patch.* New York: Duttons Children's Books, 1990.

Penner, Lucille. *A Native American Feast.* New York: Macmillan Publishing Company, 1994.

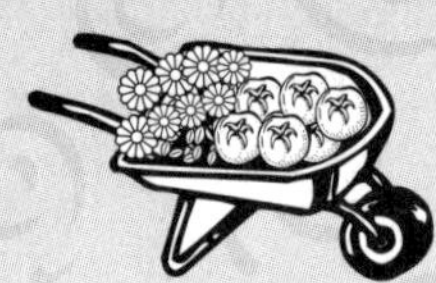

Pumpkin Seed Fun

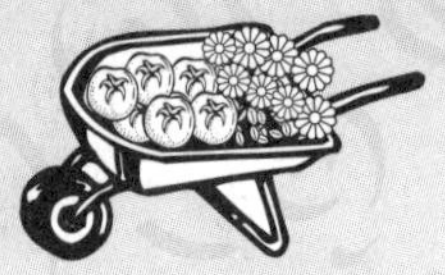

Pumpkin Seed Snack

Materials

- seeds from 1 large pumpkin
- paper towels
- 1 teaspoon salt
- shallow baking pan
- mixing bowl
- 2 tablespoons melted butter or vegetable oil
- mixing spoon

Let's Do It !

1. Remove the pumpkin seeds from the membrane and then wash and dry them using a paper towel.
2. Preheat the oven to 250°F.
3. In a bowl, mix the seeds and salt with melted butter or oil, stirring until the seeds are coated.
4. Spread seeds one layer deep in a baking pan. Bake about 45 minutes or until golden brown.
5. Allow the seeds to cool before eating them, and store extras in an airtight container.

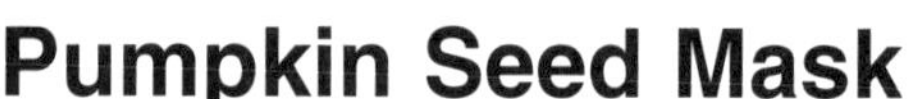

Pumpkin Seed Mask

Materials

- large paper bag
- pumpkin seeds
- markers
- glue
- pencil
- scissors
- construction paper

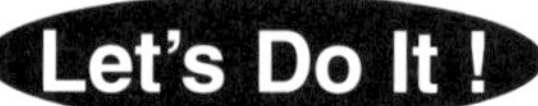

Let's Do It !

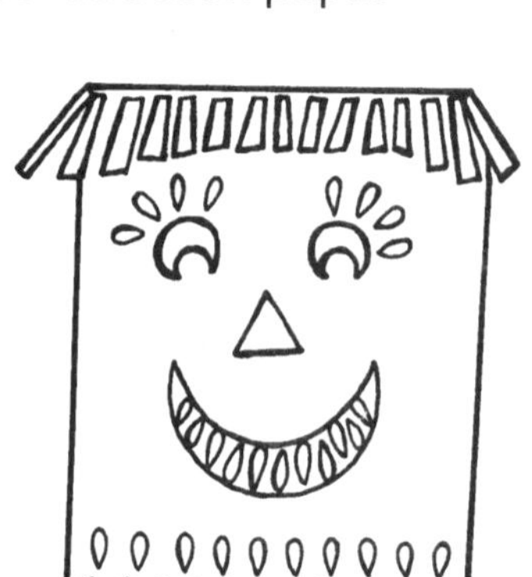

1. Draw a face on one side of the paper bag.
2. Cut out the eyes.
3. Glue pumpkin seeds on the face.
4. Use markers and construction paper to further decorate the mask.

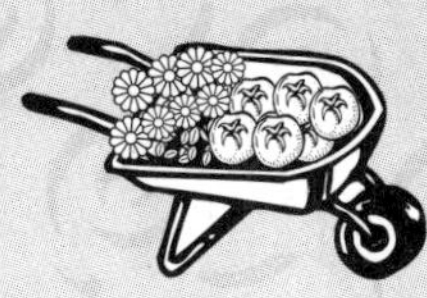

Vegetable Decorated Jack-o'-Lantern

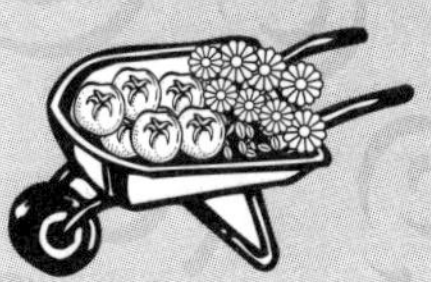

Materials

- pumpkin
- chili pepper or carrot
- red, green, or yellow bell pepper
- spoon
- leaves from celery stalks
- long-bladed knife
- toothpicks
- votive candle in holder
- paper and pencil

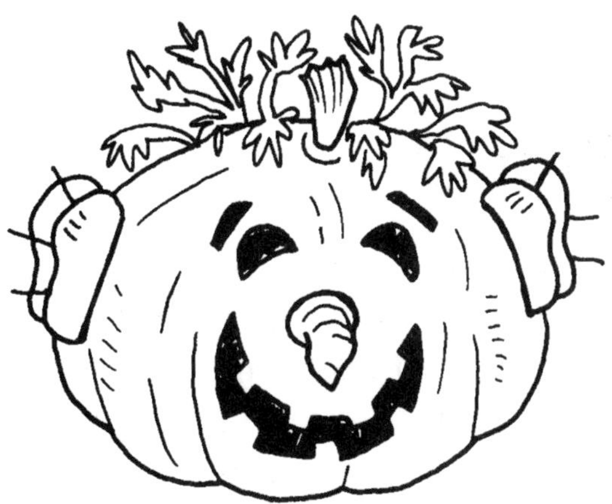

Let's Do It !

1. On paper, experiment with different designs for your pumpkin. Do you want a scary face, silly face, happy face, or sad face?
2. Cut out a "lid" from the top of the pumpkin and scoop out the seeds and membrane. Carve out the eyes and mouth.
3. Carve out a nose, or cut a hole large enough to hold a carrot or chili pepper nose.
4. Cut a bell pepper in half, and use each half for ears. Attach them with toothpicks.
5. Use toothpicks to attach celery leaves as hair.
6. Place the votive candle inside the pumpkin, and have an adult light it at night.

More Ideas

- Save the pumpkin seeds to roast or to dry and use for seed art.
- String dried pumpkin seeds on thread to make a necklace or bracelet.

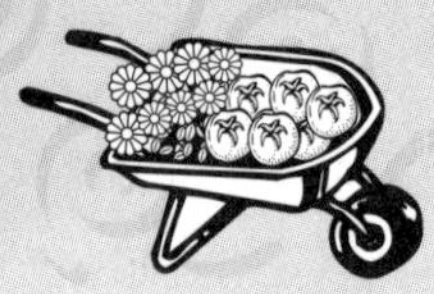

Cool Weather Theme Garden

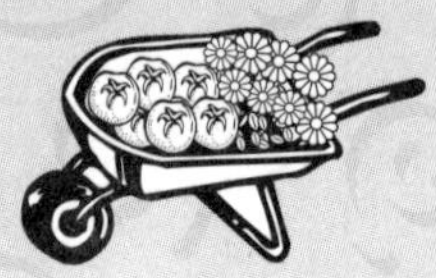

Materials

- seedlings (plant sets) for fall vegetables
- hoe
- garden rake
- trowel
- supports for plants
- fertilizer
- craft sticks
- fine-tip permanent marker
- watering can or hose

Let's Do It !

1. Plan where you will plant each vegetable and the space you need for each.
2. Work the fertilizer into well-tilled soil.
3. Water the seedlings well the day before you transplant them into the ground.
4. Make rows or hills for your vegetables and label them with the craft sticks.
5. Plant most seedlings the same depth as their containers. Plant tomatoes slightly deeper.
6. Provide support for vining vegetables.
7. Transplant the seedlings and water them thoroughly.
8. Remove weeds and look for insect pests regularly.
9. Water the garden and thin plants, as needed.
10. Harvest each crop as it matures.

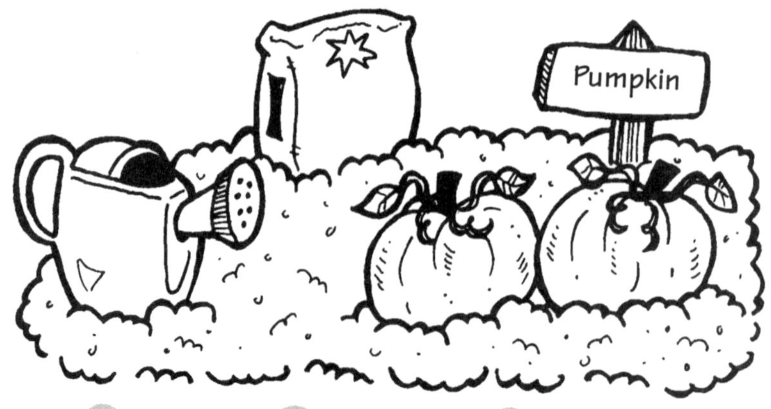

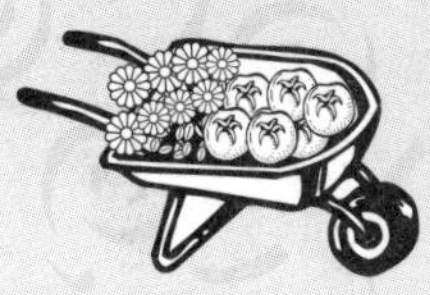

Cool Weather Theme Garden

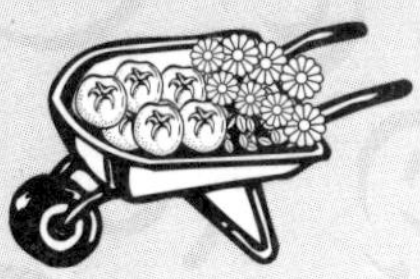

More Ideas

- For a succession of crops, plant seeds two weeks apart.
- Add cool weather flowers for color—pansies, flowering cabbage and kale, or calendula.

Tidbits

✧ Green leafy vegetables benefit from higher nitrogen while root vegetables need more phosphorous.

✧ Another type of theme garden is one whose plants start with A, B, C, etc.

✧ Some plants grow better in cool weather and can withstand light frost.

Learn More

Pohl, Kathleen. *Dandelions.* Milwaukee, MN: Raintree Publishers, 1987.

Potter, Beatrix. *The Tale of Benjamin Bunny.* New York: Crown Publishers, 1980.

Stewart, Martha. *Martha Stewart's Gardening Month by Month.* New York: Clarkson Potter Publishers, 1991.

Wilmer, Diane and Anne Currey. *Mr. Pepino's Cabbage.* New York: Gallery Books, 1989.

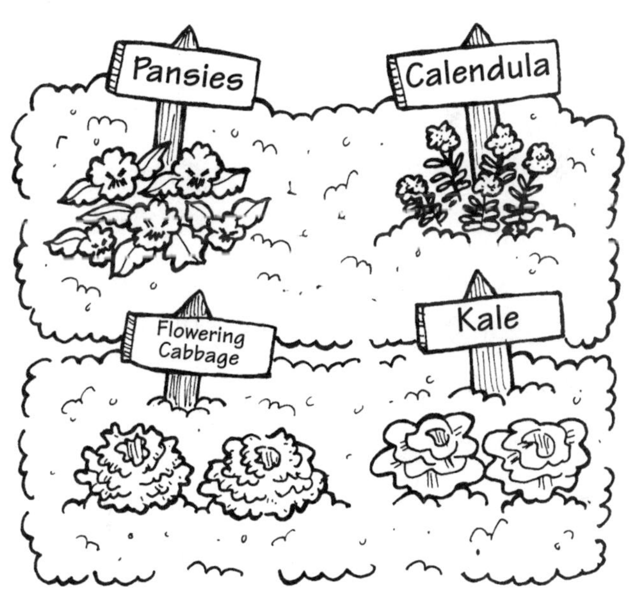

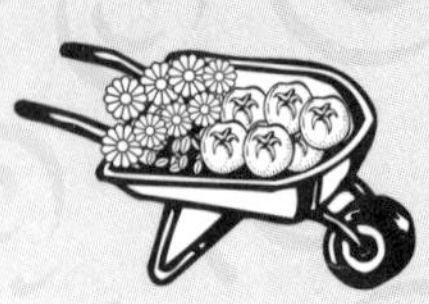

Sautéed Winter Greens

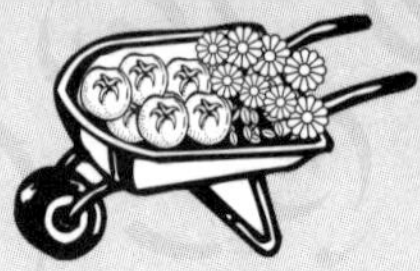

Materials

- assorted greens (cabbage, kale, spinach, Chinese cabbage)
- colander
- onion, sliced
- 1/4 teaspoon pepper
- 2 tablespoons vegetable oil
- frying pan or wok
- knife

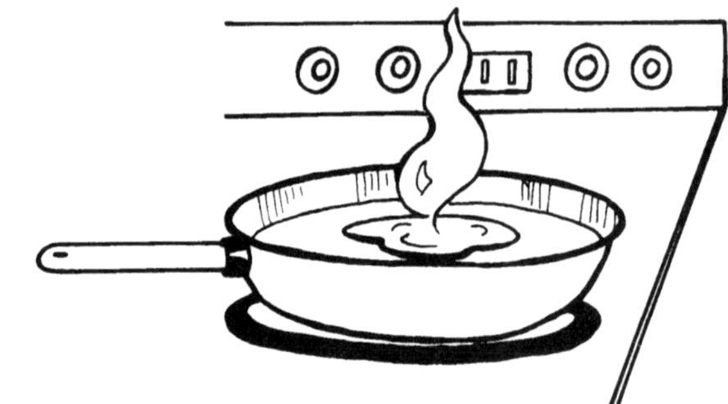

Let's Do It !

1. Wash the greens well and drain them in a colander.
2. Remove any thick stems. Remove the central core in cabbage.
3. Heat the oil in the frying pan or wok.
4. Add the onions and greens, and sauté them over a medium heat until crisply tender, stirring frequently. Add pepper to taste.
5. Serve hot.

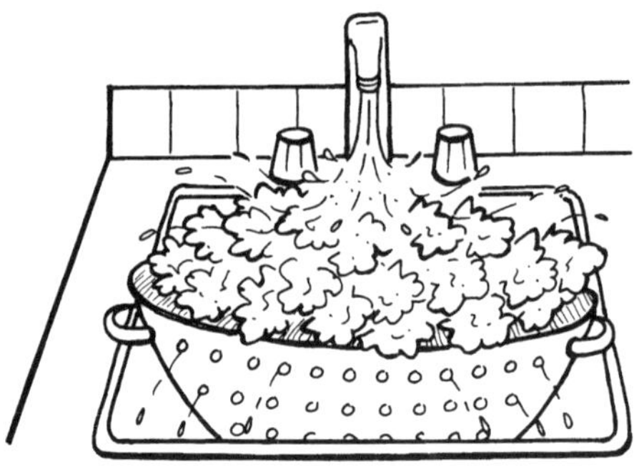

More Ideas

- Add poppy seeds or chopped hard-boiled egg after cooking.
- For color, add sautéed carrots and red or gold bell peppers.
- Serve over or mixed into a bed of rice or pasta.
- Add garbanzo beans or water chestnuts after cooking.

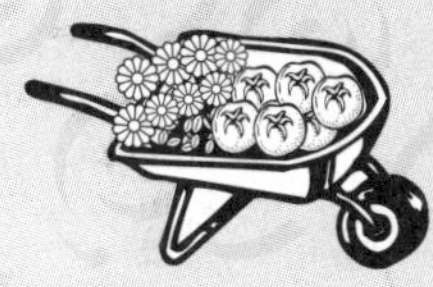

Broccoli Salad

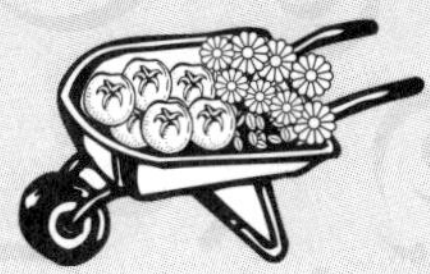

Materials

- 1 head broccoli
- 1 small yellow (Spanish) onion, chopped
- 8 pieces bacon
- 1/3 cup slivered almonds
- 1/3 cup raisins
- 1 cup mayonnaise
- knife
- 1/3 cup sugar
- 1 tablespoon vinegar
- frying pan and cooking fork
- mixing bowl
- small bowl
- paper towels
- cutting board

Let's Do It !

1. Wash the broccoli and trim off the heavy stalks. Chop up the broccoli florettes.
2. Fry the bacon until crisp, drain it on paper towels, and break it into bits.
3. In a mixing bowl, stir together the broccoli, almonds, raisins, onion, and bacon bits.
4. Prepare the dressing by combining the mayonnaise, sugar, and vinegar in a small bowl.
5. Refrigerate the broccoli salad and dressing.
6. Add the dressing to the salad and toss together just before serving.

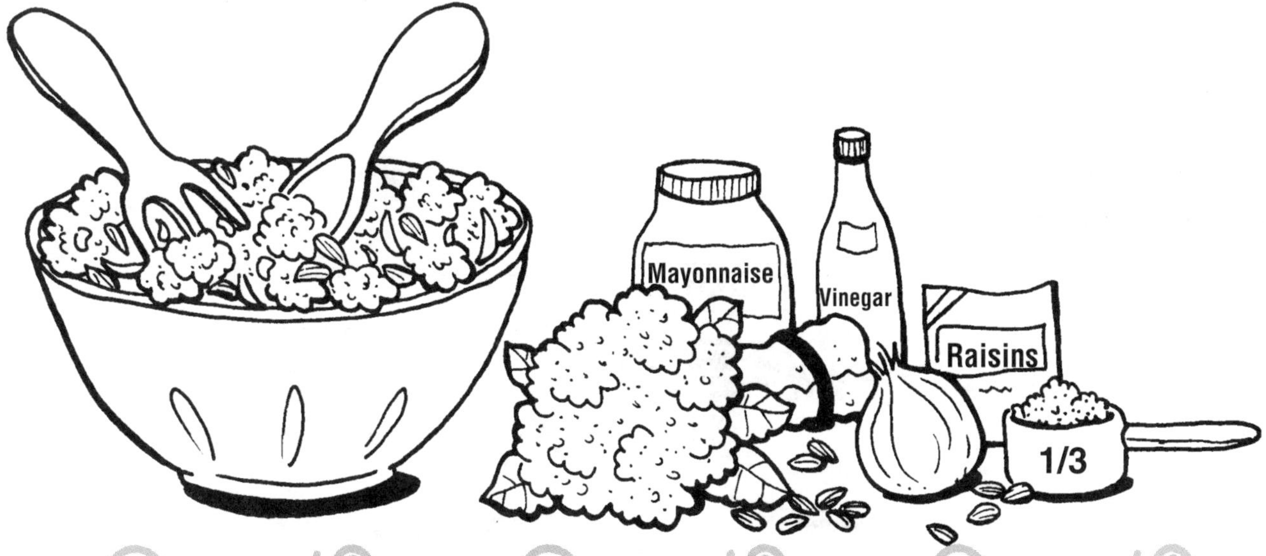

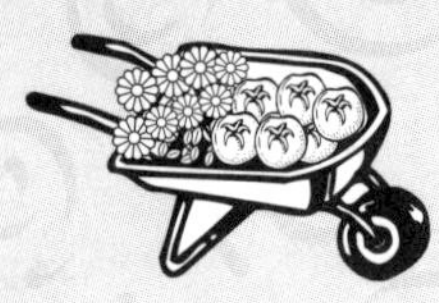

Bubble and Squeak— An English Dish

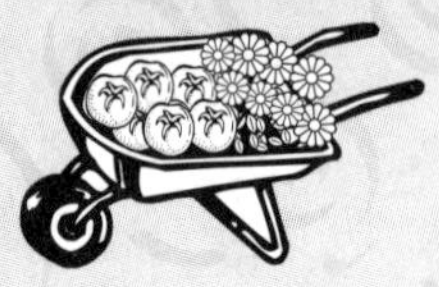

Materials

- leftover mashed potatoes
- leftover cooked cabbage or Brussels sprouts
- salt and pepper
- 2 tablespoons butter
- frying pan
- wide metal spatula
- mixing bowl

Let's Do It !

1. Mix the mashed potatoes and cabbage (and other vegetables) together in a mixing bowl and add a dash of salt and pepper.
2. Melt the butter in the frying pan and add the vegetable mixture. Press the mixture down firmly with a spatula. This will form a "vegetable pie."
3. Cook on medium heat until the pie is lightly browned on the bottom. Turn it over and brown the other side.
4. Serve hot.

More Ideas

- After cooking, add steamed turnips and sautéed leeks.

Tidbits

✧ Bubble and Squeak is named for the sounds that cooked cabbage and potatoes make when fried together in oil.

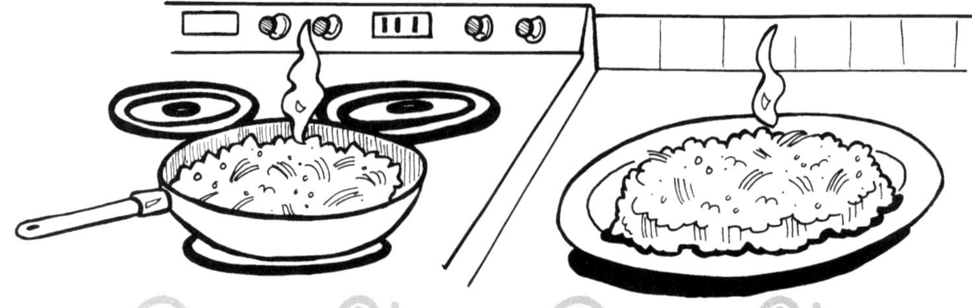

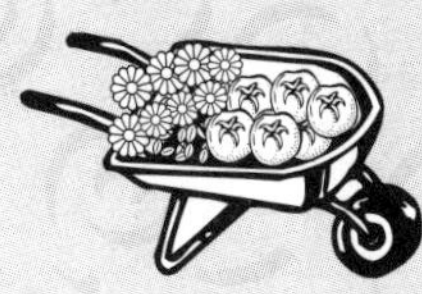

Vegetable Printers

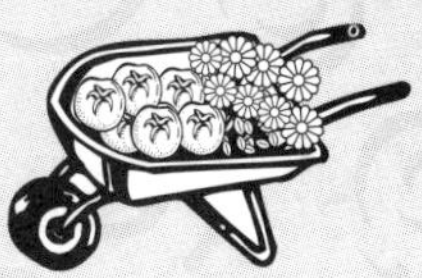

Materials

- assorted vegetables—onions, carrots, sweet potatoes, turnips, potatoes, celery
- dry corncobs
- newsprint or construction paper
- newspaper
- Styrofoam trays
- paring knife
- tempera paint or fingerpaint, assorted colors
- water and container for rinsing

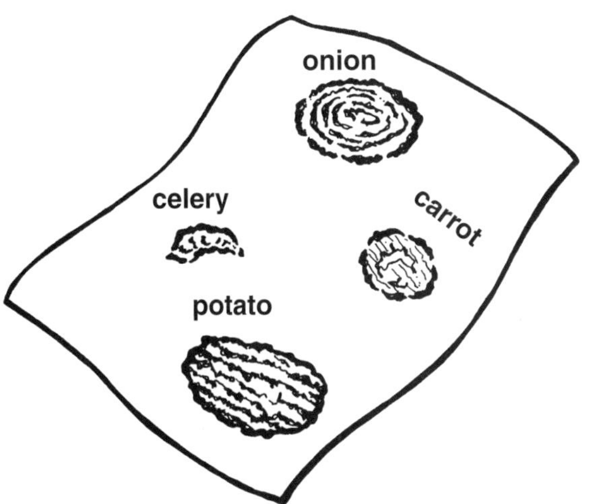

Let's Do It !

1. Cover the work area with newspaper. Pour a small amount of each paint into a Styrofoam tray.
2. Cut the onions in half so the interior circular pattern is visible.
3. Cut one end off the carrots and celery. Use the celery leaves, too.
4. Cut the turnips and potatoes in half and draw a design, letter, or shape on the cut surface. Trim the flesh away from the design.
5. Rub the corncobs to remove any loose particles.
6. Dip the vegetables in paint and press them onto a piece of paper, repeating as often as you wish.
7. Dip the corncob in paint lengthwise to capture the textured surface design and press or roll it on paper.
8. Rinse the printers in water before changing to another color of paint.

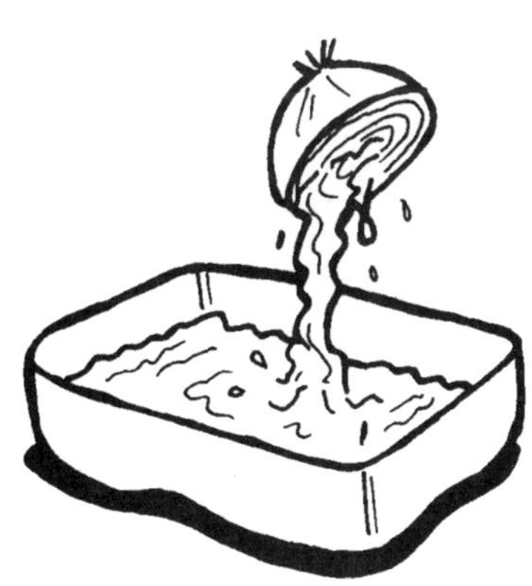

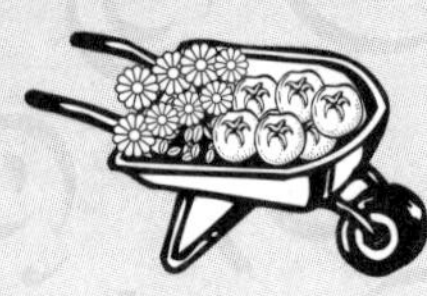

Root Gardens

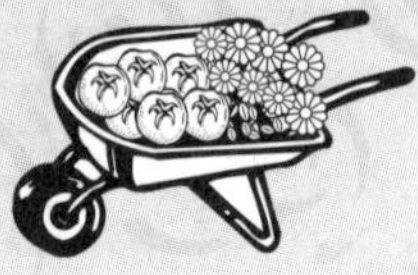

Materials

- seeds for early producing varieties of assorted root vegetables
- compost or peat
- hoe
- garden rake
- fertilizer
- craft sticks
- fine-tip permanent marker
- water hose or watering can

Let's Do It !

1. Mix compost or peat and fertilizer into well-tilled soil.
2. Follow planting directions on the seed packages. Plant tiny seeds very shallow, and tamp the soil down gently.
3. Label rows or sections with craft sticks.
4. After planting, water the seeds and plants thoroughly.
5. Thin the plants during the growing period to allow space for the roots to develop.
6. Weed and water the plants regularly. A side dressing of fertilizer rich in phosphorous can be applied to slow-growing vegetables.
7. Pull or dig the vegetables as they approach maturity. Root vegetables allowed to remain in the soil too long may get tough and/or split.

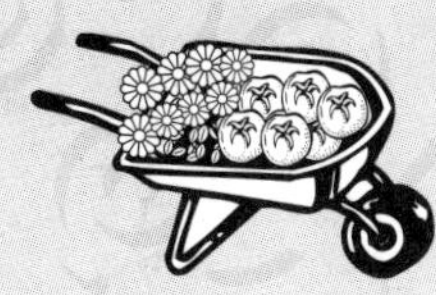

Root Gardens

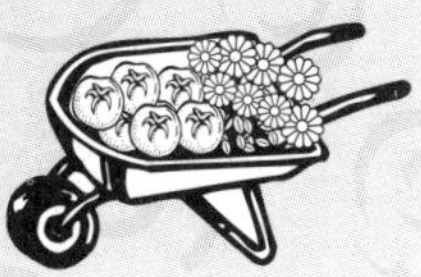

More Ideas

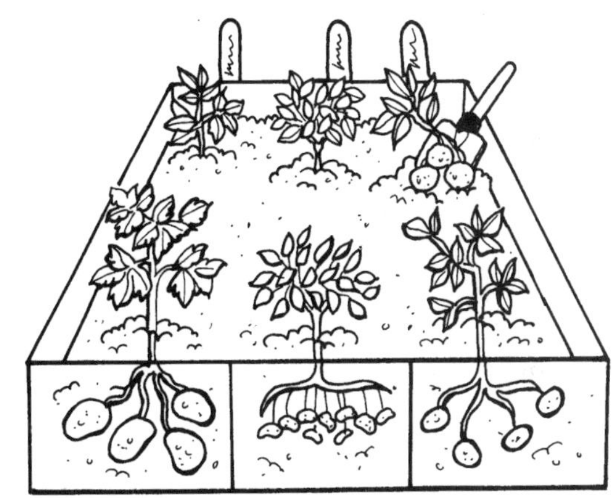

- Plant a square-foot garden with each section planted with a different root vegetable.
- Plant peanuts, sweet potatoes, and white potatoes. Dig up small, tender "new potatoes" when the plants finish flowering.
- Also cook the leaves of young root plants such as beets and turnips.

Tidbits

✧ We eat the roots of many vegetables—carrots, turnips, radishes, beets, rutabaga, kohlrabi, parsnips, onions, leeks, and potatoes.

✧ Vegetables grow at varying rates—radishes and green onions grow quickly; beets, carrots, and garlic grow slowly.

Learn More

Celfe, Albie. *My First Garden Book.* Corte Madero, CA: NK Lawn and Garden Company, 1991.

Krauss, Ruth. *The Carrot Seed.* NY: HarperCollins Publishing, 1993.

McGovern, Ann. *Stone Soup.* NY: Scholastic, Inc., 1986.

Ryder, Joanne. *First Grade Lady Bugs.* Mahwah, NJ: Troll Associates, 1993.

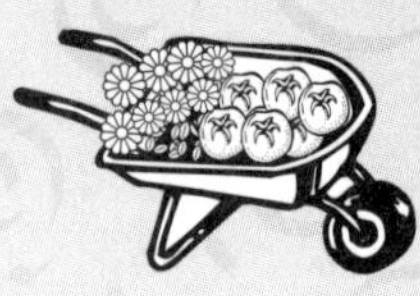

Cinnamon Carrots

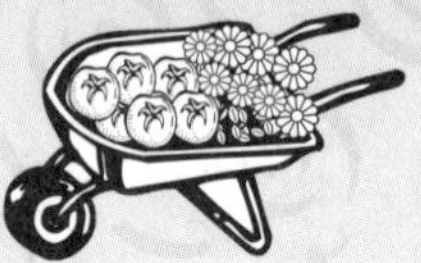

Materials

- 8 carrots
- $^{1}/_{2}$ teaspoon cinnamon
- $^{1}/_{4}$ cup butter
- $^{1}/_{4}$ cup brown sugar
- water
- vegetable peeler
- saucepan with lid
- knife
- cutting board
- colander
- mixing spoon

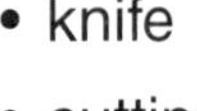

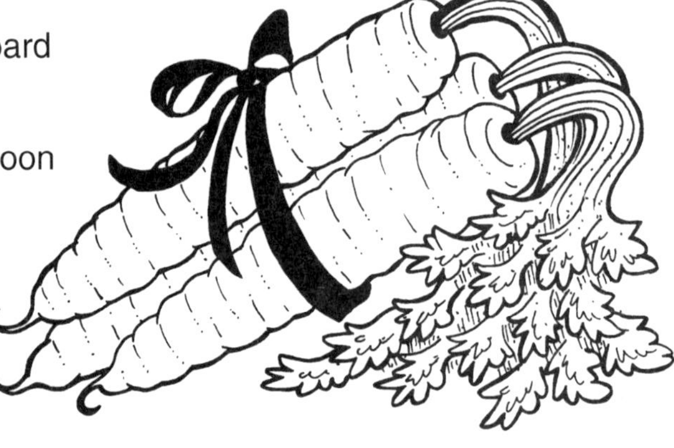

Let's Do It !

1. Wash the carrots, cut off their ends, and peel them.
2. Cut the carrots into slanted slices or strips about $^{1}/_{4}$" thick.
3. In a saucepan, add the carrots to $^{1}/_{2}$ cup water, cover the pot, and cook the carrots until they are crisply tender, about 15–20 minutes.
4. Drain the carrots and put them back into the saucepan.
5. Add the butter, cinnamon, and brown sugar.
6. Heat on low heat to melt the sugar and butter, stirring to coat the carrots.
7. Serve hot.

More Ideas

- Additional flavors that can be added to cooked carrots are allspice, brown sugar, orange juice, or maple syrup.
- Uncooked carrots can be sliced into pennies or julienned. They can also be eaten with various dips and salad dressings.

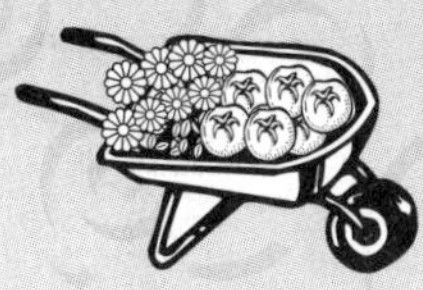

Potato Leek Soup

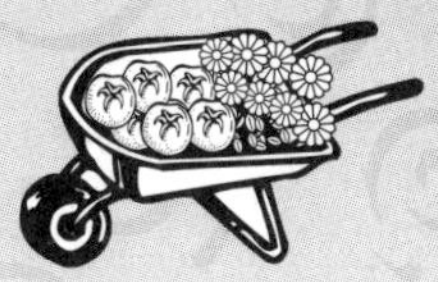

Materials

- $1\frac{1}{2}$ cups leeks, minced
- $\frac{1}{2}$ cup onion, minced
- 1 clove garlic, minced
- $\frac{1}{4}$ cup butter
- 4 cups chicken broth
- $1\frac{1}{2}$ potatoes, peeled and diced
- knife
- 1 cup whipping cream
- 1 teaspoon salt
- $\frac{1}{4}$ teaspoon pepper
- chives, chopped (optional)
- saucepan
- mixing spoon

Let's Do It !

1. Wash and trim the leeks, using the white part and 1" of the green part.
2. Sauté the leeks, garlic, and onion in butter until they are transparent.
3. Add the potatoes and chicken broth and cook until tender.
4. Add the whipping cream and seasonings and stir well.
5. Serve hot and garnish with chopped chives.

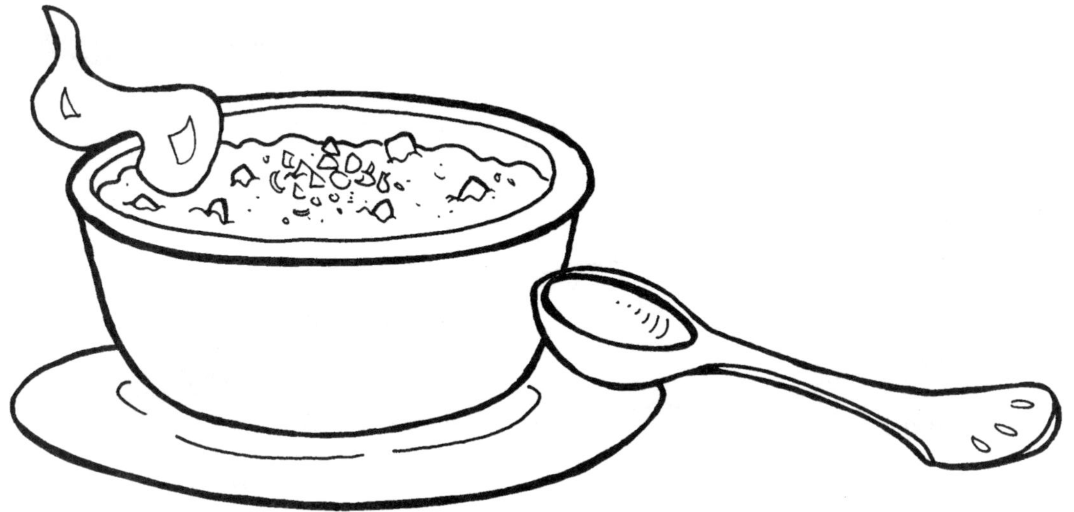

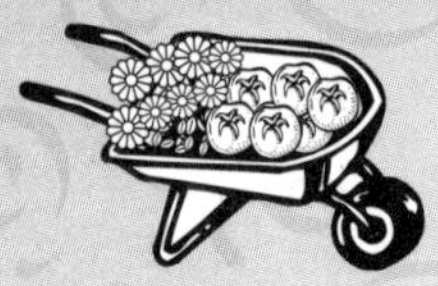

French Onion Soup

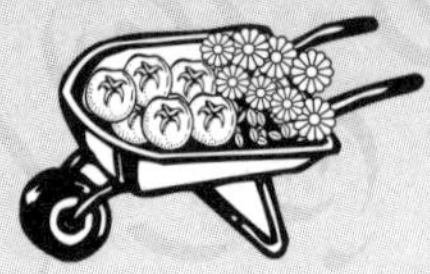

Materials

- 3 cups onions, sliced thin
- 3 tablespoons butter
- 2 cans (15 $^1/_2$ ounces each) beef broth
- 1 $^1/_2$ cups water
- 1 teaspoon Worcestershire sauce
- toaster oven
- ladle
- 1 loaf French bread
- grated Parmesan cheese
- large saucepan with lid
- soup bowls
- serrated knife
- cutting board

Let's Do It !

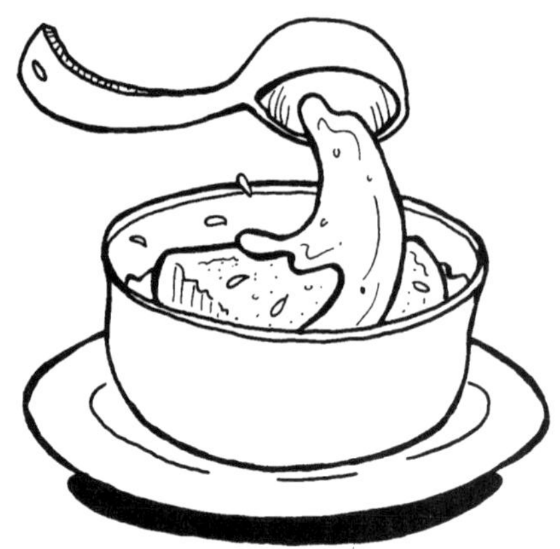

1. In a saucepan, cook the onions in butter over a low heat about 30 minutes, stirring frequently.
2. Add the beef broth, water, and Worcestershire sauce and heat to boiling.
3. Reduce heat, cover the pan, and simmer about 30 minutes.
4. Slice the French bread and toast it lightly on both sides.
5. Place 1 slice of bread in the bottom of a soup bowl, pour the hot soup over it, and sprinkle it with Parmesan cheese.
6. Serve hot.

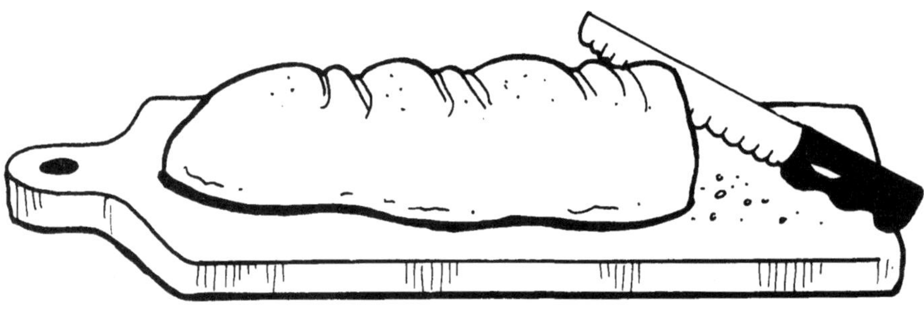

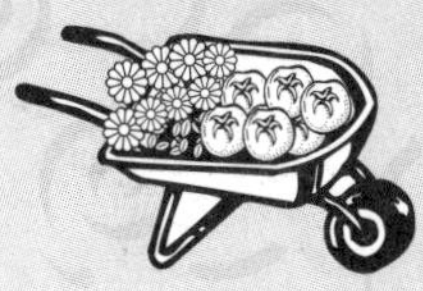

Book Fun

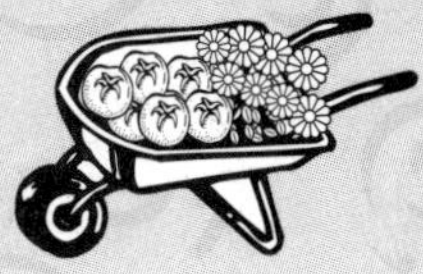

Materials

- *Stone Soup* by Ann McGovern. New York: Scholastic, Inc., 1986.
- 1 pound stew beef, trimmed and cut bite-size
- 1 clean, small, smooth stone
- 1/3 cup all-purpose flour
- 1 can of tomatoes
- 1 medium onion, chopped
- vegetable oil
- 2 large potatoes, diced
- water
- 2–3 carrots, sliced
- 1–2 turnips, diced
- 1 bay leaf
- 1–2 beef bouillion cubes, crumbled
- salt and pepper
- large pot with lid
- frying pan and wide metal spatula
- glass pie pan

Let's Do It !

1. Read the book and discuss it. Why did stone soup taste so good?
2. Put the flour into the pie pan and dredge the stew meat in it.
3. Put just enough oil in the frying pan to coat the bottom, and quickly brown the meat on all sides, turning it frequently.
4. Put the meat, bay leaf, and a dash of salt and pepper into a large pot. Cover them with water.
5. Bring the water to a boil and then reduce the heat and simmer until the beef is tender—about 30 minutes.
6. Wash and prepare the vegetables. Add them to the pot with the cooked meat and put in the tomatoes, the stone, and bouillion. Cook until the vegetables are tender, about 20 minutes.

Tidbits

✧ If the soup needs thickening, blend 1 tablespoon of cornstarch in a small amount of water, dilute it with soup broth, and stir it into the soup. Simmer 5 more minutes.

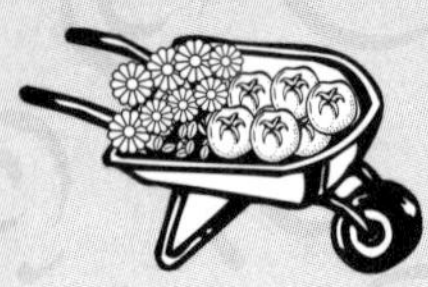

Peanuts

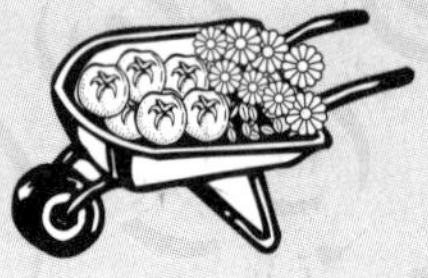

Materials

- raw peanuts, shelled
- shovel
- garden rake
- water hose
- hoe
- 8-8-8 fertilizer
- compost or peat
- mulch

Let's Do It !

1. Mix compost or peat and fertilizer into well-tilled soil.
2. Turn the soil over to a depth of 6"–8". Peanuts like loose soil.
3. Plant the peanuts in raised rows about 5" high.
4. Space seeds 36" apart and 2"–2½" deep. Water the seeds thoroughly.
5. Mulch between the rows to discourage weeds.
6. Weed and water plants regularly. Apply a side dressing of fertilizer during the summer.
7. The plants will produce small yellow-orange flowers near the leaves. Watch for tendril-like pegs that grow down from each flower into the soil. That's where the peanuts will grow! When the plants finish flowering, it will be time to harvest the peanuts.

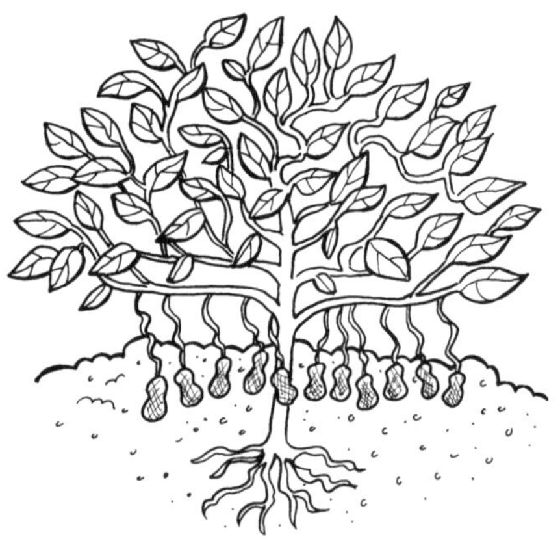

8. To harvest the peanuts, loosen the plants with a shovel. Remove the plants with peanuts attached. Turn the plants upside down and allow them to dry in the sun, or pull the peanuts off the plants and collect them.
9. Return the peanut plants to the garden and turn them under the soil, where they will decay and fertilize the garden with nitrogen. Or you can add the plants to a compost pile.
10. Wash the peanuts well, and spread them out to thoroughly dry. Keep them dry until you are ready to use them.

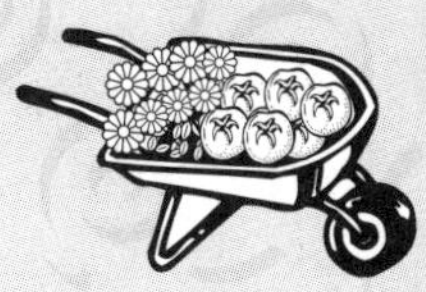

Peanuts

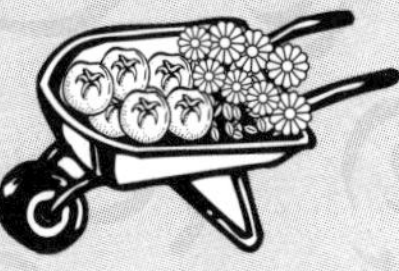

More Ideas

- Compare planting raw peanuts in the shell with peanuts removed from the shell. Plant some of each and observe to see which come up first.
- Plant a peanut garden in a ten-gallon aquarium. Provide light. Wrap dark paper around the base of the aquarium to the top of the soil line.

Tidbits

✧ Plant peanuts when the soil is warm, generally April to July.

✧ Peanuts are members of the legume family and are peas, not nuts.

✧ Peanuts are high in protein and make nutritious snacks.

✧ It takes about 120 to 150 days for the peanuts to be ready to harvest.

✧ George Washington Carver developed about 300 uses for peanuts and peanut plants.

Learn More

Andriani, Vincent. *Peanut Butter Rhino.* New York: Scholastic, Inc., 1994.

Forbes, Evan D. *Science in a Bag.* Huntington Beach, CA: Teacher Created Resources, Inc., 1995.

Robbins, Ken. *Make Me a Peanut Butter Sandwich.* New York: Scholastic, Inc., 1992.

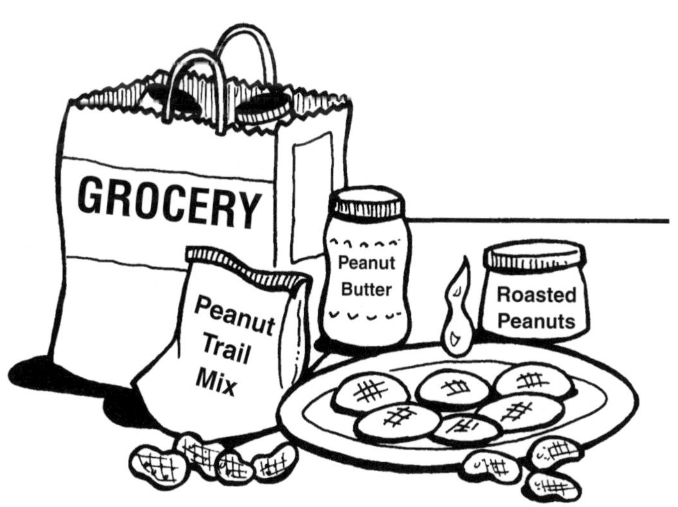

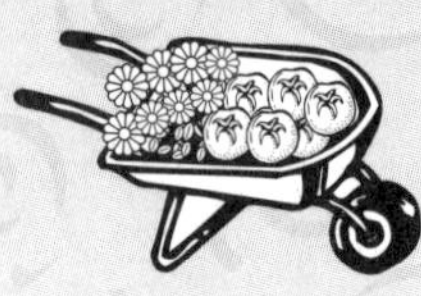

Boiled and Oven-Roasted Peanuts

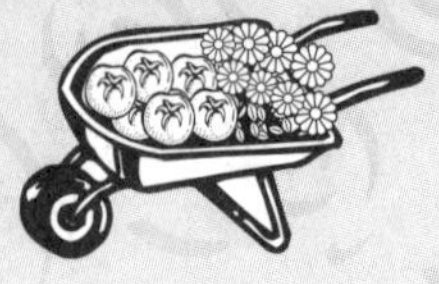

Boiled Peanuts

Materials

- 6-quart pot with lid
- colander
- 4 quarts raw peanuts in shells
- 1 teaspoon salt
- water

Let's Do It !

1. Put the peanuts and salt in the pot and cover them with water.
2. Put the lid on the pot and bring the water to a boil.
3. Reduce the heat and simmer the peanuts for about 3 hours until crisply tender.
4. Carefully pour the peanuts into a colander to drain them.
5. Remove the shells before eating the peanuts warm or cold.

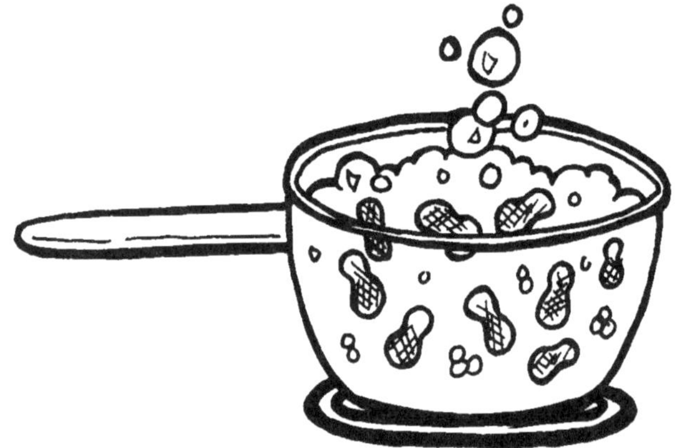

Oven-Roasted Peanuts

Materials

- raw peanuts in shells—about 2 quarts
- 13" x 9" x 2" baking pan
- spatula

Let's Do It !

1. Preheat the oven to 300°F. Put peanuts in a baking pan and roast them 30–45 minutes.
2. Turn the peanuts frequently to prevent scorching. Test for doneness by removing a shell and skin.
3. Cool the peanuts before you eat them.

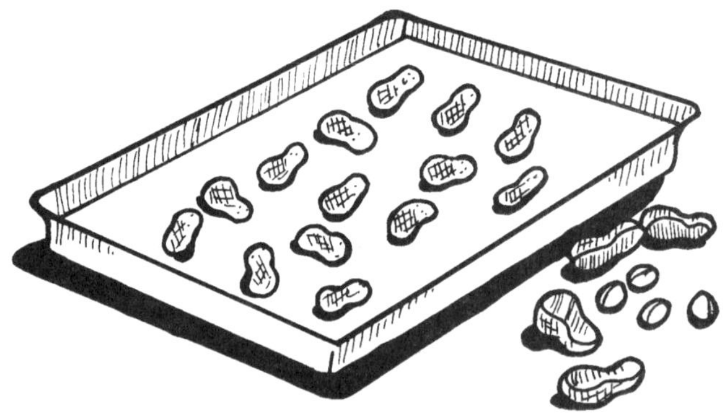

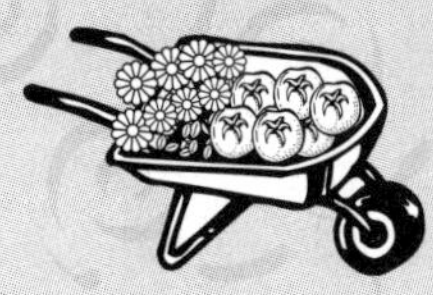

Snack Mix

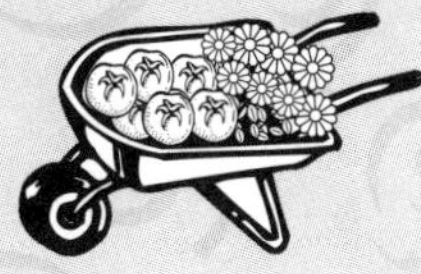

Materials

- 1 cup salted, roasted peanuts
- 1 cup pretzel sticks
- 1/4 cup butter
- 4 teaspoons Worcestershire sauce
- 2 cups each of rice and wheat cereal
- 1 cup bite-sized goldfish crackers
- 1/4 teaspoon garlic powder
- 1/2 teaspoon seasoned salt (optional)
- 2 pans 13" x 9" x 2" or large roasting pan
- paper towels
- large stirring spoon

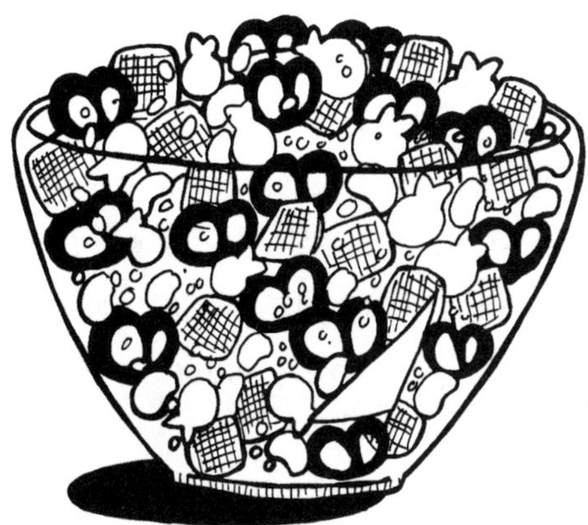

Let's Do It !

1. Preheat the oven the 250°F.
2. Melt the butter in a roasting pan and stir in the seasonings until well blended.
3. Add the peanuts, pretzels, cereals, and goldfish crackers and mix well.
4. Bake one hour, stirring well every 10–15 minutes to prevent burning.
5. Turn out the mixture onto paper towels to cool.
6. Store the snack mix in an airtight container.

More Ideas

- To make homemade peanut butter, add salted, roasted peanuts with 1 1/2 to 2 tablespoons of oil for every cup of peanuts and mix in a blender until smooth.

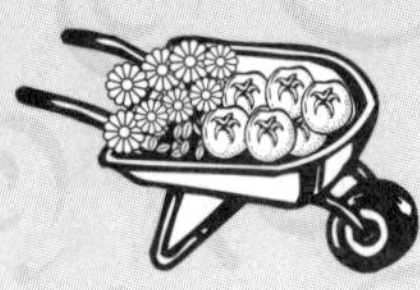

Peanut Predictions

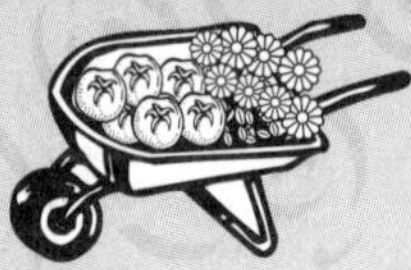

Materials

- 5 peanuts per child
- pencil and paper

Let's Do It !

1. Examine each peanut. Look at its length, width, and shape.
2. Predict (guess) how many peanuts are in each shell, and write down your prediction.
3. Remove the shells, count the peanuts inside, and compare the number with your prediction.
4. Write down the actual number of peanuts in each shell. Were your predictions accurate?
5. Find the average number of peanuts in each shell.
   - Count the total number of peanuts that came out of all the shells.
   - Divide the total number of peanuts by the number of whole shells.

   For example, if the total number of peanuts is 12 and they came out of 5 whole peanut shells, divide 12 by 5. The average number of peanuts in each shell is 2.4.

Peanut Prediction

Number of Peanuts	My Guess for Number of Peanuts	Actual Number of Peanuts

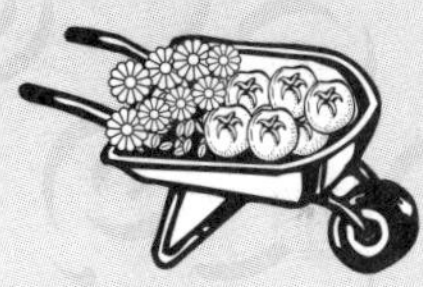

Peanut People

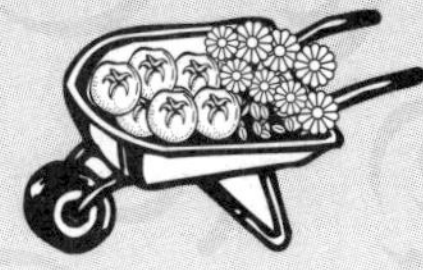

Materials

- peanuts in shells
- fine-tip markers
- bits of yarn
- pipe cleaners
- scissors
- white glue or glue gun and glue sticks

Let's Do It !

1. Draw a face on the peanut shell.
2. Glue bits of yarn on the head for hair.
3. Cut arms and legs out of pipe cleaners.
   Bend a loop at the end of each piece to form hands and feet.
4. Glue the pipe cleaners to the shell.

More Ideas

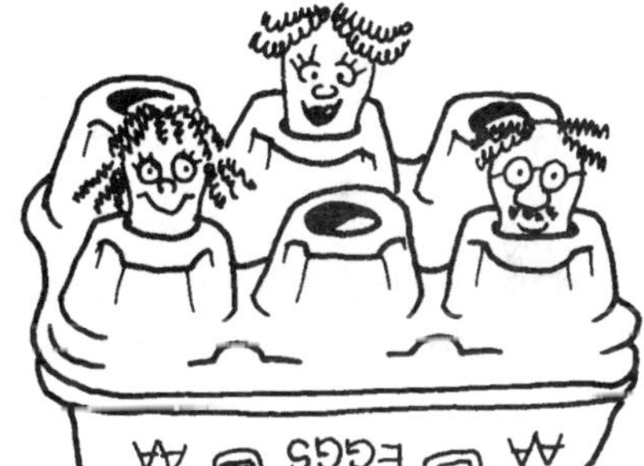

- Draw and form animal features to make peanut critters.
- Make a peanut mosaic by gluing peanut shells, whole peanuts, and shelled peanuts into a design on poster board.
- Use an empty egg carton. Turn it upside down. Poke holes in each egg cup and place the peanut people in each. Display.

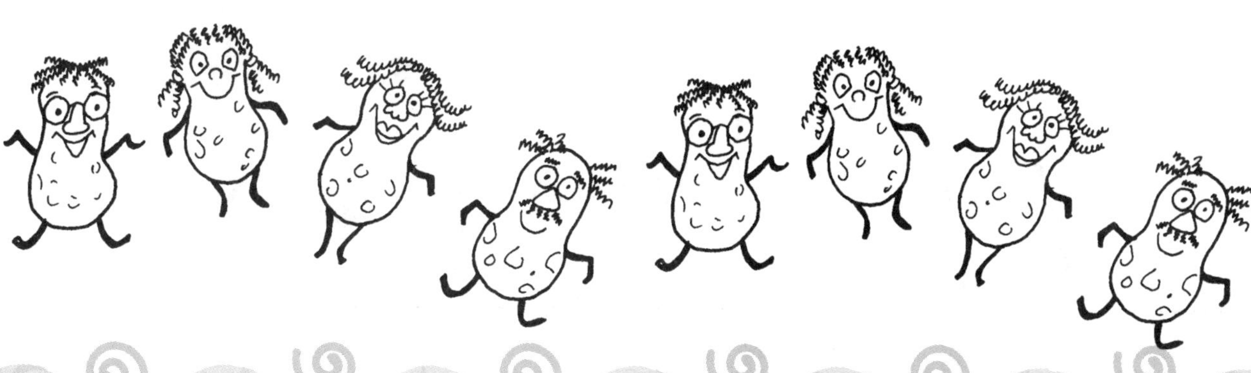

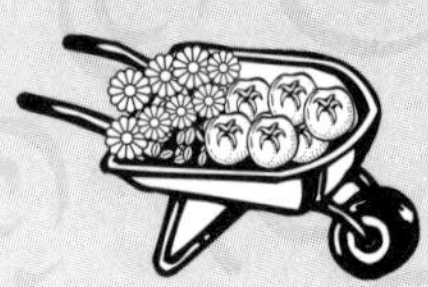

Potatoes

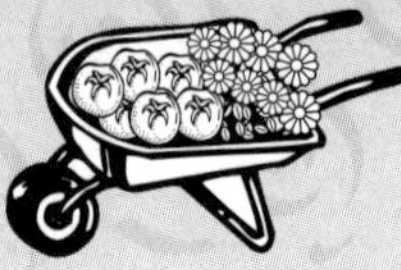

Materials

- seed potatoes
- fertilizer
- knife
- mulch
- compost or peat
- watering hose
- hoe
- shovel

Let's Do It !

1. Cut seed potatoes into chunks. Be sure there is at least one eye on each piece.
2. Work compost or peat and fertilizer into well-tilled soil.
3. Make raised rows about 3' apart for easier harvesting.
4. Plant the seed potatoes 2"–3" deep and 2' apart with the eyes or buds facing upward. Cover them with soil, add mulch, and water them thoroughly.
5. During the growing season, weed and water plants as needed.
6. Watch for insects and diseases.
7. To harvest potatoes, loosen the soil around the outer edge of the plants with a shovel. Dig up the plants, being careful to not cut into the potatoes. Harvest just enough potatoes for one meal or the whole crop.
8. Wash the potatoes well and allow them to dry thoroughly. Store them in a cool, dry place.

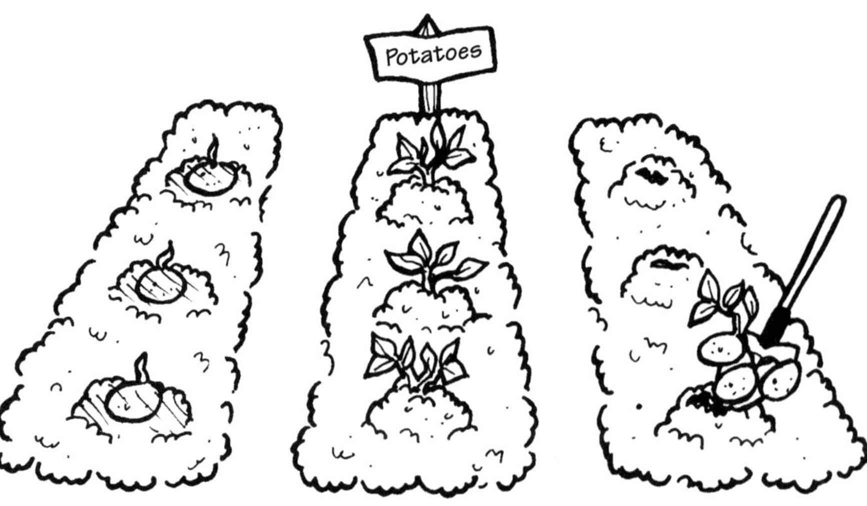

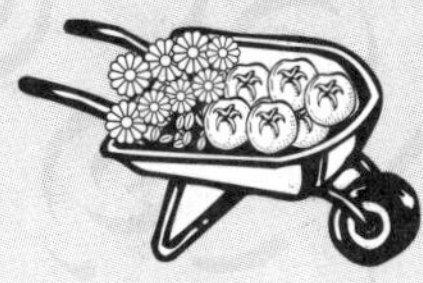

Potatoes

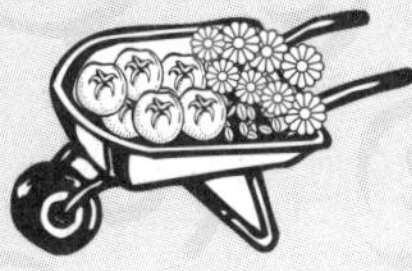

More Ideas

- Plant potatoes in cool weather before the last frost is expected.
- Plant several different types of potatoes, such as Idaho, Russet, and Red Bliss.
- With limited space, plant potatoes in a large container.

Tidbits

✧ Potatoes originated in South America.

✧ Potatoes are tubers that grow underground.

✧ The eyes and the green areas on potatoes can make you sick. Don't eat them.

Learn More

McGovern, Ann. *Stone Soup.* New York: Scholastic, Inc., 1986.

Radcliffe, Loralyn. *Creative Crafts for Clever Kids.* Huntington Beach, CA: Teacher Created Resources, 1996.

Stewart, Martha. *Martha Stewart's Gardening Month by Month.* New York: Clarkson Potter Publishers, 1991.

Walters, Jennie. *Gardening with Peter Rabbit.* London, England: F. Warne & Co., 1991.

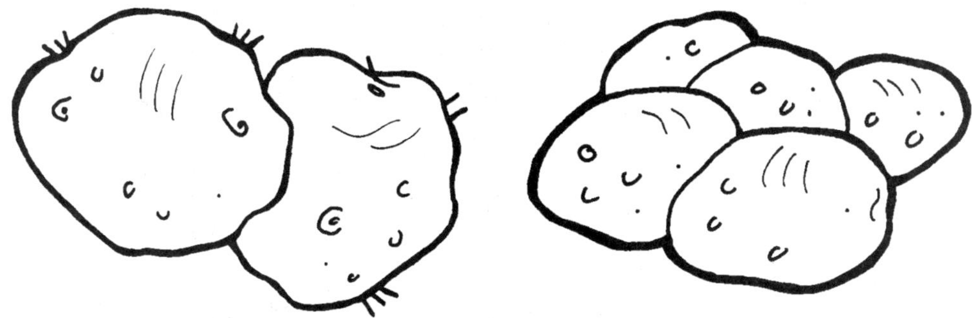

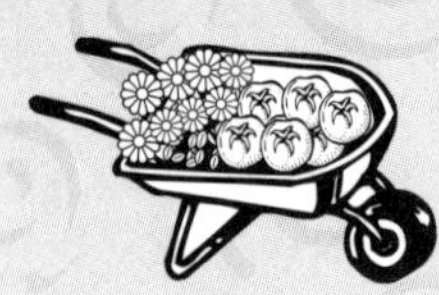

Potato Salad

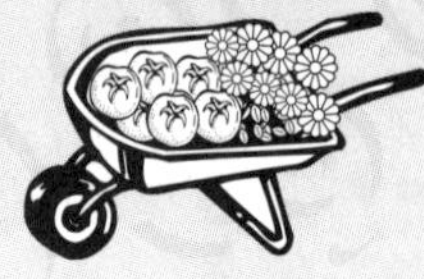

Materials

- 6 medium potatoes
- 1 medium yellow (Spanish) onion, chopped
- 1 or 2 ribs of celery, chopped
- 1 tablespoon fresh parsley
- 1 egg
- 1 tablespoon white vinegar
- 1 teaspoon sugar
- 1/2 teaspoon salt
- 1/4 teaspoon pepper
- 2-quart casserole dish with lid
- 1/3–1/2 cup mayonnaise
- 2 saucepans with lids
- mixing bowl
- vegetable peeler
- paring knife
- cutting board
- colander

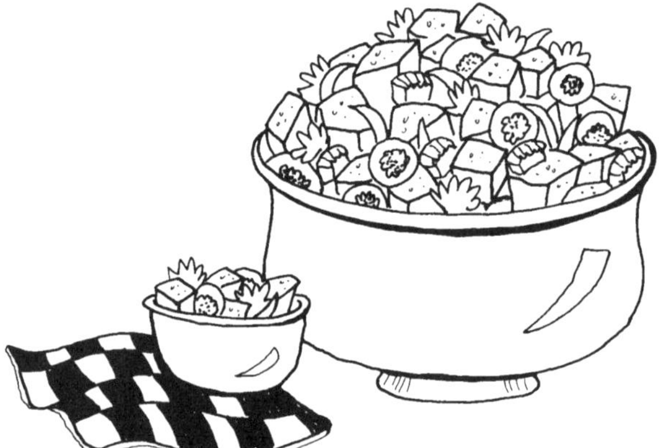

Let's Do It !

1. Wash, peel, and cube the potatoes. Rinse them and put them into a saucepan. Fill the pan with enough water to cover the potatoes.
2. Bring the water to a boil, and then reduce the heat and cook on low about 15 minutes until the potatoes are tender but firm. Drain and cool the potatoes.
3. To hard-boil the egg, put it in a saucepan and cover it with water. Bring the water to a boil, and boil the egg for 2 minutes. Then turn off the heat, put a lid on the pan, and leave the pan on the burner. When the water is cool, drain the egg and run it under cold water for 1 minute.
4. Remove shell from the hard-boiled egg and dice it.
5. Blend the mayonnaise, salt, sugar, pepper, and vinegar together in a mixing bowl.
6. Add the potatoes, egg, celery, onion, and parsley to the wet mixture. Add seasonings to taste.
7. Put the salad into a covered bowl and chill it for at least 1 hour before serving.

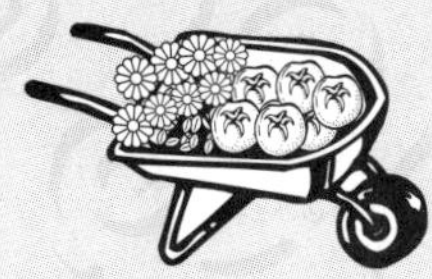

Tasty Spuds

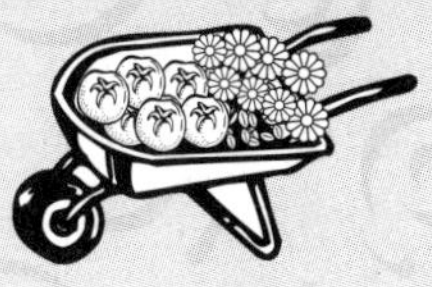

Oven Roasted Potatoes

Materials

- 4 medium potatoes
- 1 medium yellow (Spanish) onion, sliced
- $\frac{1}{2}$ teaspoon salt
- paprika
- paring knife
- 2 tablespoons butter
- 1 tablespoon vegetable oil
- baking dish or pie pan
- vegetable peeler
- cutting board

Let's Do It !

1. Preheat the oven to 375°F.
2. Wash, peel, and cut the potatoes into slices $\frac{1}{4}$" thick.
3. Lightly grease the baking dish or pie pan with vegetable oil and add the potatoes and onion slices.
4. Dot the vegetables with butter and sprinkle them with salt and paprika.
5. Bake the vegetables about 30 minutes, stirring a few times, until they are tender and a light golden color.

Crispy Baked Skins

Materials

- 2 medium potatoes
- fork
- salsa
- 2 teaspoons of butter
- baking sheet
- cheese
- ground pepper to taste
- sour cream

Let's Do It !

1. Preheat the oven to 375°F.
2. Poke holes into the potatoes with a fork.
3. Place potatoes on a baking sheet and bake for about $1\frac{1}{2}$ hours or until skin is crisp.
4. Slice the potato in half widthwise and scoop out.
5. Add $\frac{1}{2}$ teaspoon of butter on each potato and bake for 5 minutes.
6. Add pepper and serve.
7. Add sour cream, salsa, or cheese to the potatoes for additional flavor.

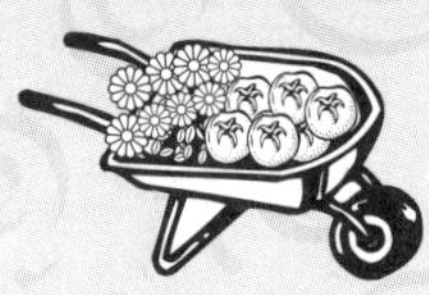

Parslied New Potatoes

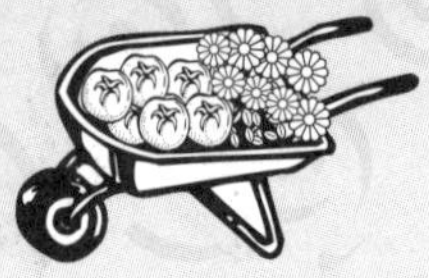

Materials

- 2 cups new potatoes the size of golf balls or larger
- 2 tablespoons butter
- 2–3 tablespoons fresh or dried parsley
- cutting board
- ½ teaspoon salt
- saucepan with lid
- kitchen scissors
- knife
- paper towels

Let's Do It !

1. Scrub the potatoes well. If potatoes differ greatly in size, cut the larger ones into chunks so they will all cook at the same rate. Leave the skins on the potatoes.
2. Put the potatoes into a saucepan and cover them with water. Put a lid on the pan.
3. Bring the water to a boil, and then reduce the heat and cook 15–20 minutes until tender but slightly firm. Drain the potatoes, and leave them in the pan.
4. Wash the fresh parsley and pat it dry using a few paper towels. Use scissors to snip the parsley into small pieces and add it to the cooked potatoes.
5. Add the butter and salt. Gently stir the potatoes to melt the butter and coat the potatoes with butter and parsley.
6. Serve hot.

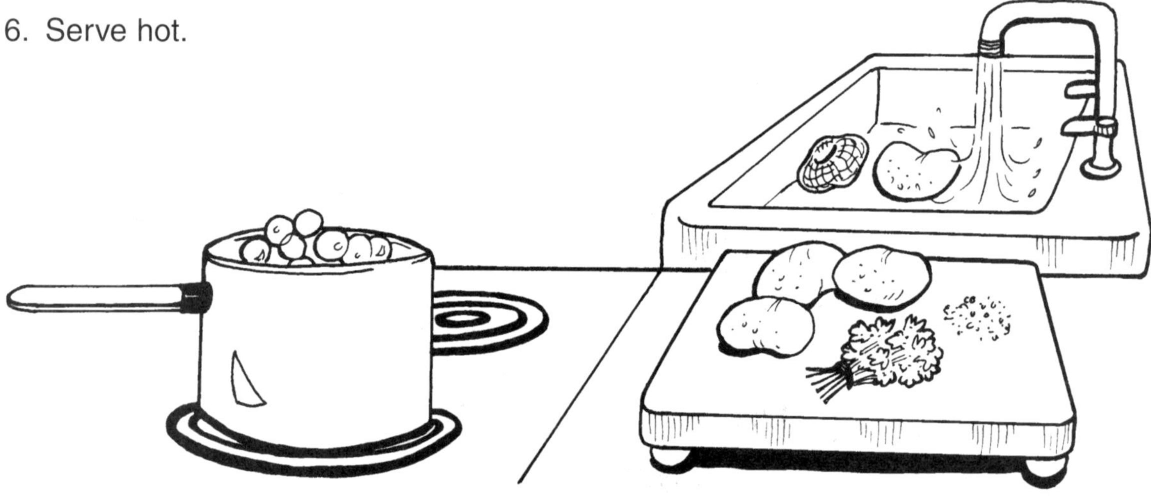

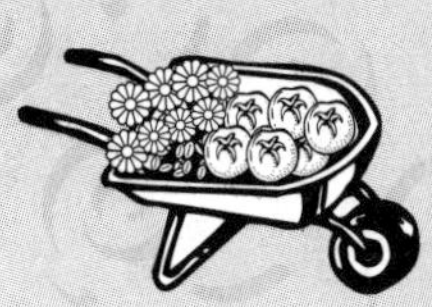

Potato Cakes–Pennsylvania Dutch Style

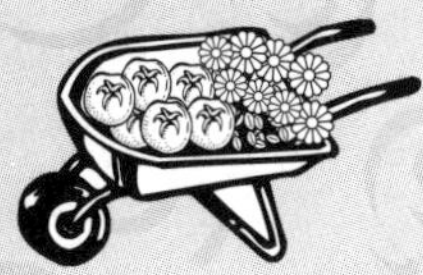

Materials

- 2 cups leftover mashed potatoes
- 1 small onion, minced, or 4 scallions, cut thin
- 2 tablespoons all-purpose flour
- 1 egg
- salt and pepper
- vegetable oil
- mixing bowl
- wire whisk
- fork
- wide metal spatula
- frying pan
- butter

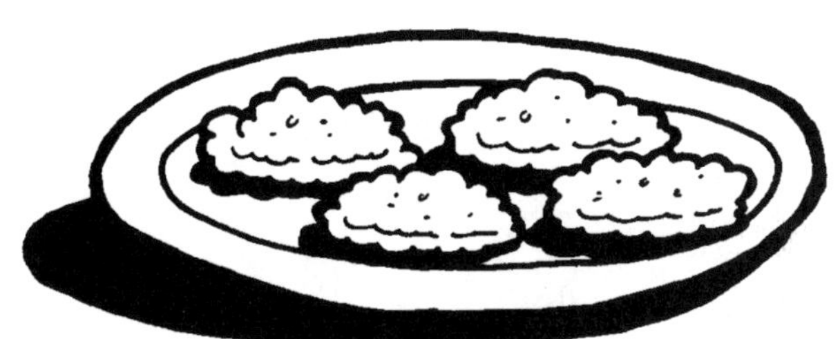

Let's Do It !

1. Place the mashed potatoes into a bowl and loosen them with the fork.
2. Add the egg, flour, salt and pepper, and onion, and blend it all together with wire whisk.
3. Coat the bottom of frying pan with oil and heat it on medium high. Add large scoops of the potato mixture and flatten with spatula to form "pancakes."
4. Cook the pancakes until they are golden brown on the bottom, and then flip them and cook the other side.
5. Serve hot with butter.

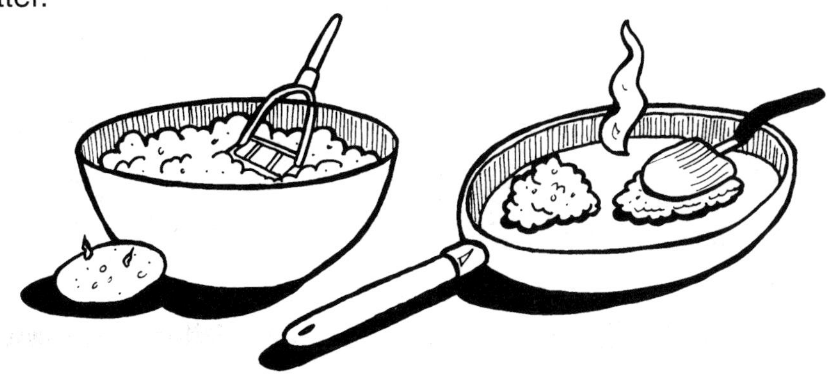

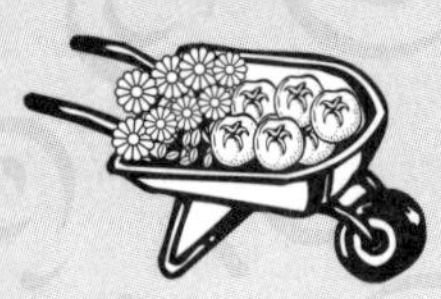

Easy Shepherd's Pie

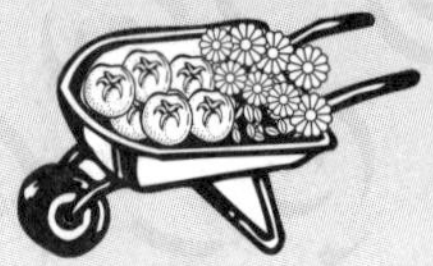

Materials

- 1 pound lean ground chuck
- 1 medium onion, chopped
- 1 package of brown gravy mix
- 2 packages of instant mashed potato mix or 1 1/2 cups leftover mashed potatoes
- 1 10-ounce package of frozen carrots and peas
- salt and pepper
- 1/2 cup of water
- 1/2 teaspoon garlic salt
- butter
- 2 slices American cheese, cut into thin strips
- frying pan
- saucepan
- glass pie pan
- 2-quart casserole dish
- paper plate
- stirring spoon

Let's Do It !

1. Put the peas and carrots in a glass pie pan, add 1/2 cup water, cover the pan with a paper plate, and cook the vegetables in a microwave oven about 5 minutes.
2. Prepare the potatoes according to the package instructions, and add extra water to make them fluffy. Blend in 2 tablespoons of butter.
3. Prepare gravy according to package instructions. Drain the vegetables and season them to taste with garlic salt, salt and pepper, and 1 tablespoon of butter.
4. Preheat the oven to 375°F.
5. In a frying pan, add the chopped onion to the ground beef and cook them until onions are transparent and the beef is brown. Drain off the liquid and then stir in the seasonings and gravy mixture.
6. Spoon the meat and gravy mixture into a casserole dish and top it with the peas and carrots.
7. Spread the mashed potatoes on top of it all, sealing the edges of the dish. Bake 25–30 minutes or until the potato peaks begin to brown lightly.
8. Remove the dish from the oven and sprinkle the strips of cheese on the top.
9. Return the dish to the oven and bake it just until the cheese melts (about 5 minutes).

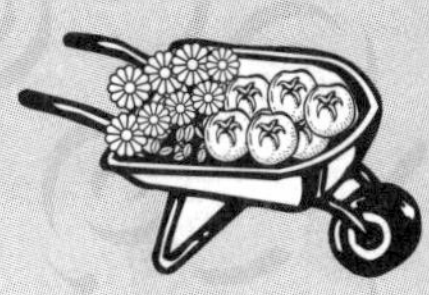

Hairy Potato Head

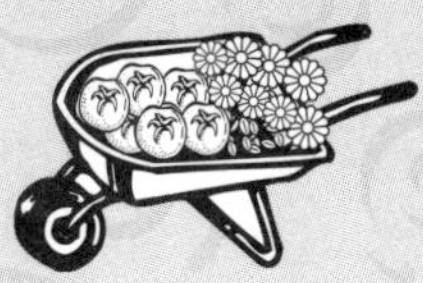

Materials

- potato
- cotton balls
- radish seeds
- construction paper
- pins or glue
- scissors
- knife
- toothpicks
- cup

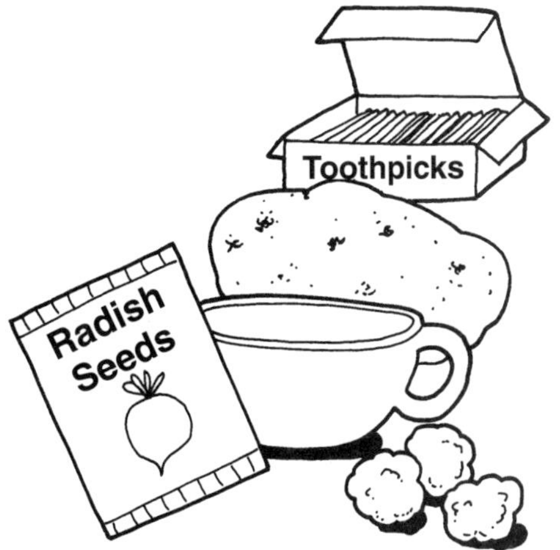

Let's Do It !

1. Slice the top off a potato and carve out a hole in the potato large enough for the cotton balls.
2. Create facial features out of construction paper and glue or pin them in place on the potato.
3. Fill the hole with cotton balls, moisten them, and sprinkle them with the radish seeds.
4. Poke three toothpicks into different sides of the potato and place it in a cup on a windowsill.
5. Keep the cotton moist so the seed hair sprouts and grows.

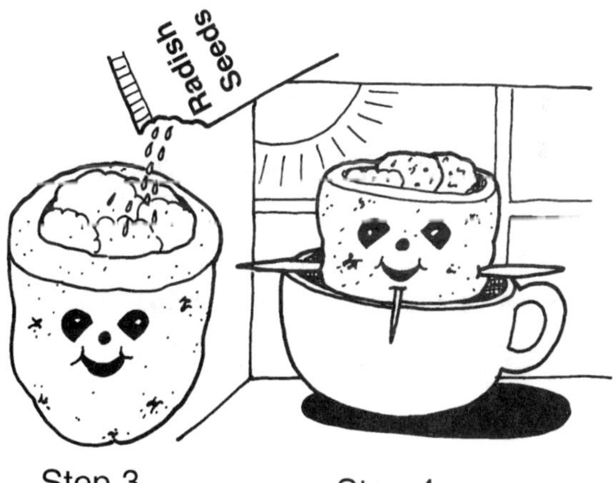

Step 3 Step 4

More Ideas

- Use other quick-sprouting seeds such as watercress, rye grass, alfalfa, or marigold.
- Make hairy eggheads by emptying and thoroughly cleaning an eggshell and following the procedures above.

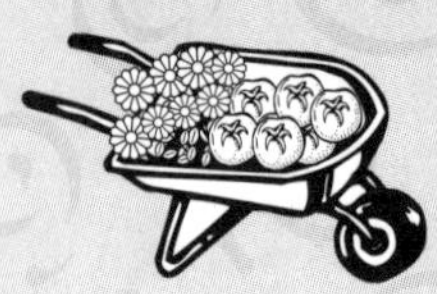

Sweet Potatoes

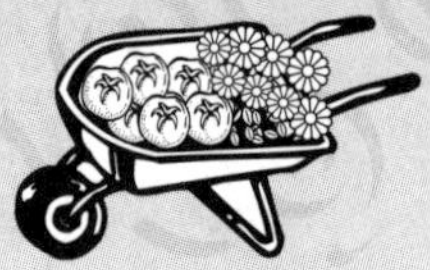

Materials

- disease-free sweet potato pieces or certified plants
- shovel
- hoe
- compost
- fertilizer high in phosphorous
- garden rake

Let's Do It !

1. Work compost and fertilizer into well-tilled soil.
2. Create raised hills or rows 5" to 10" high and 12" wide.
3. Make furrows 4" deep, and set the plants 3" deep and 12" apart. Plant the pieces of sweet potato with the bud or eye upward, and cover them with 1" of soil. Water well.
4. Weed the plants weekly and cultivate around them to keep the nodes on the vines from sprouting roots.
5. Harvest sweet potatoes prior to the first frost. You can harvest sweet potatoes when they are at least 1" thick or wait until they are larger.
6. Loosen the soil with a shovel around the main section of the plants. Carefully dig up the sweet potatoes and shake off the dirt.
7. Air dry them and store them in a cool place.

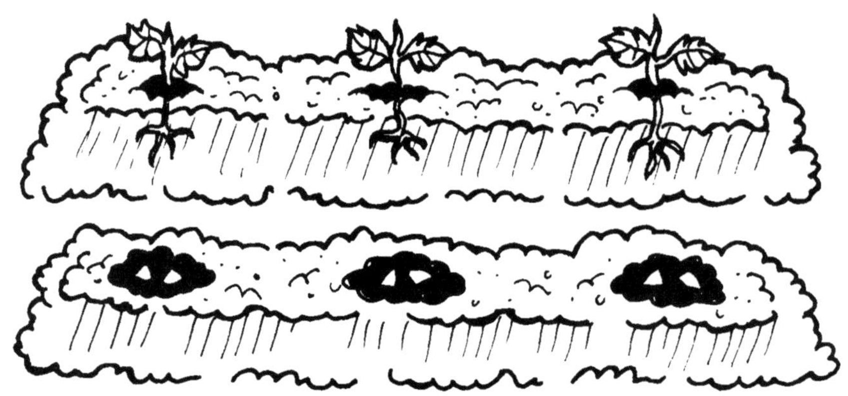

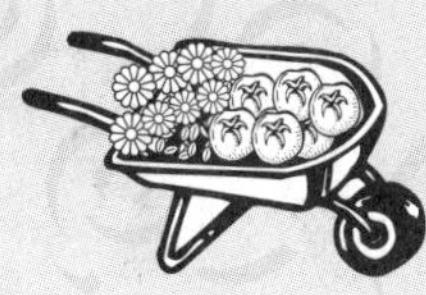

Sweet Potatoes

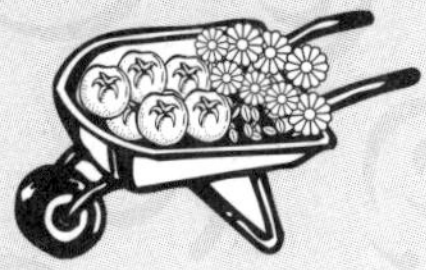

More Ideas

- If your growing season is short, try planting sweet potatoes in a large aquarium under lights.
- Grow a sweet potato in a jar with water and watch its "hair" grow. Push toothpicks into the sweet potato to form supports around it 2"–3" from the top. Fill the jar with water and put the sweet potato in it so the bottom of it is submerged. Add water to the jar as needed as the vine grows.

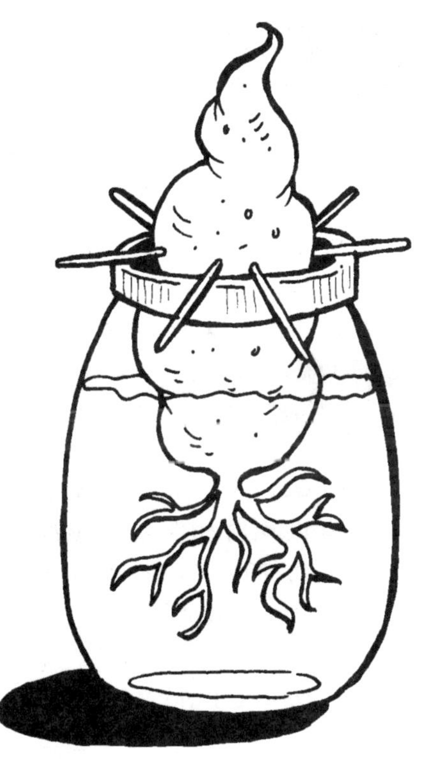

Tidbits

✧ Sweet potatoes require 100 to 150 days to mature. Be patient!

✧ Sweet potatoes are an excellent source of vitamins A and C.

Learn More

McMillan, Bruce. *Growing Colors.* New York: HarperTrophy, 1994.

Wiesner, David. *June 29, 1999.* New York: Clarion Books, 1992.

Rockwell, Anne. *Sweet Potato Pie.* Step Into Reading. New York: Random House Books for Young Readers, 1996.

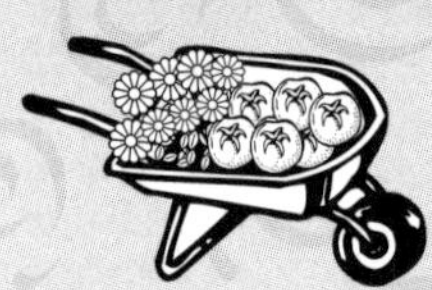

Sweet Potato Casserole

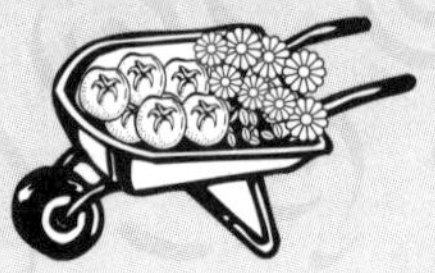

Materials

- 1 can (1 pound 13 ounces) sweet potatoes or 2 pounds of fresh, peeled and cooked sweet potatoes
- 3/4 cup butter plus some to grease casserole dish
- 1 cup canned milk
- 1/2–2/3 cup sugar
- 2 eggs, beaten
- coconut, flaked
- 1/8 teaspoon ground cloves
- 1/4 teaspoon nutmeg
- 1/4 teaspoon cinnamon
- mixing bowl and electric mixer
- rubber spatula
- 2-quart casserole dish with lid
- small bowl

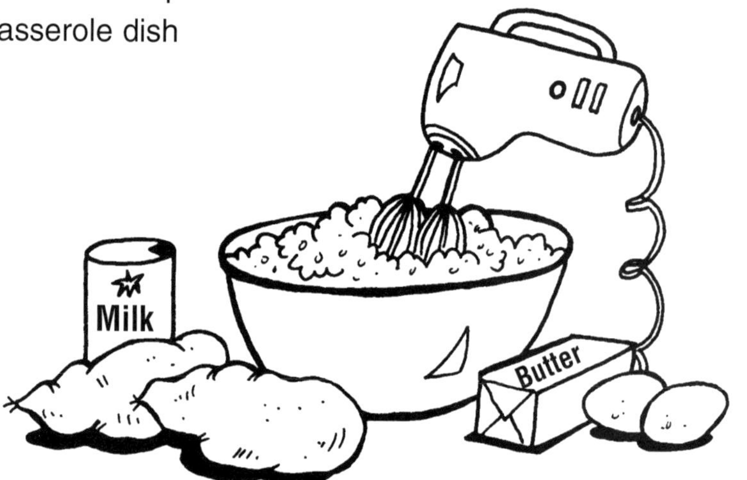

Let's Do It !

1. Preheat the oven to 350°F.
2. Drain and mash the sweet potatoes with electric mixer in a mixing bowl.
3. Melt the butter in a small bowl in a microwave oven.
4. Combine all the ingredients (except coconut) in the mixing bowl. Blend well until all the lumps are gone and the mixture is light.
5. Grease a casserole dish with butter and pour the sweet potato mixture into it. Cover the dish and bake the casserole 30 minutes.
6. Sprinkle the casserole with coconut and bake it another 15–20 minutes, uncovered, until the coconut browns.

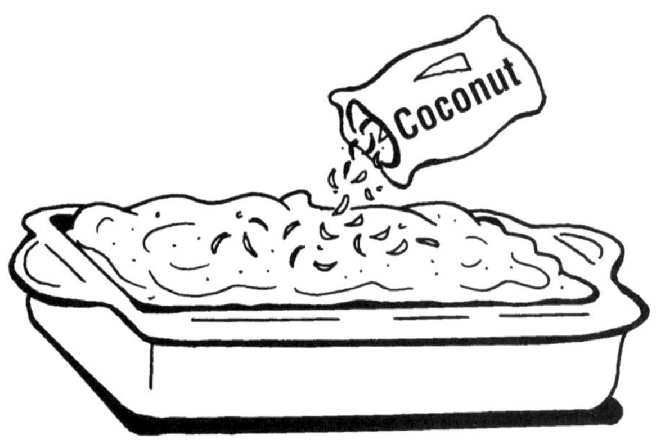

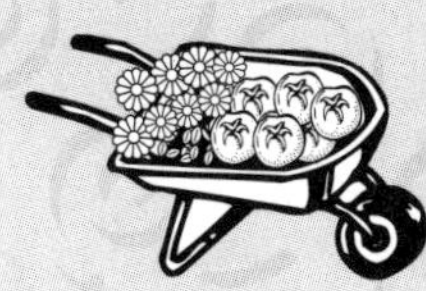

Sweet Potato Critters

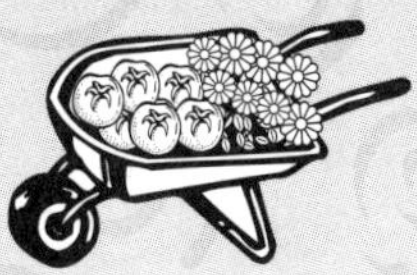

Materials

- sweet potatoes, small to medium
- tempera paints and small brushes
- toothpicks
- raisins
- carrots
- celery
- knife

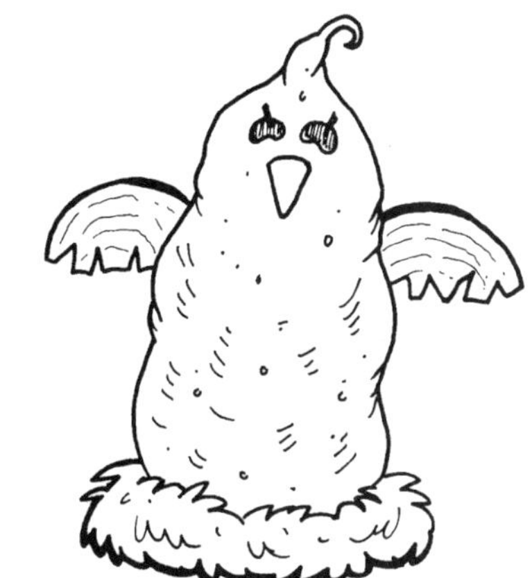

Let's Do It !

1. Create critters by pushing toothpicks into the potatoes for legs.
2. Use short broken pieces of toothpicks to hold raisins for eyes or a nose.
3. Use bits of carrots for a nose, ears, fangs, ridges, or wings.
4. Shred a rib of celery and attach it for a tail, or use celery leaves.
5. Add details by carving the sweet potatoes, or paint your critters.

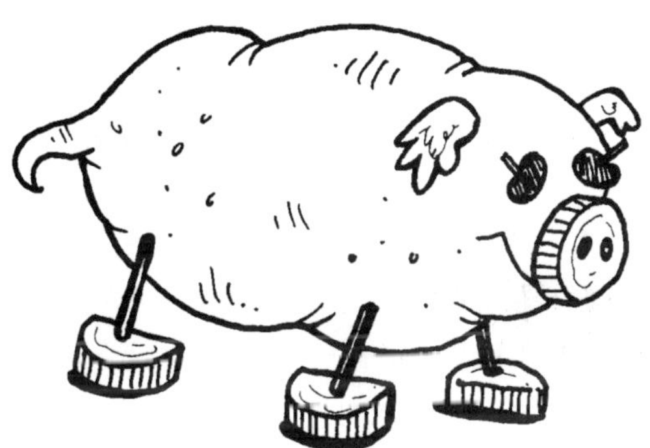

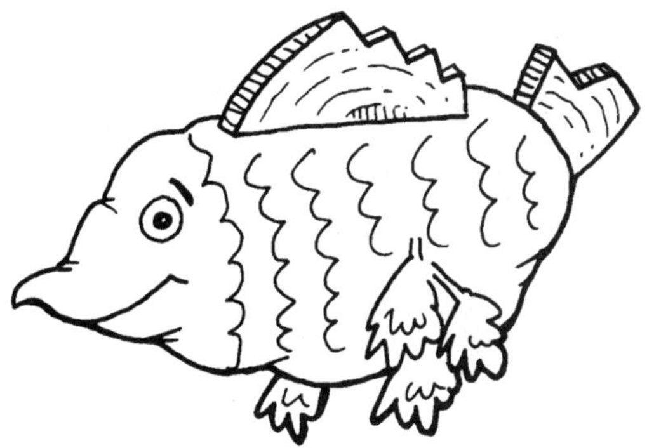

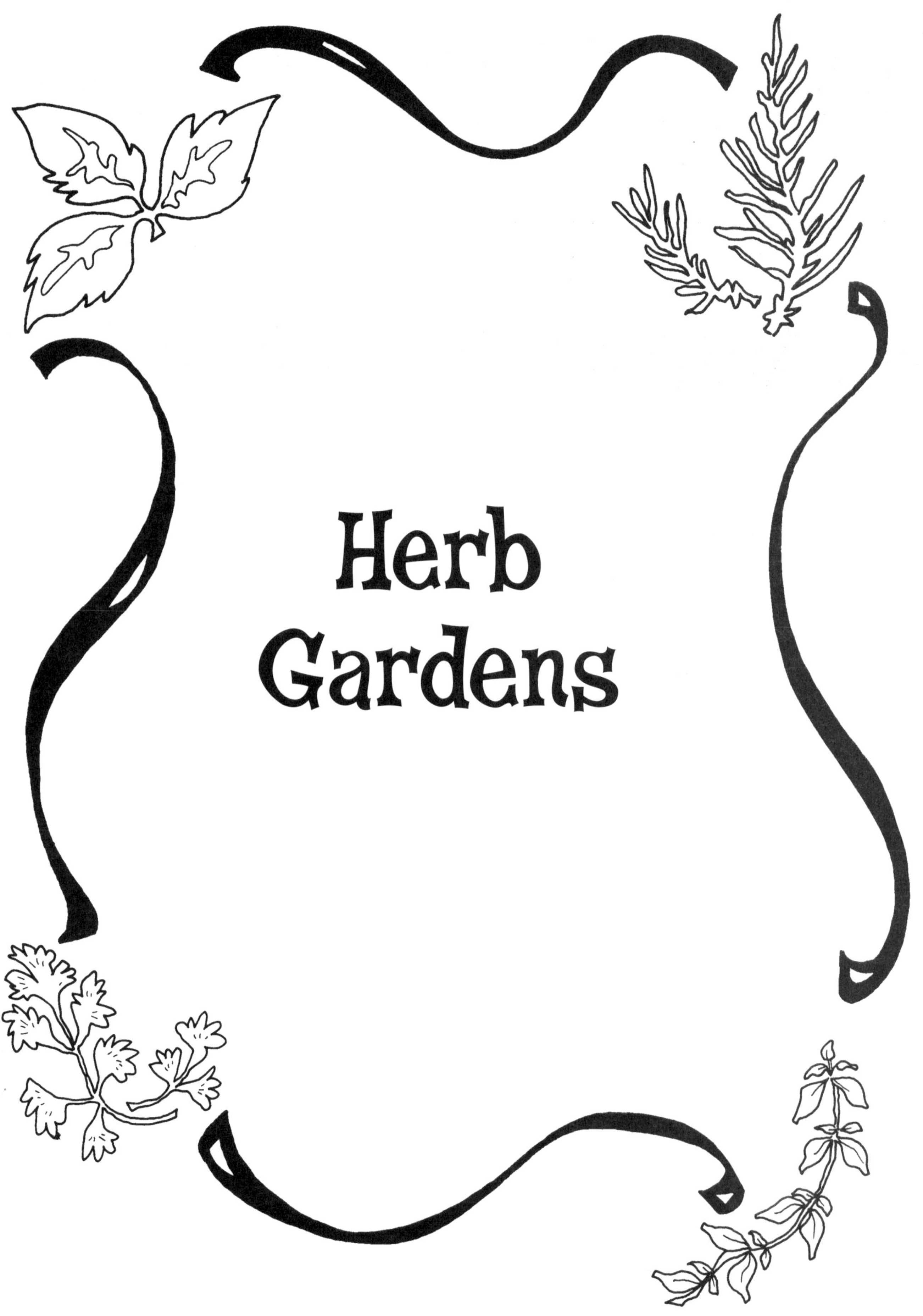

Herb Gardens

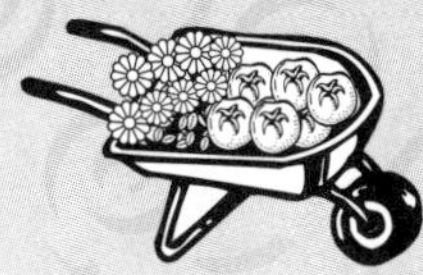

What's in Your Kitchen?

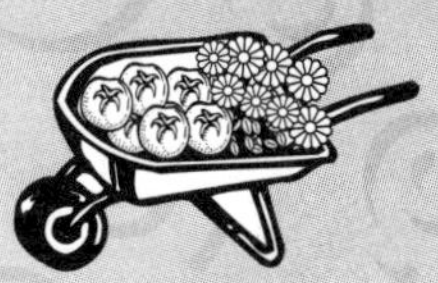

Spices, herbs, and other seasonings are used to add flavor to foods, and some are used as preservatives. Use the checklist below to find out what is in your kitchen and to record what herbs you are growing in your garden. Mark an X by the ones you find. Mark an * by your favorite herbs, spices, and seasonings.

Herbs, Spices, and Seasonings		
allspice	garlic powder	tarragon
anise	garlic salt	thyme
basil	horseradish powder	turmeric
bay leaf	lemon extract	vanilla
black pepper	lemon pepper	Others:
caraway seed	mace	
cardamom	marjoram	
cayenne pepper	mint	
celery salt	mustard, dry	
celery seed	nutmeg	
chives	oregano	
cinnamon	paprika	
cloves	parsley flakes	
cumin	poppy seed	
curry powder	rosemary	
dill	sage	
dill seed	salt	
garlic cloves	sesame seed	

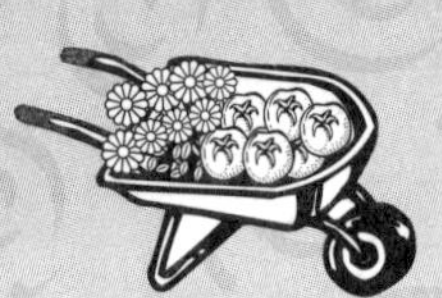

Herbs

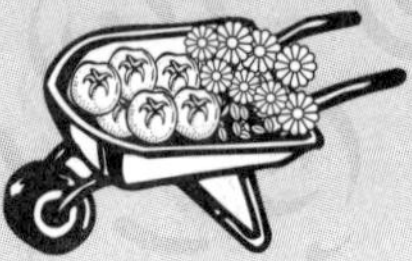

Materials

- trowel
- baking sheet
- potting soil and sand
- balanced fertilizer and compost
- packages of seeds and/or small herb plants
- tightly covered containers
- paper towels
- hoe
- garden rake

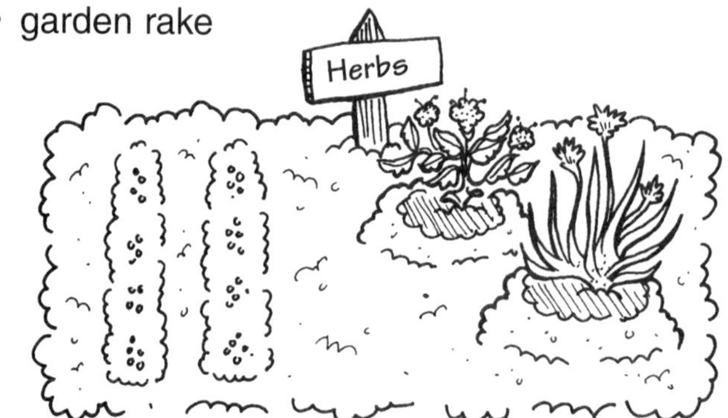

Let's Do It !

1. Herbs need full sun and well-drained soil. Construct raised gardens or plant herbs in pots. If the ground soil is hard, work in compost and sand well, and mix in a balanced fertilizer.
2. Make furrows for seeds and holes for plants. Pat the soil firmly in place and water the plants or seeds.
3. Weed and water the herbs regularly. Pick the leaves before the plants bloom for more fragrant herbs.
4. Thin plants grown from seeds.
5. Wash and dry the leaves on paper towels to retain more flavor. You may oven-dry them, but they tend to lose flavor if they are oven-dried. To oven-dry herbs, heat the oven to 200°F, and then turn it off and place the leaves inside on a baking sheet until they are dry.
6. Store herbs in tightly covered containers away from light.

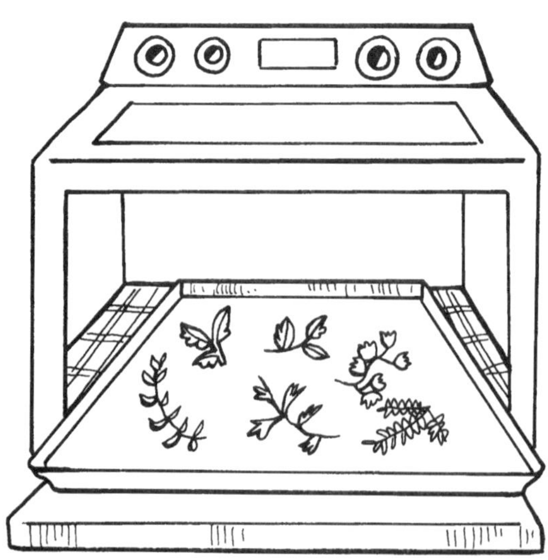

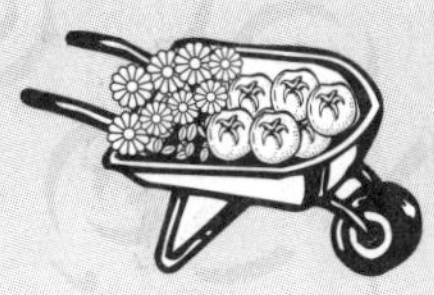

Herbs

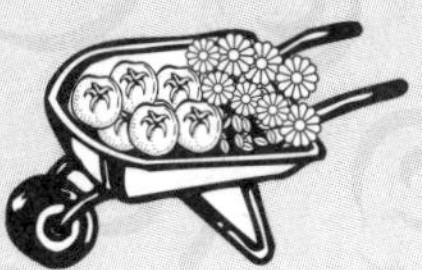

More Ideas

- Tie small bunches of herbs together with string and hang them in a cool, dry, well-ventilated place such as an attic or breezeway.
- Plant a small raised herb garden designed to show off the contrasting colors and textures of the plants. Consult books on herb gardening for ideas and pictures.
- Grow a few plants of different herbs in a design pattern.

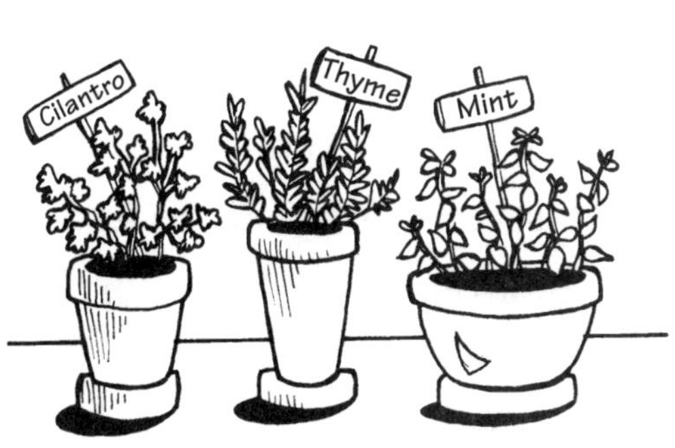

- Transplant extra herb plants into pots and give them as gifts.

Tidbits

- ✧ Herbs have been used throughout history for flavoring foods, medicinal purposes, and as aromatic fragrances.
- ✧ Fresh herbs are more delicate in flavor than crushed or powdered dry herbs. Use $\frac{1}{3}$–$\frac{1}{2}$ teaspoon of dried herbs in place of one tablespoon of fresh herbs. If you are increasing a recipe, do not increase the herbs proportionately. Instead, season to taste.
- ✧ Grow herbs on a sunny windowsill, among vegetables or flowers in the garden, or in formal herb gardens.

Learn More

Casely, Judith. *Grandpa's Garden Lunch*. New York: Greenville Books, 1990.

Cleaver, Bill. *Where the Lillies Bloom*. Philadelphia, PA: Lippincot, 1989.

George, Jean Craighhead. *My Side of the Mountain*. New York: Puffin Books, 2001.

"Growing Ideas," Volume 7, Number 3, September, 1996. National Gardening Association, 180 Flynn Avenue, Burlington, VT 05401.

Laird, Elizabeth and illustrated by Satomi Ichikawa. *Rosy's Garden.* New York: Philomel Books, 1990.

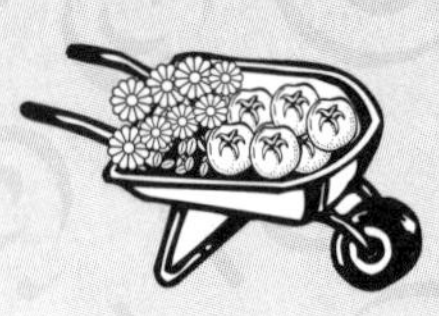

Grilled Cheese and Herb Sandwich

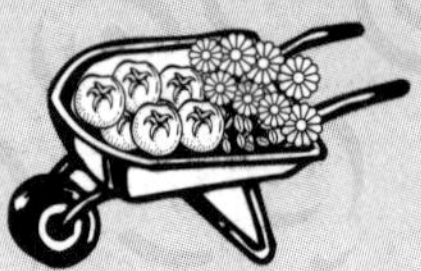

Materials

- 2 slices of bread
- 1 medium tomato, sliced thin
- fresh or dried oregano, chopped
- 1 slice of American cheese
- 1 medium onion, sliced thin
- cutting board
- butter, softened to room temperature
- 1 thin slice of low-fat ham
- paring knife
- frying pan
- wide spatula

Let's Do It !

1. Spread softened butter on the outside of each slice of bread.
2. Place one piece of bread buttered side down in the frying pan. On top of it place a slice of cheese, a slice of onion, a slice of ham, and a slice of tomato. Sprinkle it with oregano. Top it with the other slice of bread, buttered side up.
3. Heat the frying pan and brown the sandwich on both sides.
4. Cut the sandwich in half and serve it hot.

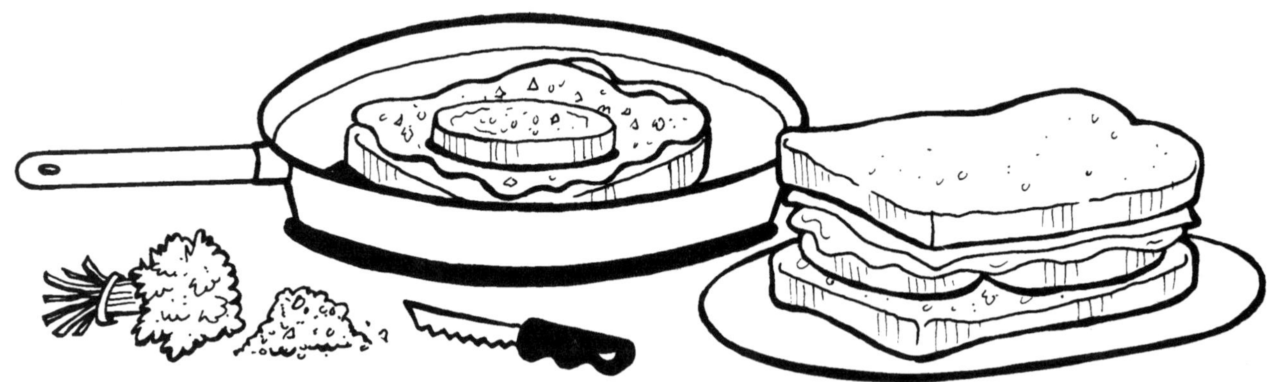

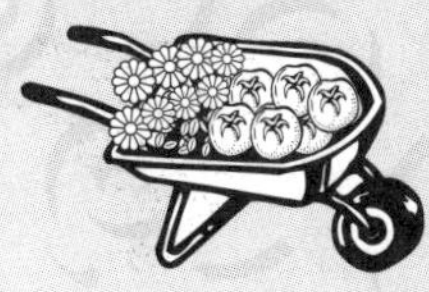

Toasted Herb Bread

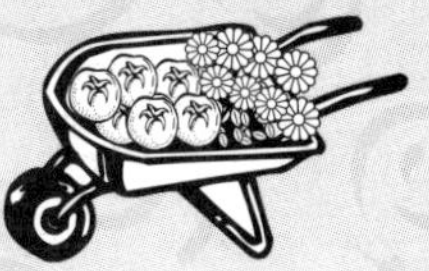

Materials

- 1 loaf French or Italian bread
- $^{1}/_{2}$ cup butter
- $^{1}/_{4}$ cup Parmesan cheese
- table knife
- serrated knife
- cutting board
- small bowl
- mixing spoon
- $1^{1}/_{2}$ teaspoons Italian herbs (marjoram, thyme, rosemary, sage, oregano, basil)

Let's Do It !

1. Slice the bread into pieces 1" thick.
2. In the broiler of your oven, or in a toaster oven, toast the slices on one side.
3. Blend the butter, cheese, and herbs together into a paste.
4. Spread the herb paste on the untoasted sides of the bread and toast until light tan.

More Ideas

- Make toasted croutons by cutting slices of bread into cubes and sauté in butter until they are an even brown. Add salt, paprika, and herbs to a bag with hot croutons and shake until they become evenly coated.
- Add croutons to different soups, noodles, and salads.

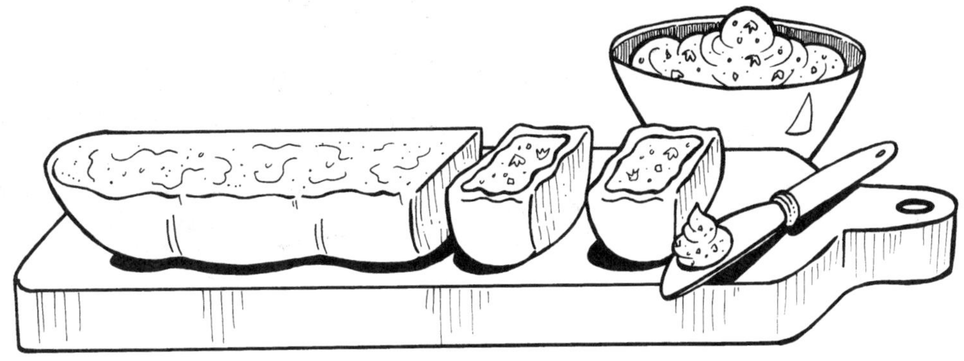

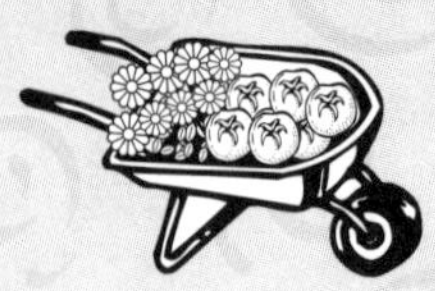

Herb Salad Dressing

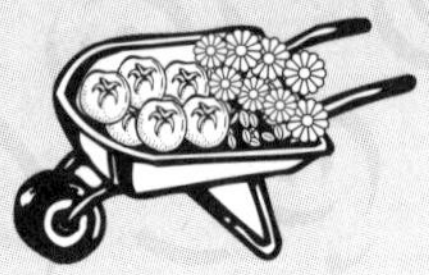

Materials

- $1\frac{1}{2}$ teaspoon salt
- 1 teaspoon oregano
- 1 teaspoon pepper
- 1 teaspoon dill weed
- $\frac{1}{2}$ cup parsley, minced
- 2 tablespoons Dijon mustard
- 1 tablespoon sugar
- $\frac{1}{2}$ cup vinegar
- $\frac{3}{4}$ cup vegetable oil or olive oil
- blender or shake bottle with lid

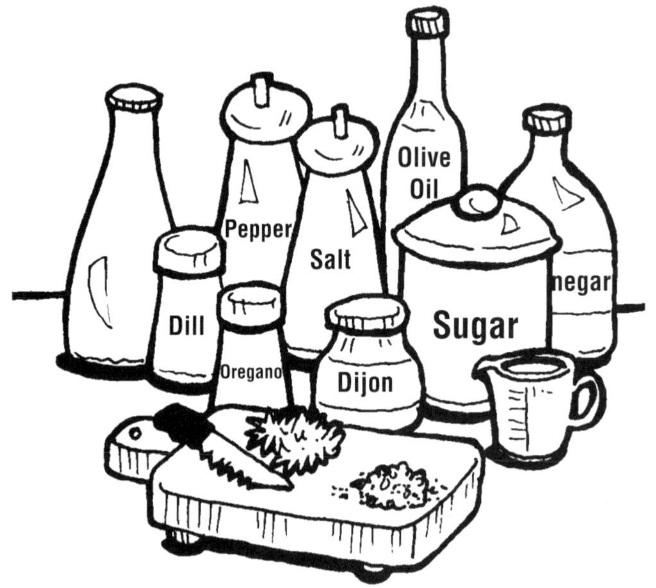

Let's Do It !

1. Blend all the ingredients together in a blender or bottle.
2. Shake the mixture well, and chill it in the refrigerator.
3. Shake it well again before using.

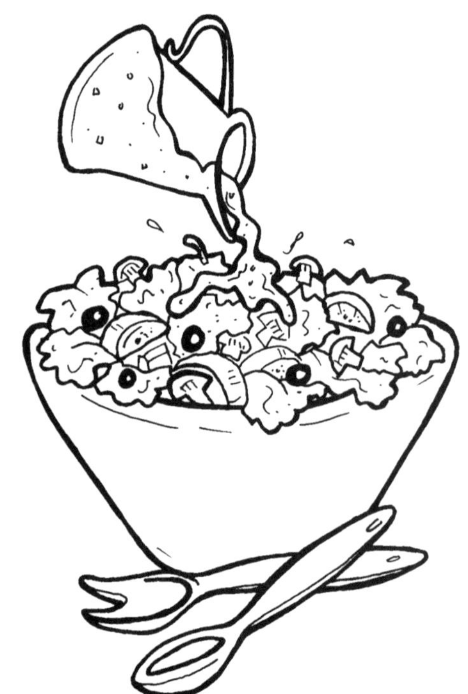

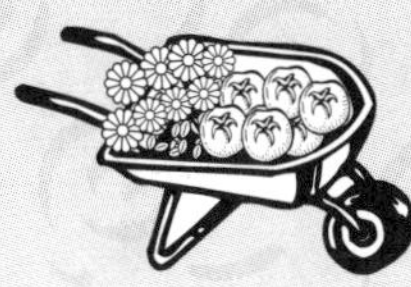

Herb Wreath

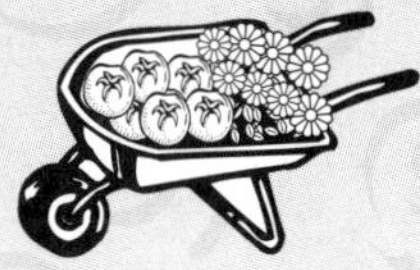

Materials

- wooden or wire wreaths, 6" diameter or greater
- small bunches of dried herbs (lavender, rosemary, yarrow, thyme)
- glue
- florist wire
- ribbon or raffia
- shears
- clippers
- greenery (boxwood, pine, cedar, eucalyptus)
- wire

Let's Do It !

1. Buy wreath frames or make your own:
   - Gather woody vines from grapes or honeysuckle or use slender pliable willow tree branches.
   - While the vines are green and pliable, remove the leaves and twine them into a wreath shape, tucking in the ends.
   - Hang the wreaths in a clean, dry place to dry.
2. Make small bunches of dried herbs at least 4" long. Tie them together with raffia or florist wire.
3. Arrange the bunches one at a time on the wreath, overlapping the bunches to hide the ends. Glue and tie the bunches in place.
4. Glue small lengths of greenery onto the wreath to complete the arrangement.
5. Add a ribbon or raffia bow.
6. To create a hanger for the wreath, cut a piece of wire about 6" long. Insert it into the wreath at the back of the top and bend the ends to secure it to the wreath.
7. Small bunches of herbs can be arranged individually and tied on with narrow ribbon or raffia.

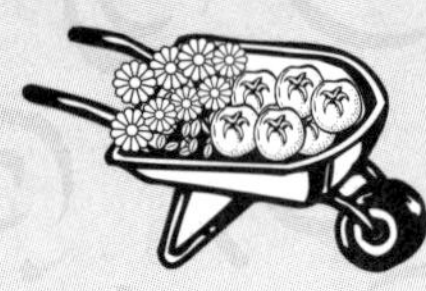

Lavender Sachet

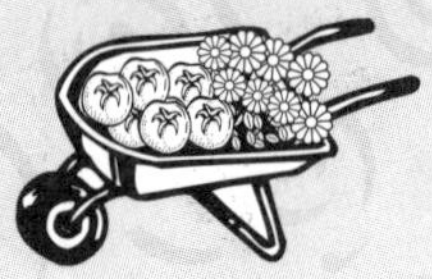

Materials

- sachet patterns (page 123)
- dried lavender flowers (about 1 cup for each sachet)
- assorted fabric pieces
- thread
- narrow ribbon
- needle and straight pins
- fusible, non-woven interfacing
- fabric glue (optional) or sewing machine
- iron and ironing board
- fabric paint
- shears

Let's Do It !

1. Make a copy of the pattern pieces on page 123. Use the heart and bear or make your own pattern.
2. Cut the pattern pieces out of the fabric of your choice, making two fabric circles for each sachet.
3. Cut a bear and a heart (or your patterns) out of fabric and fusible interfacing.
4. Lay the fabric patterns on top of one of the sachet pieces and iron them together, following the directions that come with the interfacing.
5. Seal the raw edges of the bear (or your pattern) with zigzag stitching or fabric glue, and add features or decorate with fabric paint.
6. Pin the two sachet pieces together with the fabric's right sides facing each other and sew them together, leaving part of the sachet open.
7. Clip the seam allowance, being careful not to cut through the stitching, and turn the sachet right sides out. Smooth the seam and press the sachet.
8. Fill the sachet with the dried lavender.
9. Make a hanging loop out of a 6" length of narrow ribbon. Insert both ends of the ribbon into the opening of the sachet and pin them in place. Then pin the opening shut and sew it together by hand.

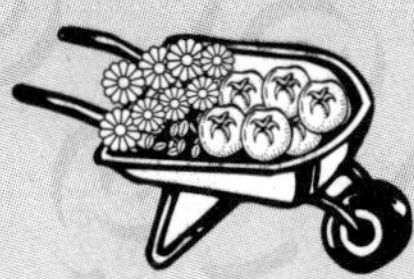

Sachet Patterns

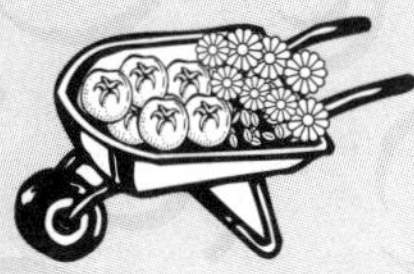

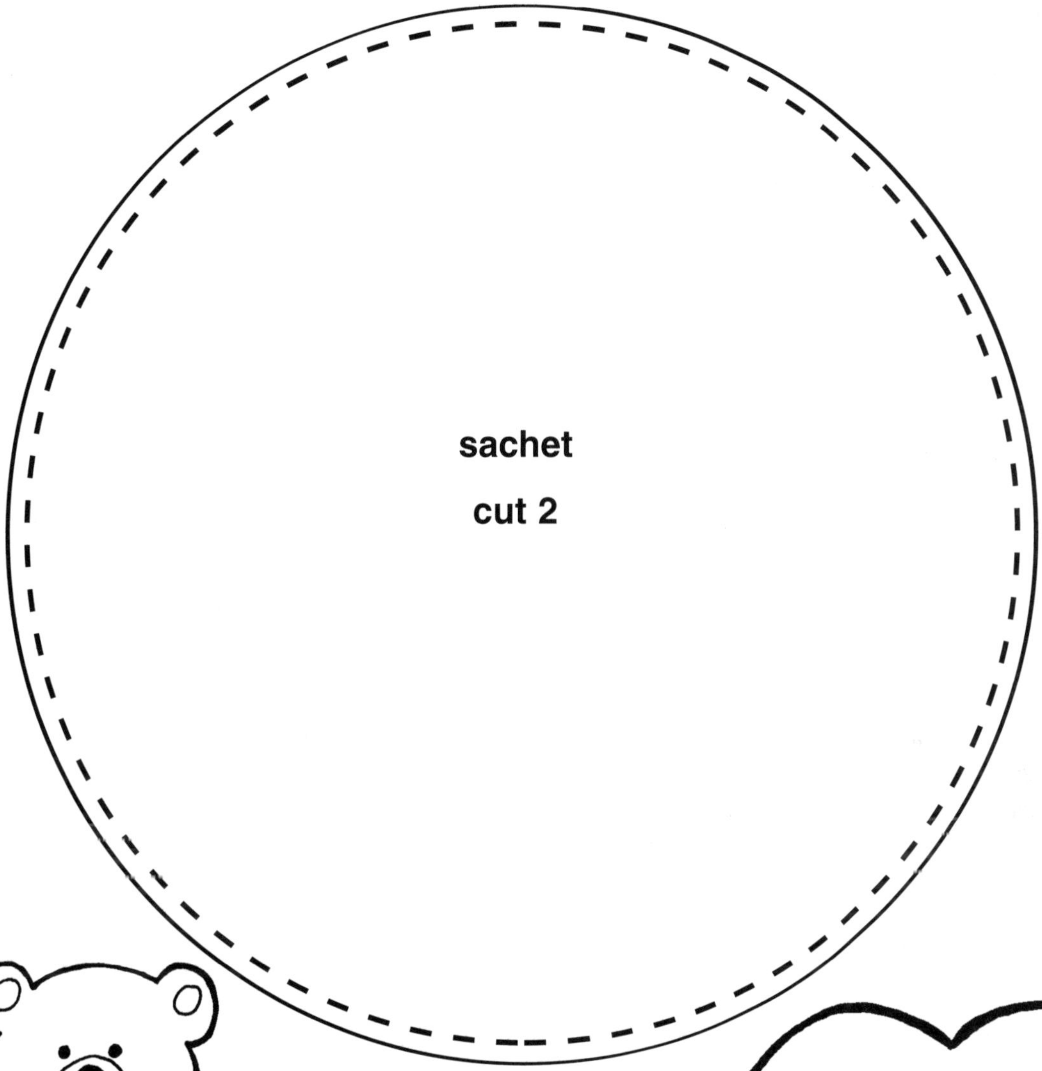

sachet

cut 2

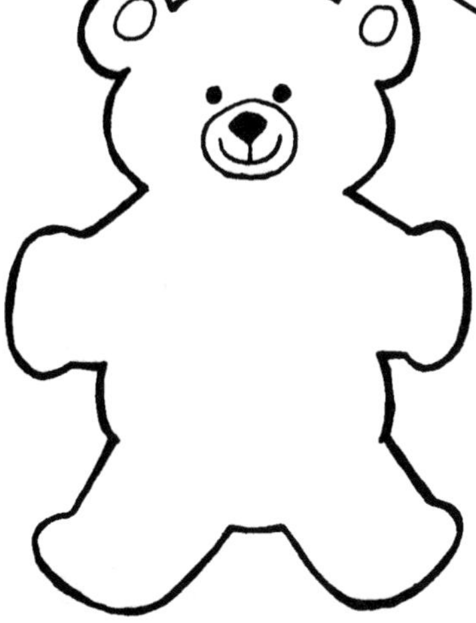

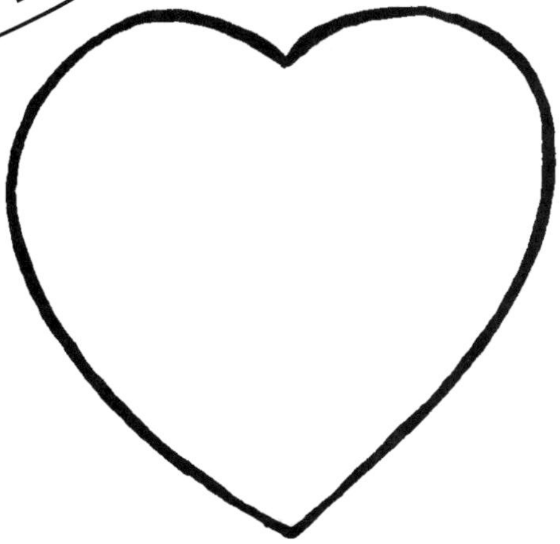

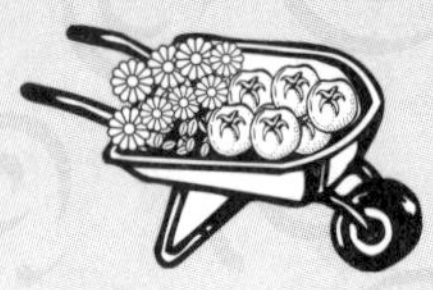

Herb Mask

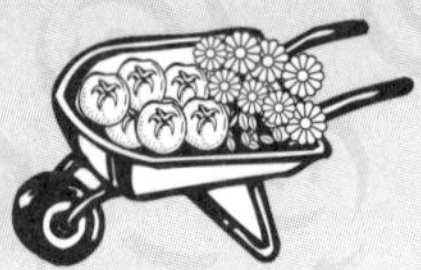

Materials

- paper plate
- stapler
- scissors
- large rubber band
- herbs
- glue

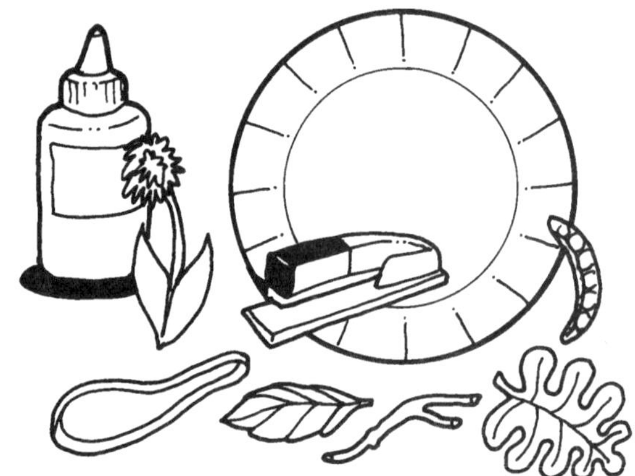

Let's Do It !

1. Cut mouth, eye, and nose holes in the paper plate.
2. Staple the rubber band to the sides of the plate.
3. On the front of the plate, glue the herbs.

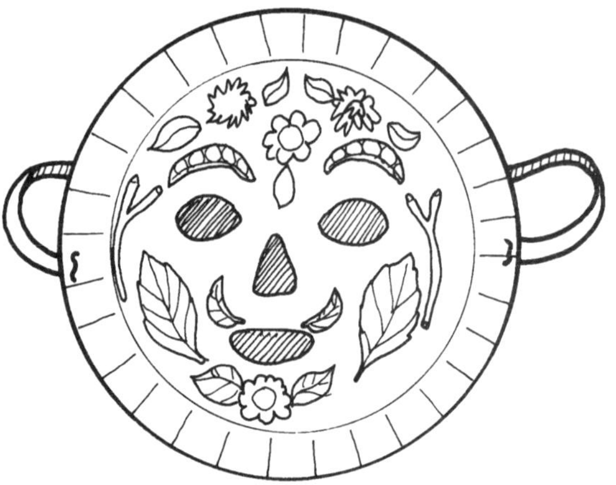

More Ideas

- Make your mask look like a specific animal. Use construction paper to help you make its features.
- Make a nature headband. Cut a construction paper strip to fit around your head. Glue on leaves and feathers and let the glue dry. Then, staple the ends together to form a headband.
- Using the same process as for the headband, make a nature bracelet and choker necklace. Wrap the paper bands around your neck or wrist and staple the ends together.

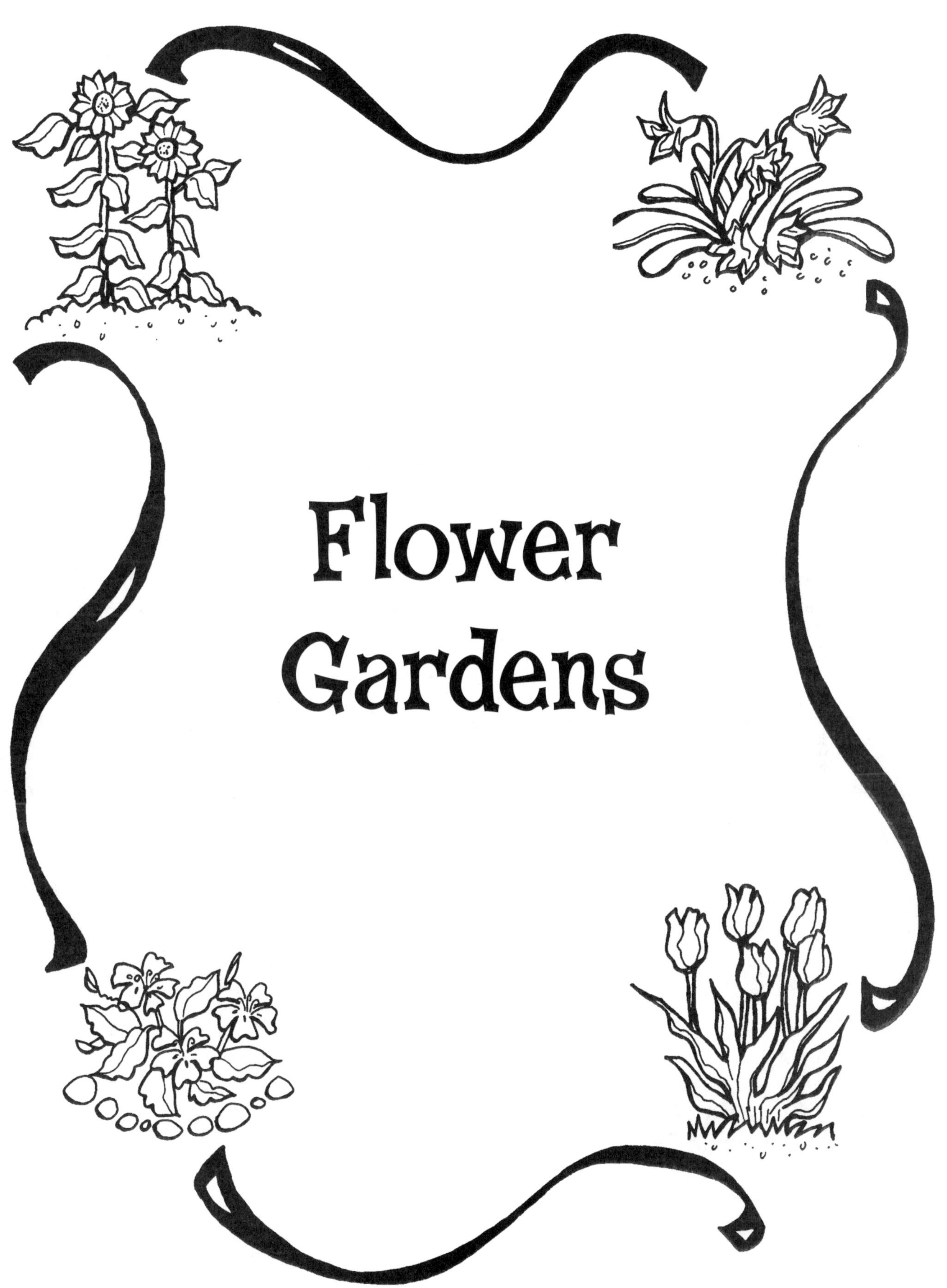

Flower Gardens

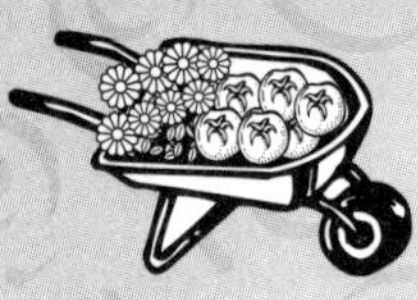

Annuals and Perennials

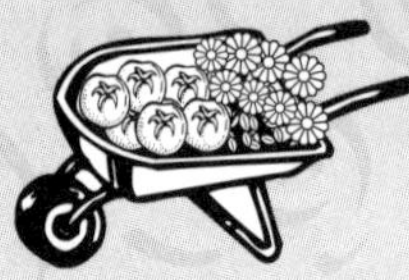

Materials

- flower seeds and/or plants
- bedding mix or slow-release fertilizer for flowers
- compost
- trowel or bulb planter
- hoe
- garden rake
- watering can or hose

Let's Do It !

1. Work fertilizer and compost into well-tilled soil.
2. Use a trowel or bulb planter to dig holes for small plants, and space plants according to container directions to allow for mature size. If planting seeds, follow the package directions, and thin plants as they grow.
3. Firm the soil around the plants or seeds, and water them thoroughly and regularly.
4. When the plants reach a height of about 3", pinch off the growing tip. This will promote side branching and fuller plants.
5. Keep dead blooms pinched or cut off so the plant's energy goes to making more flowers.
6. Apply a side dressing of bedding mix fertilizer during the growing season.

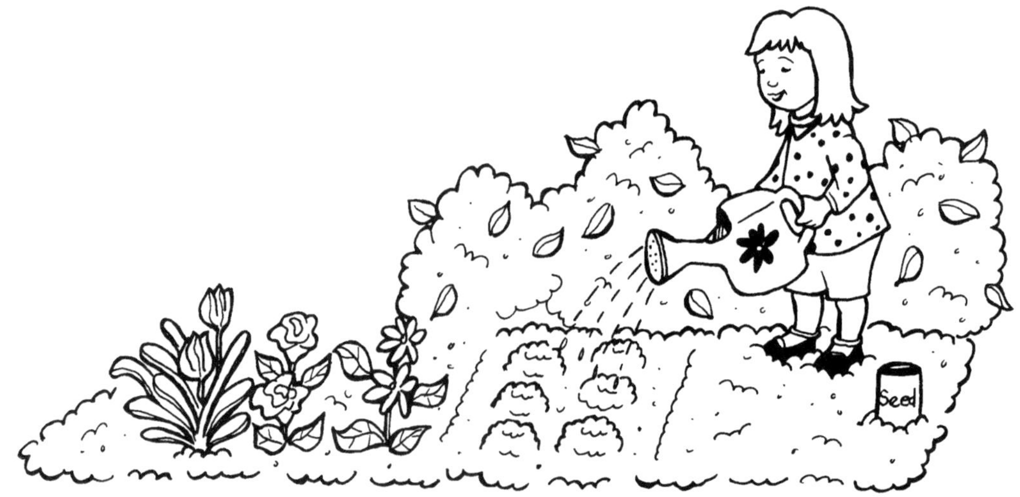

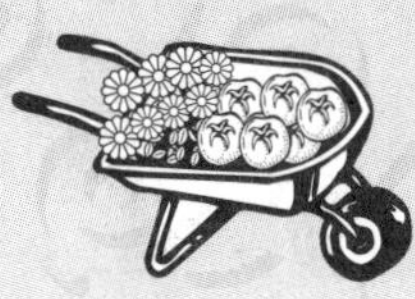

Annuals and Perennials

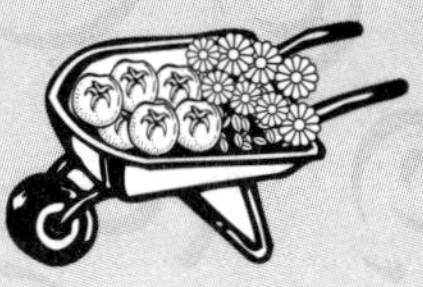

More Ideas

- Consider the mature height and size of plants, as well as the color of flowers and foliage. Place tall plants behind shorter plants. Dwarf varieties are nice for borders or in front of taller plants.
- Vining flowers are lovely in rock gardens, terraced beds, or hanging baskets.
- Sunflowers and marigolds brighten a vegetable garden, and marigolds help discourage insect pests.
- Mass several kinds of flowers in a wide container to provide color on a sunny doorstep or patio.
- Use a border or edging of rocks, bricks, or stones to keep grass out of flower beds.
- Most flowering plants require full sun for at least five to six hours a day to provide an abundance of flowers. Without enough sun they grow leggy and produce few blooms. However, some varieties do best in the shade or partial shade.

Tidbits

✧ Annuals must be planted each year, but perennials come back year after year.

✧ The flowers, leaves, and seeds of some plants are edible.

✧ You get quicker results by setting out flower plants rather than planting seeds.

Learn More

Burnett, Frances Hodgson. *The Secret Garden.* New York: HarperCollins, 1992. (also available in videotape)

Cooney, Barbara. *Miss Rumphius.* New York: Puffin Books, 1985.

de Paola, Tomie. *The Legend of the Bluebonnet.* New York: Putnam Juvenile, 1996.

Ehlert, Lois. *Planting a Rainbow.* San Diego, CA: Voyager Books, 1992.

Forte, Imogene. *Nature Craft: Simple Pleasures with Natural Treasures.* Nashville, TN: Incentive Publications, Inc., 1985.

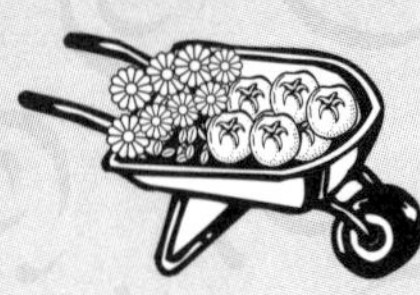

Dried Flowers

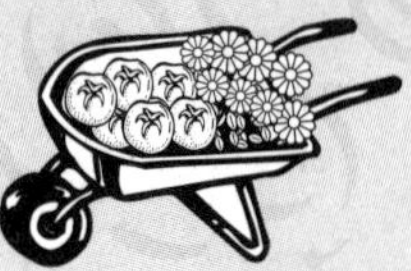

Materials

- flowers
- scissors
- clips
- string
- clothesline

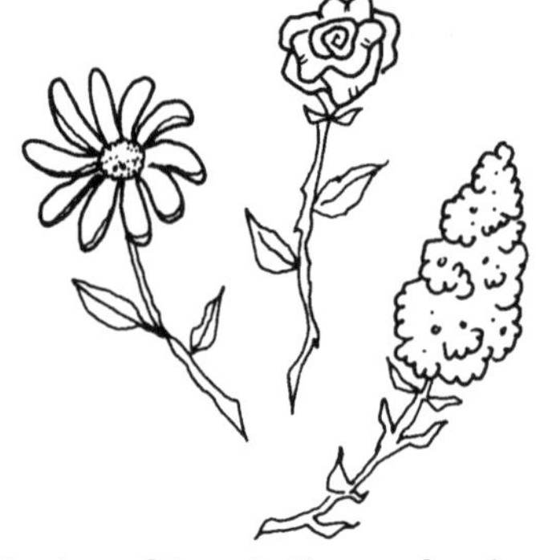

Let's Do It !

1. Cut the flowers before they reach full maturity or begin to fade. Check them for insects and plant disease. Remove any damaged or diseased leaves or stems.
2. Tie string to the flower stems individually or in small bunches. Tie them upside down on a line in a dry, well ventilated place indoors.

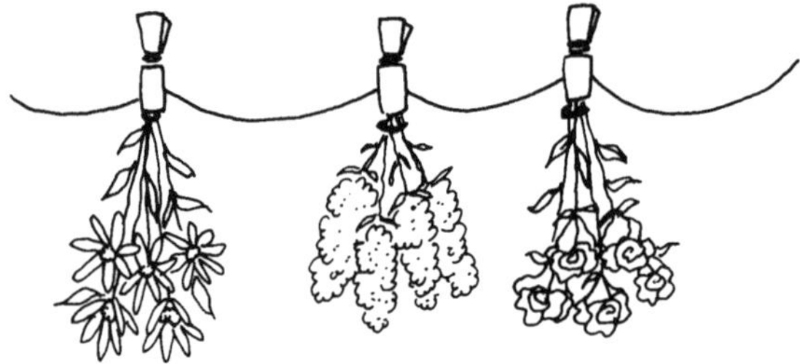

3. Cut the dried flowers to a desired length and arrange them in a vase, or glue them in wreaths or wall hangings.

More Ideas

- Use dried flowers in a picture or greeting card.
- Use the flower petals to make potpourri.
- Other dried objects to use are wildflowers that dry on the stalk and seed pods.

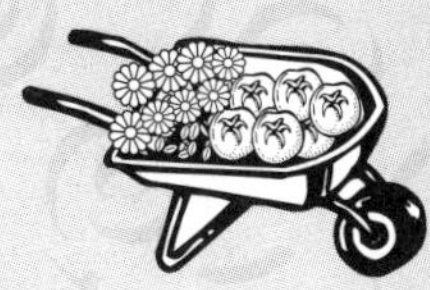

Pressed Flowers

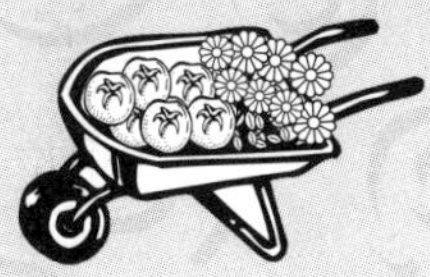

Materials

- flowers
- twine
- scissors
- white copy paper
- 8–12 pieces of cardboard the same size, 12" x 12" or larger

Let's Do It !

1. Cut the flowers you want to press, and remove any excess leaves.
2. Place a piece of copy paper on top of a piece of cardboard, and lay one flower on the paper.
3. Put another piece of cardboard on top of the flower and another piece of copy paper on the cardboard. Layer cardboard/paper/flower in this manner until you have sandwiched all your flowers.
4. Tie the stack together tightly with twine and put it in a cool, dry place. Check your flowers weekly until they are dry.

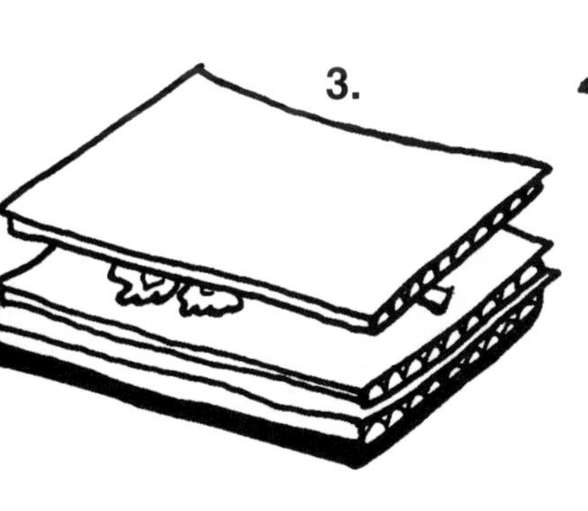

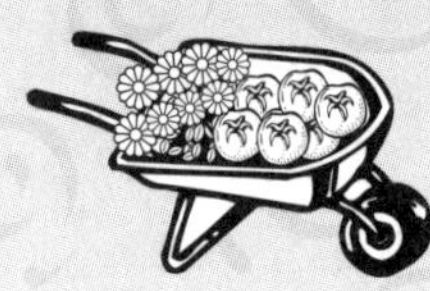

Bright Bouquets

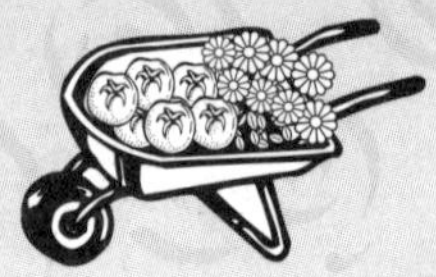

Materials

- packets of seeds (marigolds, petunias, zinnias, spider plant, bachelor buttons, Johnny-jump ups, pansies, salvia, nasturtiums, red salvia, snapdragons)
- germinating mix or potting soil
- peat pots, seed starter kits, peat discs
- clean half-pint milk or juice cartons
- trowel
- craft sticks
- fine-tip permanent marker
- newspaper
- clear plastic wrap

Let's Do It !

1. See the general information about growing annuals and perennials on pages 126–127.
2. Select the type of containers and soil mixture you will need for starting your seeds indoors.
3. Cover the work area with newspaper.
4. Dampen the soil mixture ahead of time. Fill the containers with soil and press it down gently.
5. Plant the seeds to the depth recommended on the seed packets, and water the seeds lightly.
6. Write the names of the seeds on the craft sticks and put them with the containers. Cover the containers with plastic wrap to retain moisture until the plants sprout.

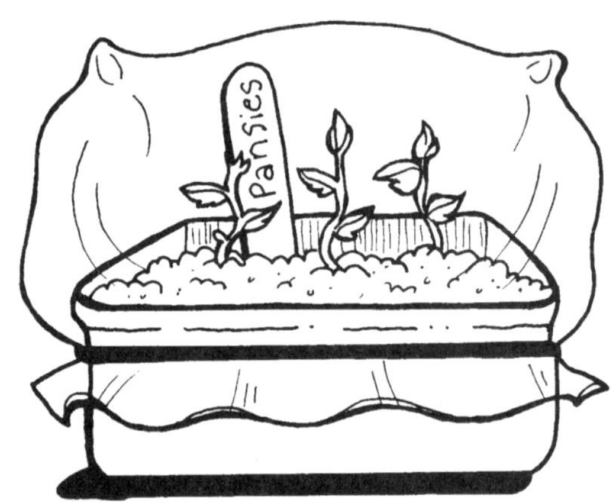

7. When the plants have sprouted, remove the plastic covering. Put the plants in a sunny location where they will receive sunlight 6–8 hours a day.
8. Check your plants every 2–3 days, and water as needed to maintain damp but not soggy soil.
9. When plants are 3" tall, pinch off the growing tip to encourage branching and fuller plants.
10. Set plants outside in a sheltered spot for a few days before transplanting into the garden or outdoor containers.

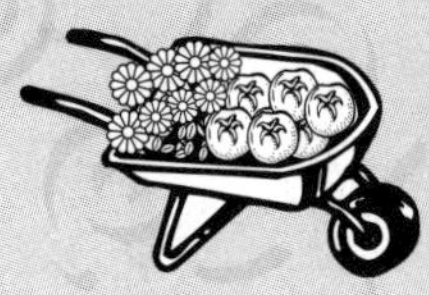

Bright Bouquets

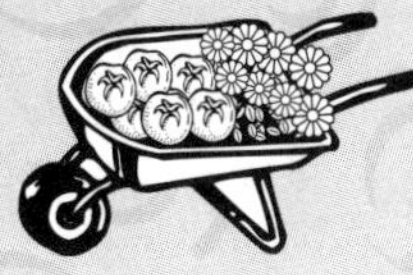

More Ideas

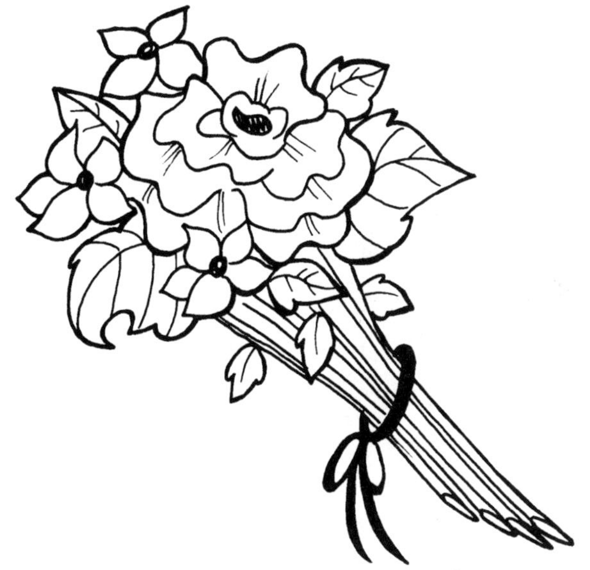

- Grow flowers you can eat, such as daylilies, violets, nasturtiums, and dandelions.
- Grow flowers in window boxes or other containers placed where they receive six to eight hours of sunlight a day.
- Cut flower stems at an angle to provide more surface for absorbing water.
- Carry a bucket of water to put flowers in as you cut them.
- Cut flowers in the early morning or late afternoon when it's cool.
- Select flowers that are beginning to open rather than ones that are mature.
- Remove diseased, damaged, and excess leaves and those that will be under water in a vase.
- Use a flower preservative to help flowers last longer. A teaspoon each of sugar and liquid bleach works for this.
- Change the water in your flower arrangement every two or three days. Trim the ends of the stems again, and remove any dead blooms.

Tidbits

✧ Many flowers can be started indoors when it's too cold to plant outside. They can be transplanted to window boxes or the garden later.

✧ Lovely flowers also grow on bushes and trees and from bulbs, rhizomes, and tubers.

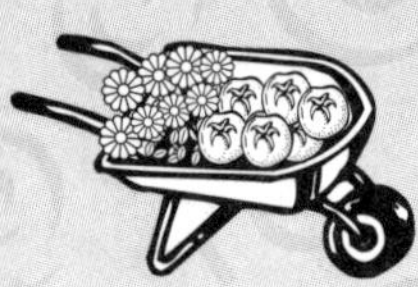

Braided Flower Crown

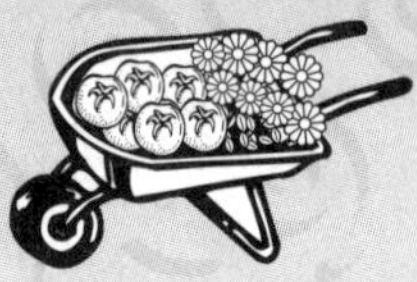

Materials

- fresh cut flowers with stems at least 5"–6" long
- scissors
- narrow ribbon *(optional)*

Let's Do It !

1. Cut single stems of flowers and remove the leaves.
2. Begin braiding three flowers as you would braid hair, and add flowers as you go.
3. Loop each stem around the preceding one, and go through to form a loose knot.
4. When you are finished, connect the end stems into the beginning part of the braid. Trim off excess stems.
5. Add a pretty narrow ribbon.

1.

2.

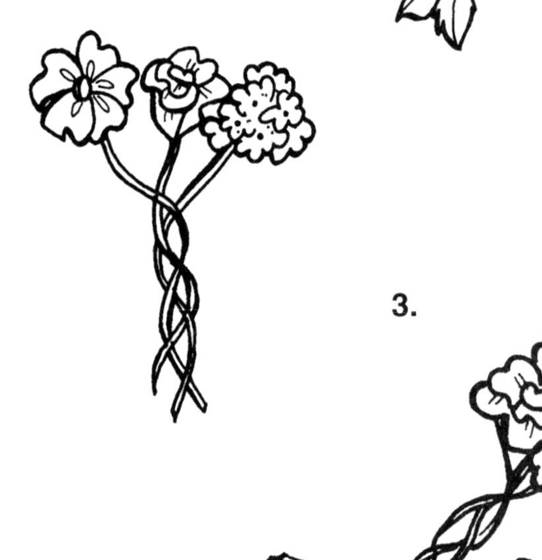

3.

4.

5.

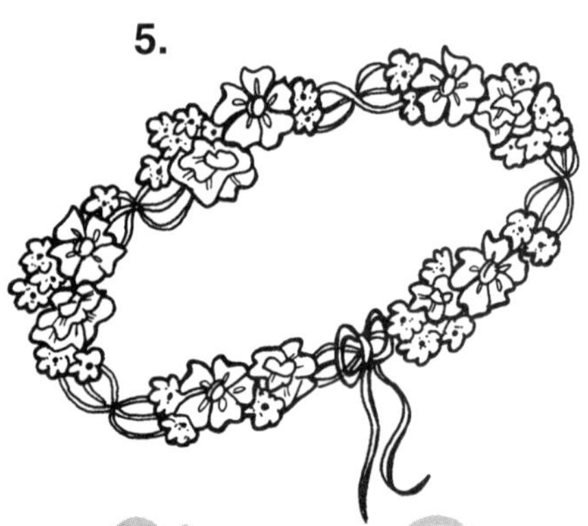

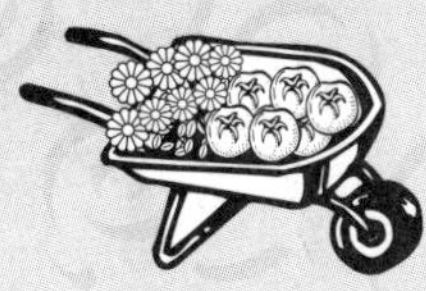

Flower Jewelry

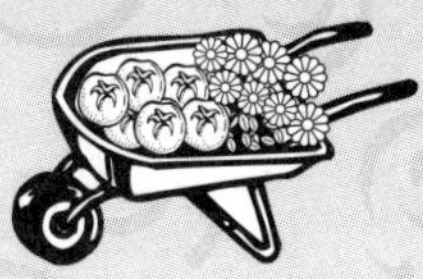

Materials

- cut flowers
- dental floss
- blunt-tip tapestry needle
- scissors

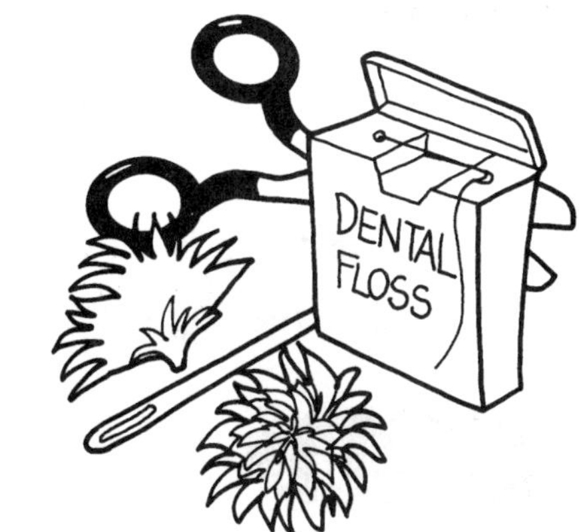

Let's Do It !

1. Thread the needle with dental floss. Double the floss, make sure it fits around your neck or wrist, and knot the ends together, leaving a dental floss tail.
2. String flower heads onto the floss until the floss is nearly covered.
3. Cut the needle off the floss and tie the dental floss tails together to form a necklace.

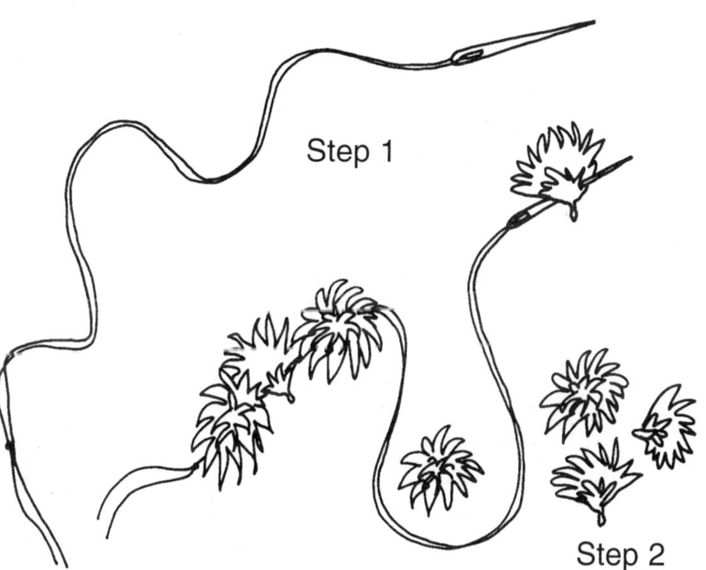

More Ideas

- Pin a flower head on your shirt.
- Alternate flower heads with leaves. (Get permission to pick them!)
- Read *Amy Loves the Sun* (Harper, 1988) by Julia Hoban.

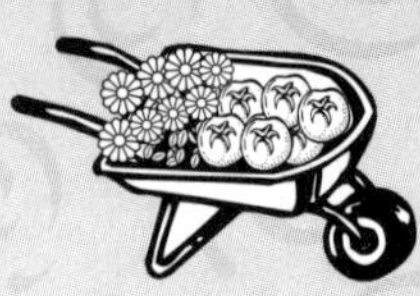

Sunflowers

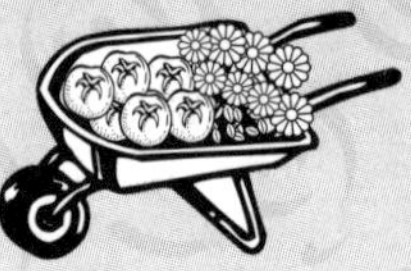

Materials

- sunflower seeds or seedlings
- hoe
- bloom booster fertilizer or bedding mix
- 1/2" mesh screening *(optional)*

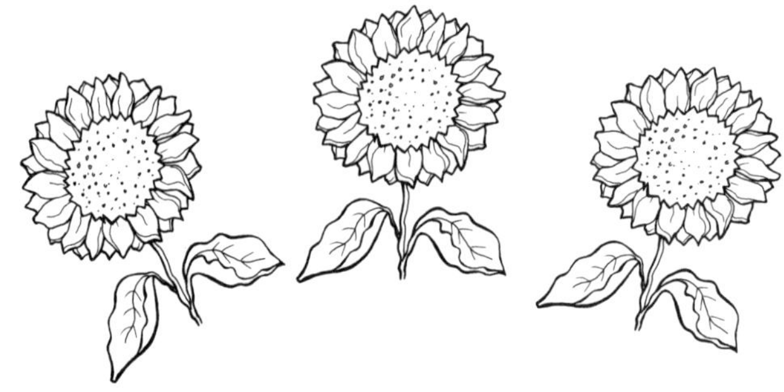

Let's Do It !

1. Work the fertilizer into well-tilled soil.
2. Plant seeds or seedlings when there is no danger of frost. Follow the package directions for planting.
3. If animals start to eat your planted seeds, protect them with a cover of 1/2" mesh screening until they reach at least 1" in height.
4. The sunflower head consists of florets surrounded by a ray of yellow petals. Harvest the flowers.
   - When the florets in the center have dried and the petals turn brown, cut off the flower heads and hang them upside down in a dry, well ventilated area for a week or two.
   - Brush the dried florets off the seeds. Cut apart the flower head and remove the seeds.

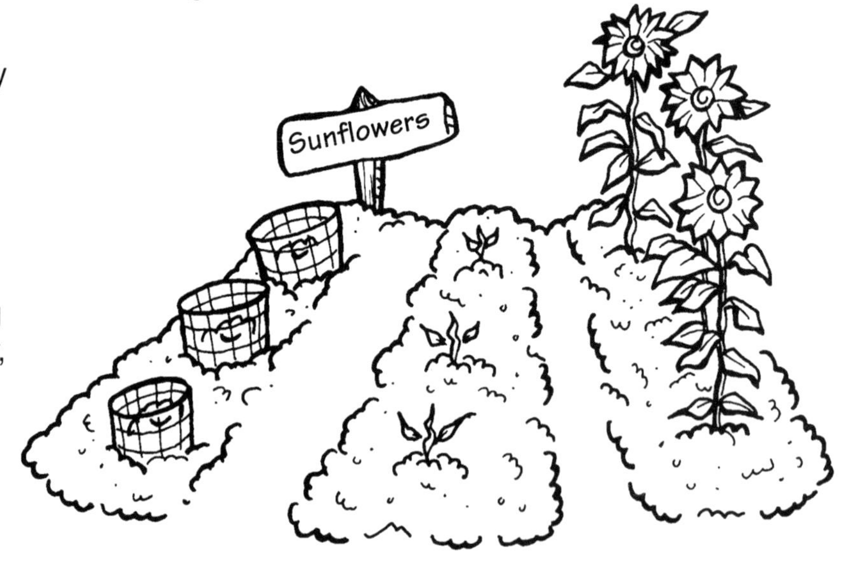

5. After harvesting, chop up the dead stalks and turn under in the soil, or add them to a compost pile.

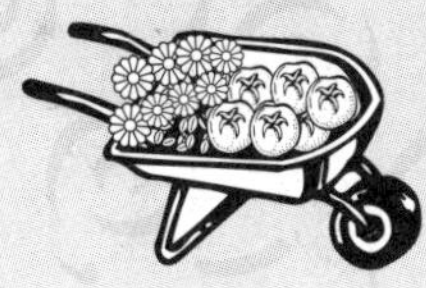

Sunflowers

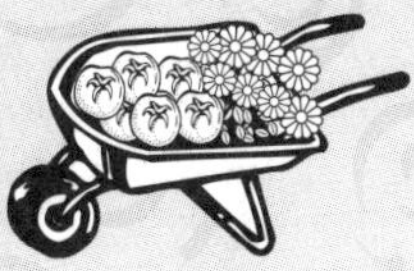

More Ideas

- Try several varieties of sunflowers and compare their flowers and seeds.
- Plant giant sunflowers.
- Grow seeds indoors and transplant them outside when the seedlings are about three inches tall.

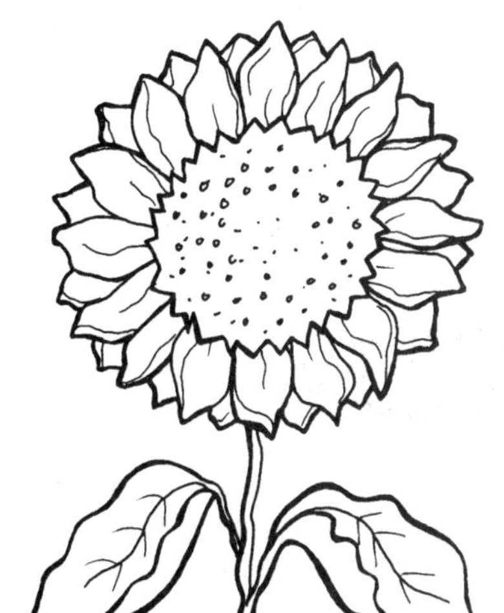

Tidbits

✧ Giant sunflowers grow quickly, can reach ten feet in height, and produce hundreds of seeds—sometimes over 1,000 seeds.

✧ Sunflower plant leaves, stalks, and flower heads can be prickly. Wear gloves.

✧ Sunflower seeds make a nourishing snack; they can be added to salads; and their oil is used in dressings and for cooking.

Learn More

Anholt, Laurence. *Camille and the Sunflowers: A Story About Vincent Van Gogh.* London: Barron's, 1994.

Celfe, Albie. *My First Garden Book.* Corte Madera, CA: NK Lawn and Garden Co., 1991.

Penner, Lucille R. *A Native American Feast.* New York: Macmillan Publishing Company, 1994.

Welch, Martha McKenn. *Sunflower!* New York: Dodd, Mead, and Company, 1980.

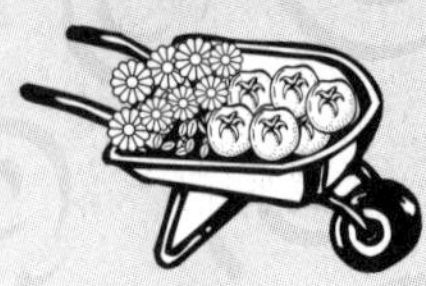

Seed to Sunflower

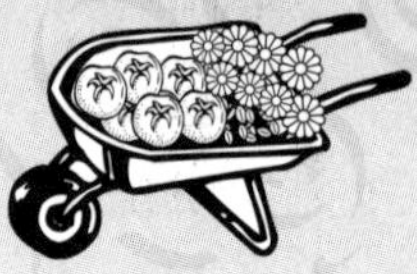

Materials

- planted sunflowers
- notebook or the log on page 137
- pencil or pen
- camera and film *(optional)*
- drawing paper
- yardstick
- magnifying lens

Let's Do It !

1. Use the notebook or log on page 137 to keep a record of your sunflower gardening project.
2. Draw pictures or take photographs of the sunflowers showing their stages of growth. Add the pictures to the logs and note the date you drew or photographed them.
3. Measure the width of the flowers from the tips of the yellow petals across to the tips on the other side.
4. Use a magnifying lens to examine the leaves and stems.
5. Note the different insects that visit your sunflowers.
6. Observe the pattern of the seeds.

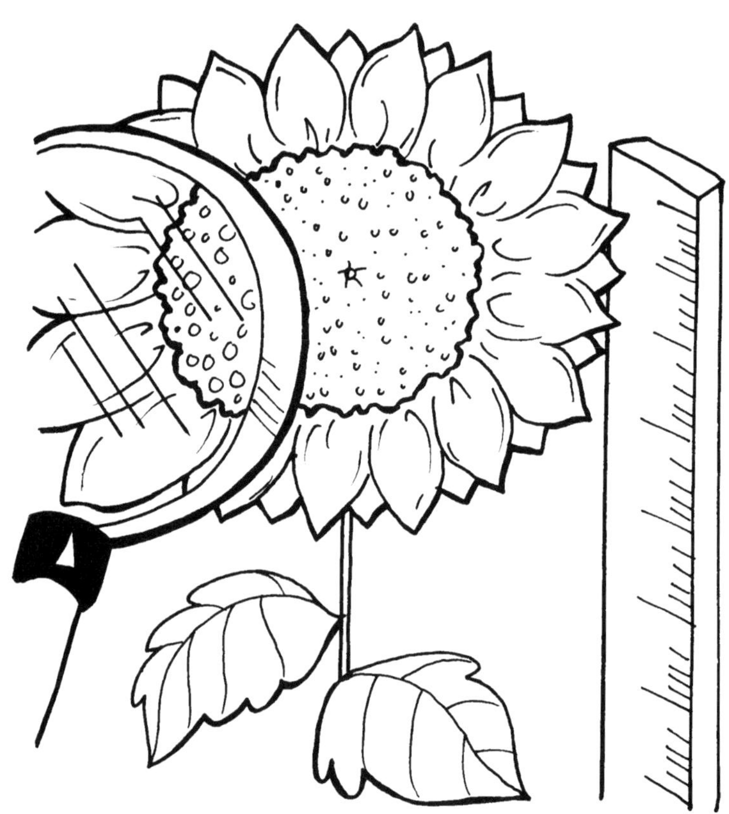

Seed to Sunflower Log

Date I planted seed	Days it took for seed to sprout	Seeds that sprouted	Number of days for flower head to begin to develop
Number of days until flower head harvested	Height of the plant when flower head harvested	Number of seeds in flower head	Seed pattern in flower head

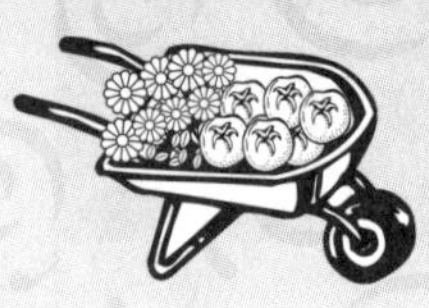

Sunflower Math

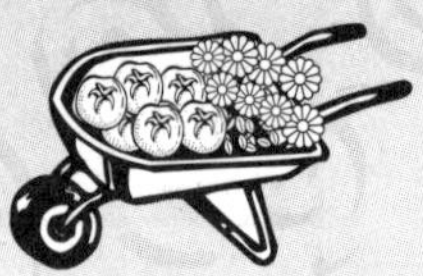

Materials

- dried sunflower heads with seeds
- newspaper
- kitchen scissors
- resealable plastic bags or clean containers with lids
- pencil and paper
- gardening gloves *(optional)*

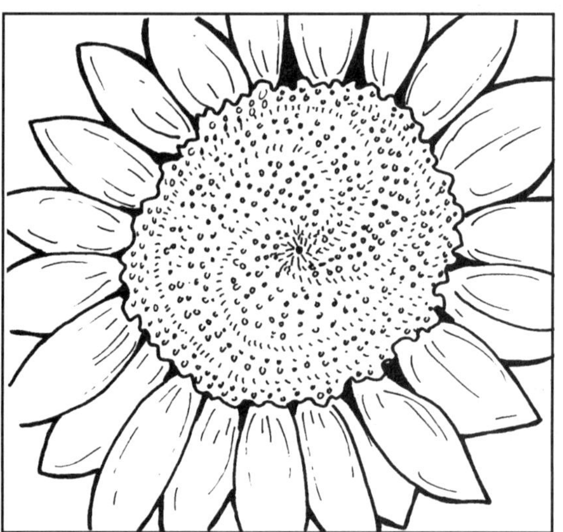

Let's Do It !

1. Examine the swirling pattern of the seeds in the flower head. Guess how many seeds are in each flower head, and write down your guess. Cover the table with newspaper.
2. Work with a partner, and cut the flower head into 4 or 5 sections. If the flower head is prickly, you may want to wear gloves. Remove the seeds and count them in piles of 10, 20, or 25. Add the total number of seeds for each flower head. Was your guess correct?
3. Compare the amount of seeds from the sunflowers.
   - What was the greatest number of seeds on one flower?
   - What was the least number of seeds on one flower?
   - What was the total number of seeds for the sunflowers harvested?
4. Store the seeds in resealable plastic bags or covered containers.

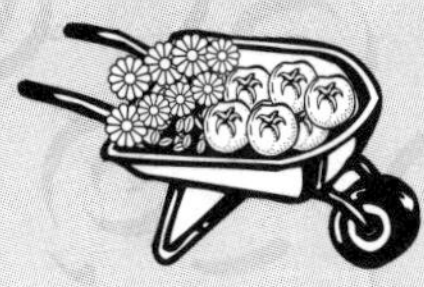

Sunflower Seed Snack

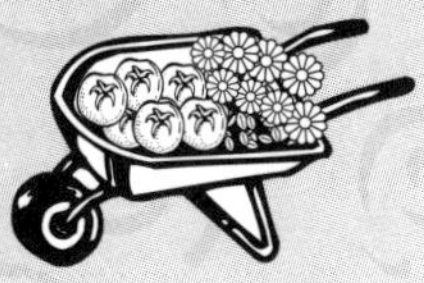

Materials

- raw sunflower seeds
- salt
- vegetable oil
- baking sheets with sides
- measuring spoons
- colander
- mixing bowl
- mixing spoon
- paper towels
- measuring cup

Let's Do It !

1. Wash and drain the sunflower seeds in a colander.
2. Dry them on paper towels.
3. In a mixing bowl, put 2 tablespoons of oil for each cup of seeds, and toss the seeds until they are coated. Add 1/2 teaspoon of salt for each cup of seeds, and stir to mix well.
4. Turn the seeds out on baking sheets and spread them apart in a thin layer.
5. Preheat the oven to 250°F, and roast the seeds for 10–15 minutes, stirring them frequently so they brown evenly.

More Ideas

- After washing and draining seeds, heat a heavy skillet with 2 tablespoons of oil per cup of seeds. Add the seeds and stir them constantly for 3 minutes. Turn the seeds out onto paper towels to drain, and sprinkle them with salt while they're still hot.

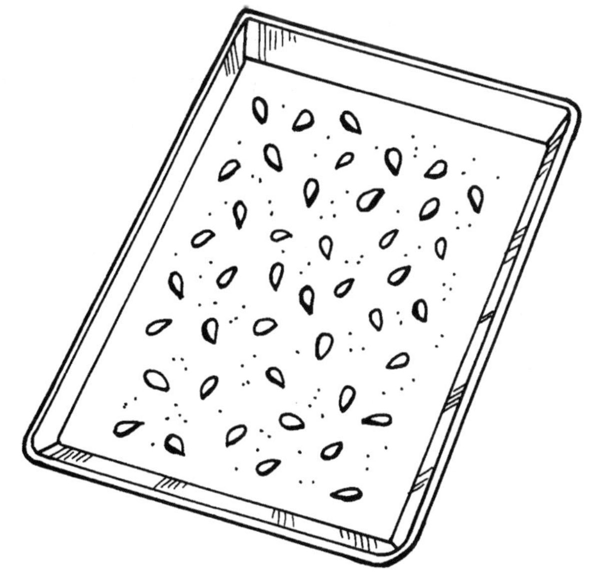

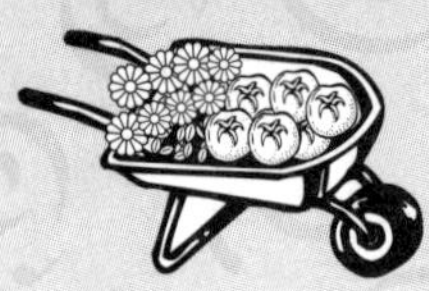

Flowers from Bulbs

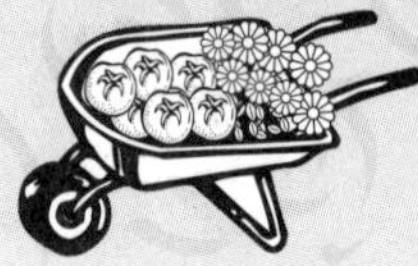

Materials

- flower bulbs
- bulb planter or trowel
- bone meal
- balanced fertilizer or bedding mix

Let's Do It !

1. Work the bone meal and fertilizer into well-tilled soil.
2. Use the bulb planter or trowel to make holes the specified depth for your bulbs. Place a bulb in each hole, with the pointed end upward.
3. Cover the bulbs with soil and water them thoroughly.
4. Weed and water the plants regularly.
5. When bulbs finish blooming, cut off the stems and allow the bulbs to continue to grow until the leaves die.
6. Dig up the bulbs and store them in a cool, dry place to replant the next year.

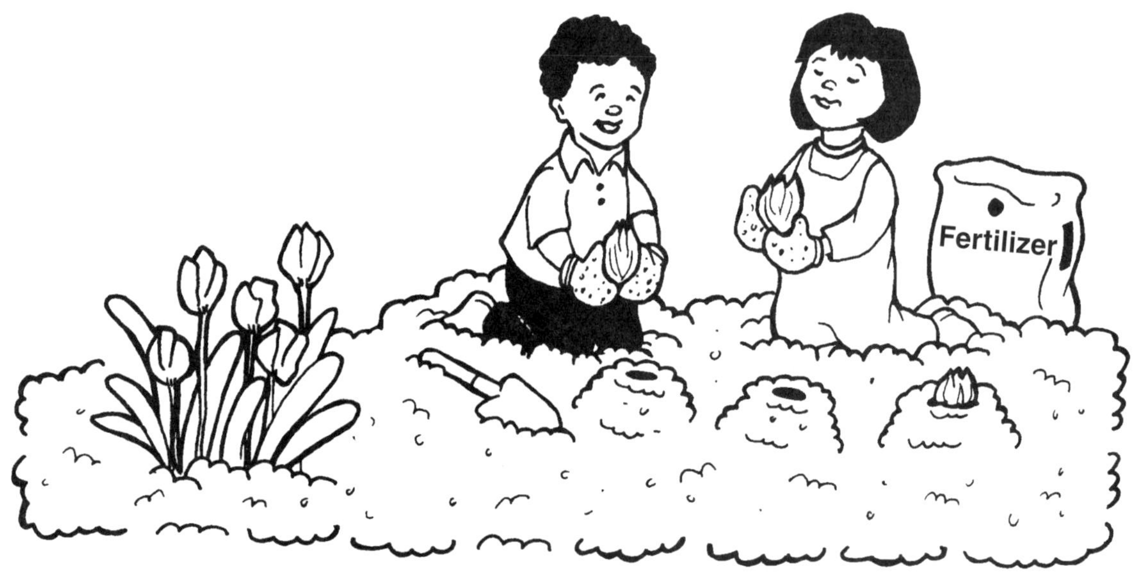

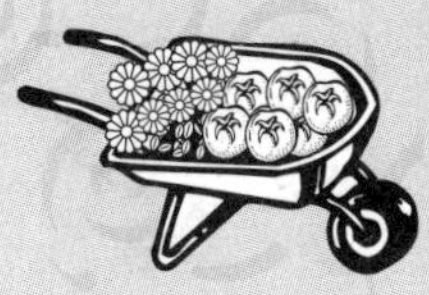

Flowers from Bulbs

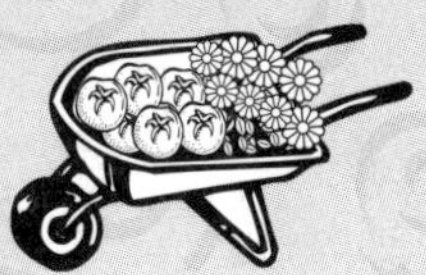

More Ideas

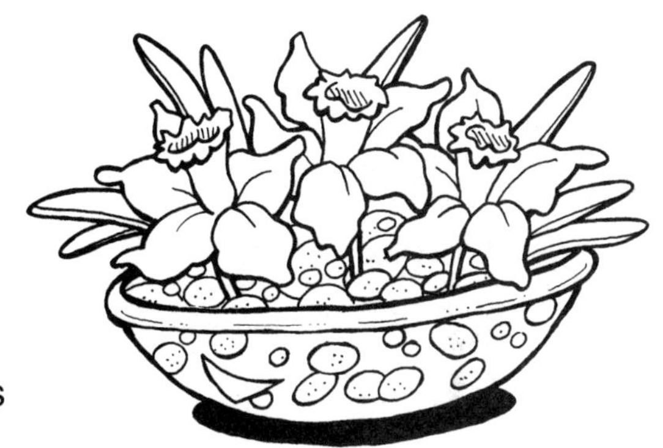

- Plant a dish garden. Refrigerate the bulbs for 2–3 weeks. Place about 1" of sand or stones in a shallow planter dish. Arrange the bulbs close together on top of the sand or stones and press them down gently to anchor them in place. Pour water in the dish until it reaches the top of the stones Put the dish garden in a sunny or well-lit place. When growth emerges from the bulbs, rotate the dish every few days so each bulb gets the same access to light. Add water to the dish as needed to keep the garden damp.
- Plant a dozen or more bulbs close together in your sunny flower garden for a mass of color. Find out which bulbs will naturalize in your area.

Tidbits

✧ Most flowers that grow from bulbs are perennials.

✧ Bulbs contain the undeveloped plant surrounded by layers of fleshy leaves that provide food for the plant.

Learn More

Forbes, Evan D. *Science in a Bag.* Huntington Beach, CA: Teacher Created Resources, Inc., 1995.

Pohl, Kathleen. *Tulips.* Milwaukee, MN: Raintree Publishers, 1982.

Robbins, Ken. *A Flower Grows.* New York: Dial Books, 1990.

Stout, A. B. *Daylilies.* Sagaponak, NY: Sagapress, 1986.

Walters, Jennie. *Gardening with Peter Rabbit.* London: Penguin Books, 1992.

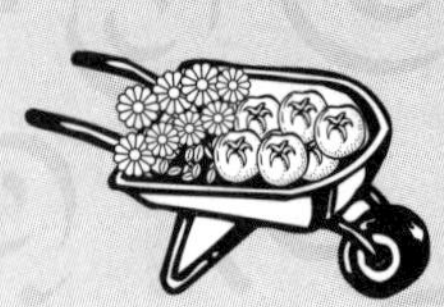

Butterfly and Bird Theme Garden

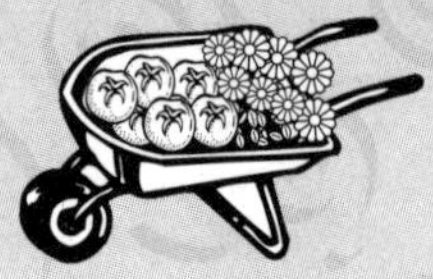

Materials

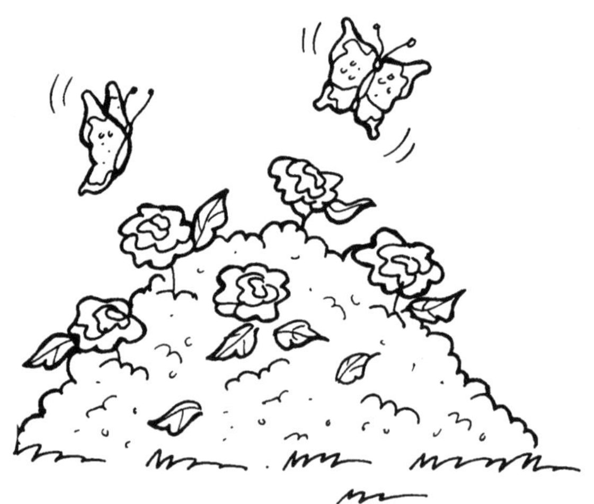

- seeds or plants
- shovel
- trowel
- garden rake
- bedding mix fertilizer
- birdbath and bird feeder
- water

Let's Do It !

1. Pick an area that gets full sun most of the day.
2. Work the fertilizer into well-tilled soil.
3. Plant the seeds or plants randomly together to fill the prepared area.
4. Water the plants regularly.
5. Add a bird feeder and a birdbath and clean and refill them regularly.
6. Put fresh water in the birdbath daily.

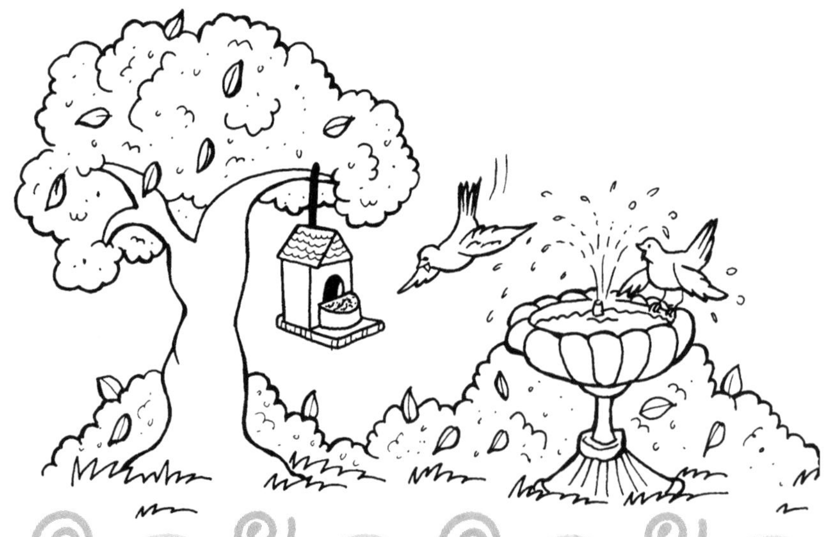

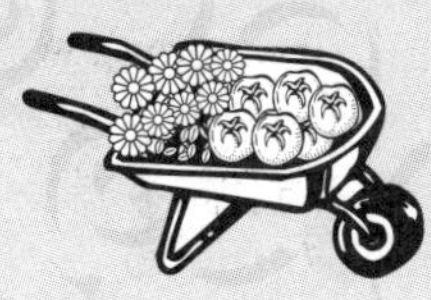

Butterfly and Bird Theme Garden

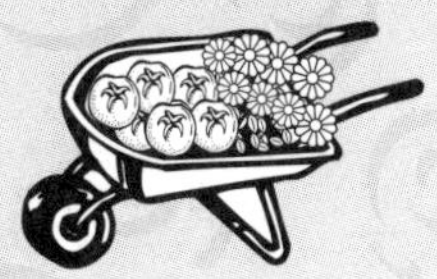

More Ideas

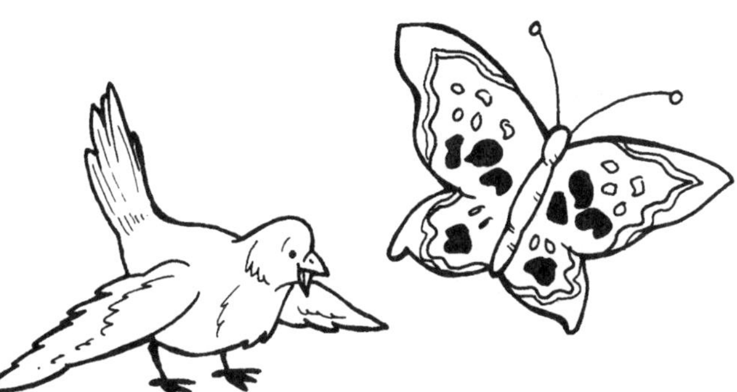

- Use binoculars for a closeup look at birds and butterflies. Draw and color pictures or take photographs of the ones you see to help you identify them in guidebooks.
- Keep a log of your observations on each species.
- What dates did you see each species?
- How many of each did you see at a time? Total?
- What time of day does each usually appear?
- What attracted each species—water? flowers? food?
- Record birds' songs and try to imitate them.

Tidbits

✧ Plants that draw birds and butterflies are blueberries, butterfly bush, pentas, salvia, lantana, Mexican heather, zinnias, cosmos, parsley, fennel, milkweed, and coral honeysuckle.

✧ Check with your local nursery for native plants that grow well in your area.

Learn More

Cherry, Lynne. *Flute's Journey: The Life of a Wood Thrush.* San Diego, CA: Gulliver Green, 2001.

Curran, Eileen. *Birds' Nests.* Mahwah, N.J.: Troll Communications, 1985.

Daly, Kathleen. *The Big Golden Book of Backyard Birds.* New York: Golden Books, 1991.

Julivert, Angels. *The Fascinating World of Butterflies and Moths.* Hauppauge, NY: Barron's Educational Series, Inc., 1991.

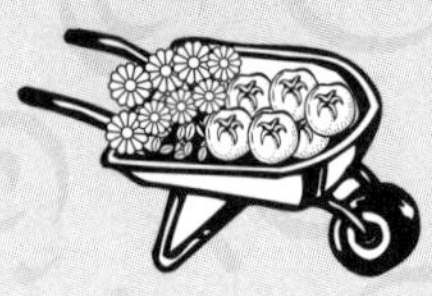

Pine Cone Bird Feeder

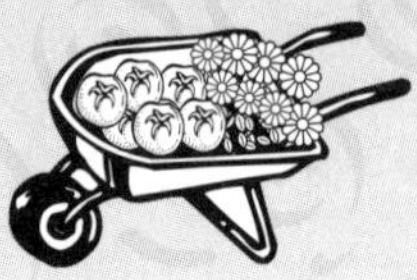

Materials

- large pine cones
- smooth peanut butter
- dried corn, sunflower seeds, and bird seed
- heavy string or narrow ribbon
- newspaper
- scissors
- spoon
- Styrofoam tray

Let's Do It !

1. Cut a length of string about 12"–18" long and tie it to the top of a large pine cone. Cover the table with newspaper.
2. Mix corn, wild bird seed and sunflower seeds together in a Styrofoam tray.
3. Use a spoon to spread peanut butter on the pine cone and use your fingers to push it in between the petals.
4. Roll the cone in the seed mixture. Use your fingers to add seeds in bare spots.
5. Hang the bird feeder in a tree or from the overhang of your house so you can easily watch the birds eat.

2.

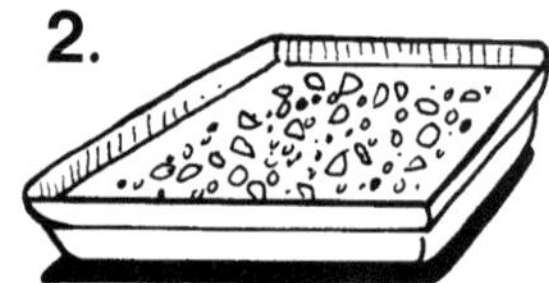

3.

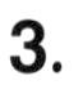

4.

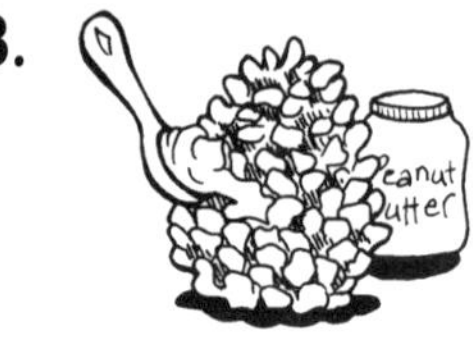

5.

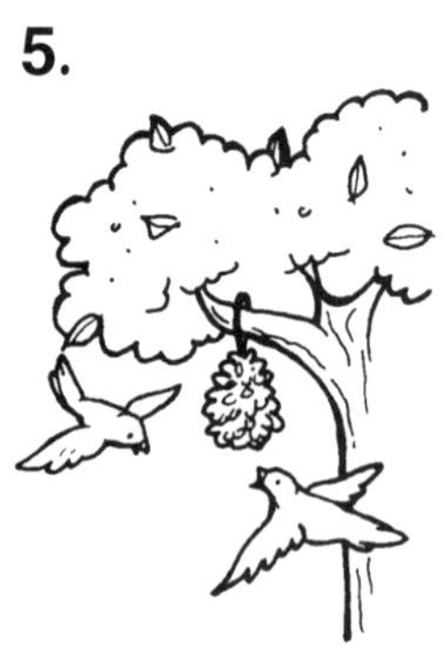

More Ideas

- Make a painted butterfly with identically marked wings. Fold pieces of construction paper in half lengthwise. Draw an outline of half of a butterfly on one side of the folded paper. Cut out the folded butterfly and open it up. Paint on one side of the inside and refold the butterfly. Open the butterfly and see the same pattern on both wings.

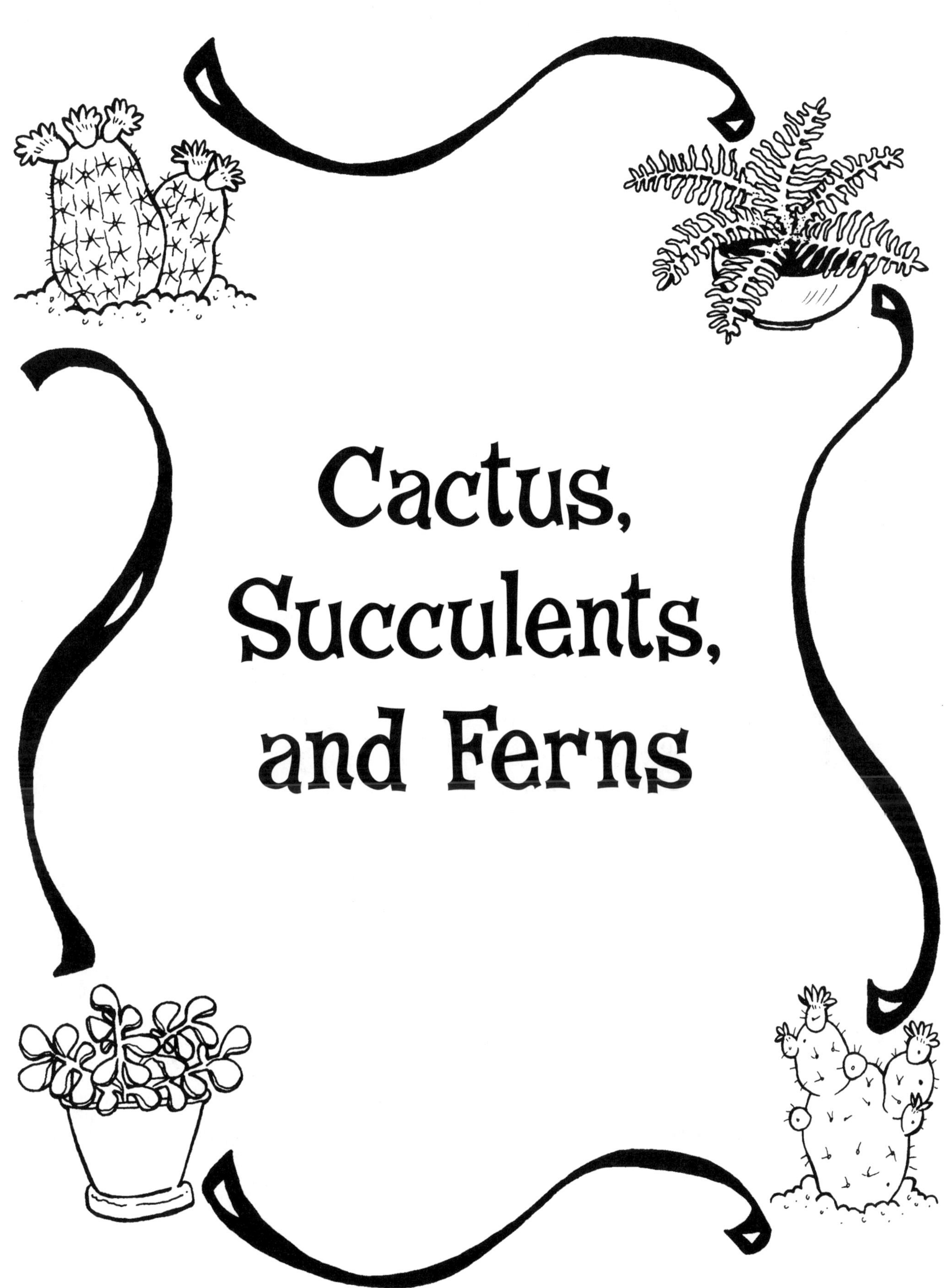

Cactus, Succulents, and Ferns

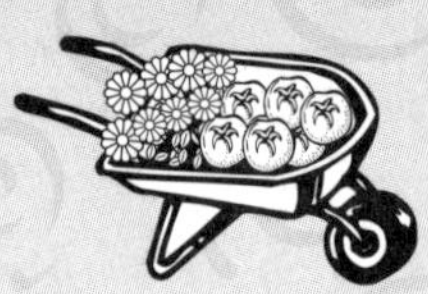

Cactus and Succulents

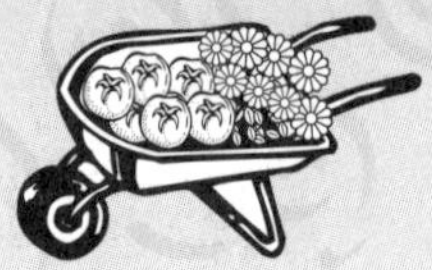

Materials

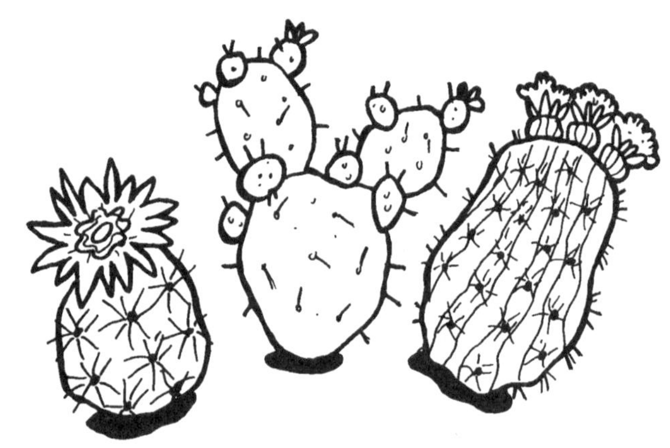

- variety of cactus plants
- shallow planting dish or small clay pots
- potting soil and sand to mix in the soil
- small trowel
- newspaper
- gardening gloves

Let's Do It !

1. Spread newspaper on your work surface.
2. Mix sand in with the potting soil. Fill the planting dish or pot to within 1" of the top.
3. Wear gloves while handling cactus or fold a piece of newspaper into a loop to place around the cactus to hold it.
4. Cactus roots spread out, so allow plenty of room for them as you arrange the plants in the dish. Make a hole deep enough for the roots, put the cactus in the hole, and firmly press the soil around it. Repeat with each plant.
5. Water the garden and place it in a spot where it will receive sunlight most of the day.
6. Rotate the pot several times a week. Be careful not to overwater!

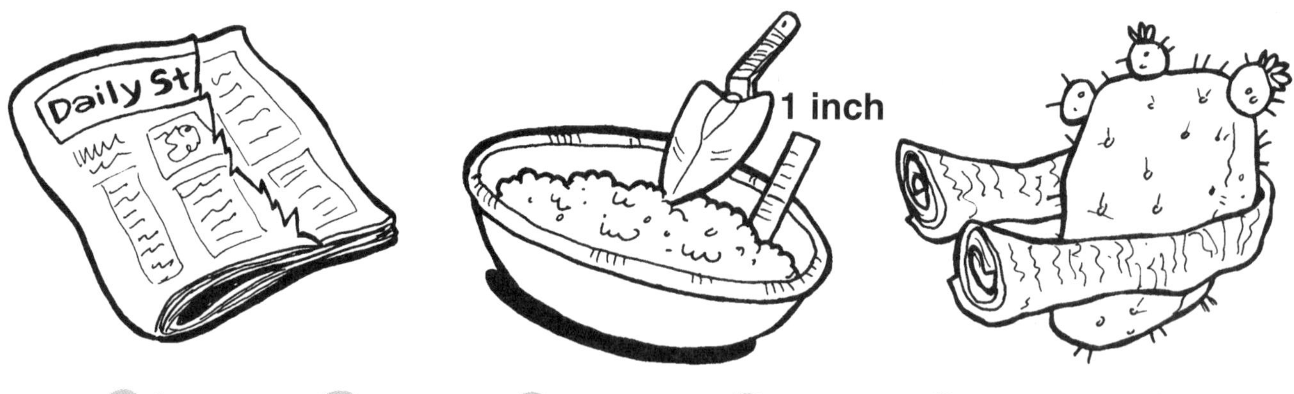

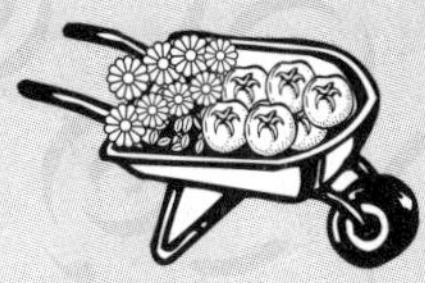

Cactus and Succulents

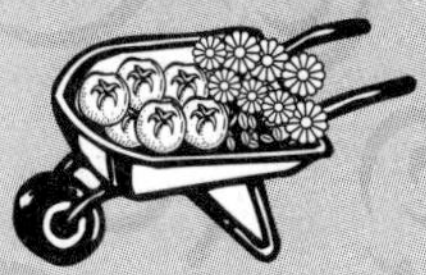

More Ideas

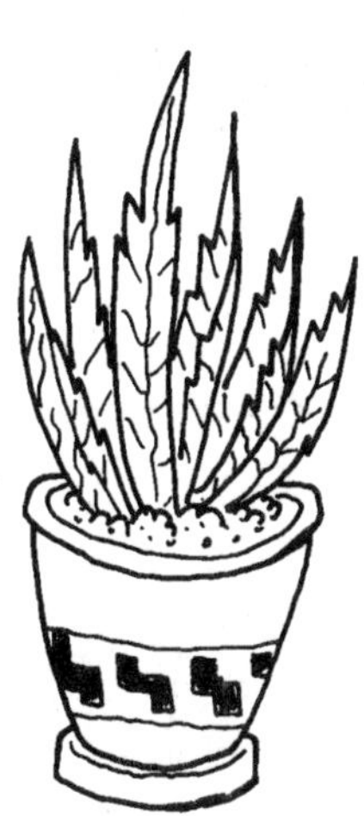

- Grow an aloe vera in a pot for home use. The sticky inside juice eases burns and scrapes, sunburn, and other skin irritations.
- Fine gravel can be used at the bottom of the pot and on top of the soil to aid in drainage.
- If you live in a tropical climate, plant succulents and cactus outside in a sunny spot.
- You can root cuttings of Christmas cactus or Easter cactus in water or moist soil.

Tidbits

✧ Cacti are succulents that hold moisture in their stems, and they have spines.

✧ Cacti come from desert areas and don't need much water. They need a lot of sun and well-drained soil.

✧ Most cacti come from the North American continent.

Learn More

Amsel, Sheri. *Deserts (Habitats of the World).* Austin, TX: Raintree Steck-Vaughn Publishers, 1992.

Keen, Bill. *Cacti and Succulents: Step-by-Step to Growing Success.* Ramsbury, Marlborough, UK. The Crowood Press Ltd., 1991.

Lerner, Carol. *Cactus.* Minneapolis, MN: HarperCollins, 1992.

Markmann, Erika. *Grow It! An Indoor/Outdoor Gardening Guide for Children.* New York: Random House, 1989.

Storad, Conrad J. *Saguaro Cactus.* Minneapolis, MN: Lerner Publications Co., 1992.

Wright-Frierson, Virginia. *A Desert Scrapbook.* New York: Turtleback Books, 2002 (hardcover).

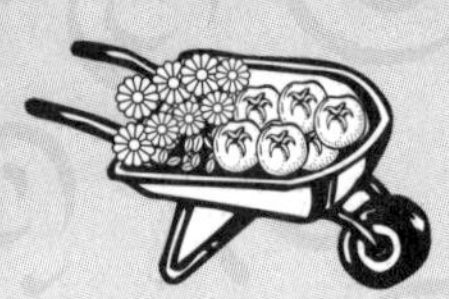

Ferns

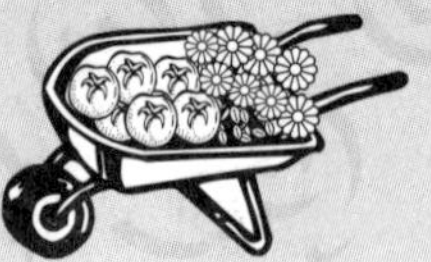

Materials

- potted fern plants
- shovel
- compost or peat
- mulch

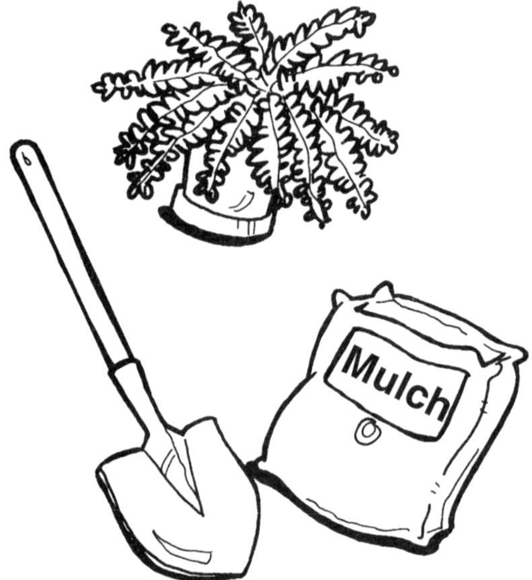

Let's Do It !

1. Ferns like shade and dampness, so choose a planting area that gets little or indirect sun.
2. Work compost or peat into well-tilled soil. Peat will help retain water.
3. Dig a hole slightly larger than the plant's container and plant the fern to the same depth as it was in the pot. Firm the soil around the plant.
4. Mulch your fern bed, and water and weed it regularly.
5. Most ferns freeze back in the winter, so cut off the dead leaves. Ferns are perennials, so they will grow back in the spring.

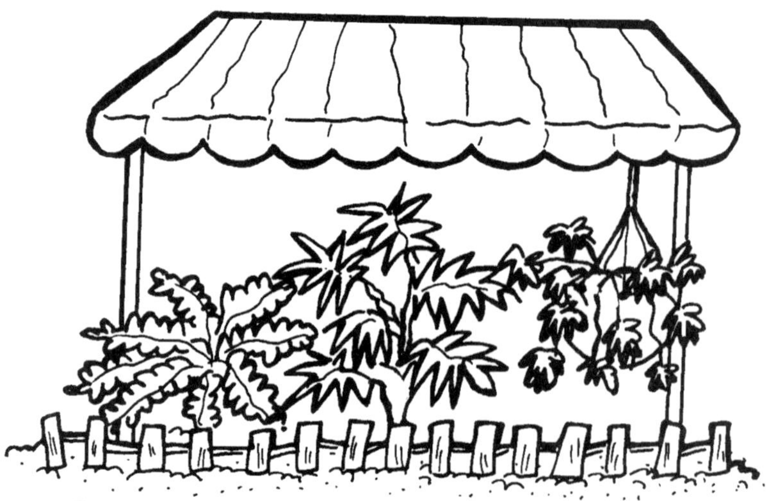

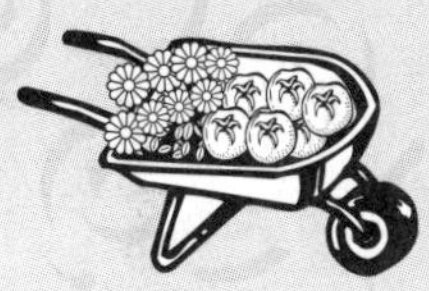

Ferns

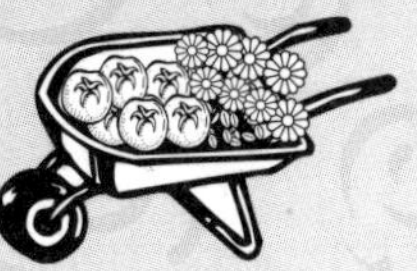

More Ideas

- Plant a Boston fern in a pot to enjoy indoors during the winter months.
- Grow a variety of ferns and use them in cut-flower arrangements.
- You can easily divide ferns into more fern plants. Gently separate the roots by pulling the roots and crowns of the ferns apart. Plant each subdivided plant in a separate spot or pot.

Tidbits

- ✧ Ferns are flowerless, seedless plants that produce spores that make new plants.
- ✧ There are about 10,000 kinds of ferns. They grow almost everywhere in the world.
- ✧ Some ferns grow to 40 feet tall, while others are as tiny as moss.

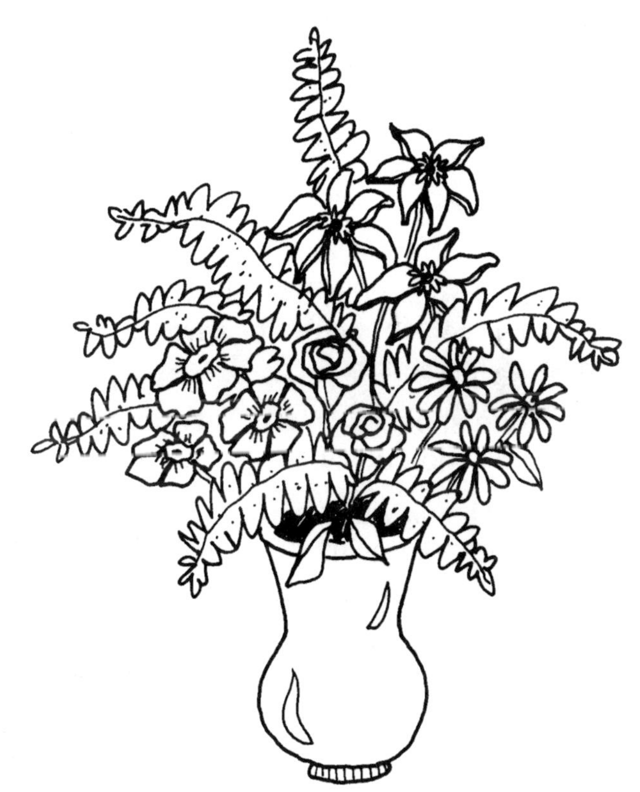

Learn More

Foster, F. Gordon. *Ferns to Know and Grow.* Portland, Oregon: Timber Press Inc., 1984.

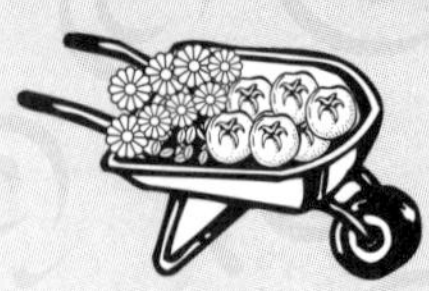

Fern-Covered Box

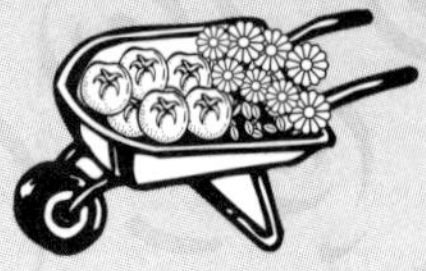

Materials

- shoe box with lid
- tempera paint
- assortment of fern leaves
- wax paper
- stacks of books
- glue
- water
- paintbrush
- bowl

Let's Do It !

1. Place the fern leaves between two pieces of wax paper and press them under a stack of books for several days to flatten them.
2. Paint the shoebox and the lid and let them dry thoroughly.
3. In a bowl, mix water and glue to the consistency of paint.
4. Place a fern leaf on the box and brush on glue to attach the leaf.
5. Continue adding leaves until the box and lid are covered.

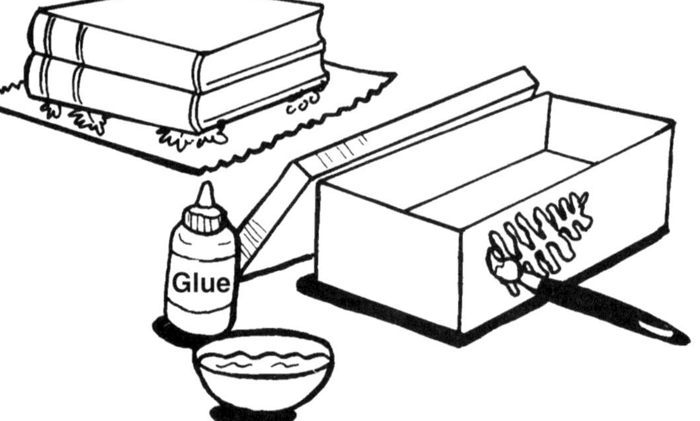

More Ideas

- Make paper bows to decorate the box.
- Paint the leaves.
- Spatter-paint the box, using a toothbrush.

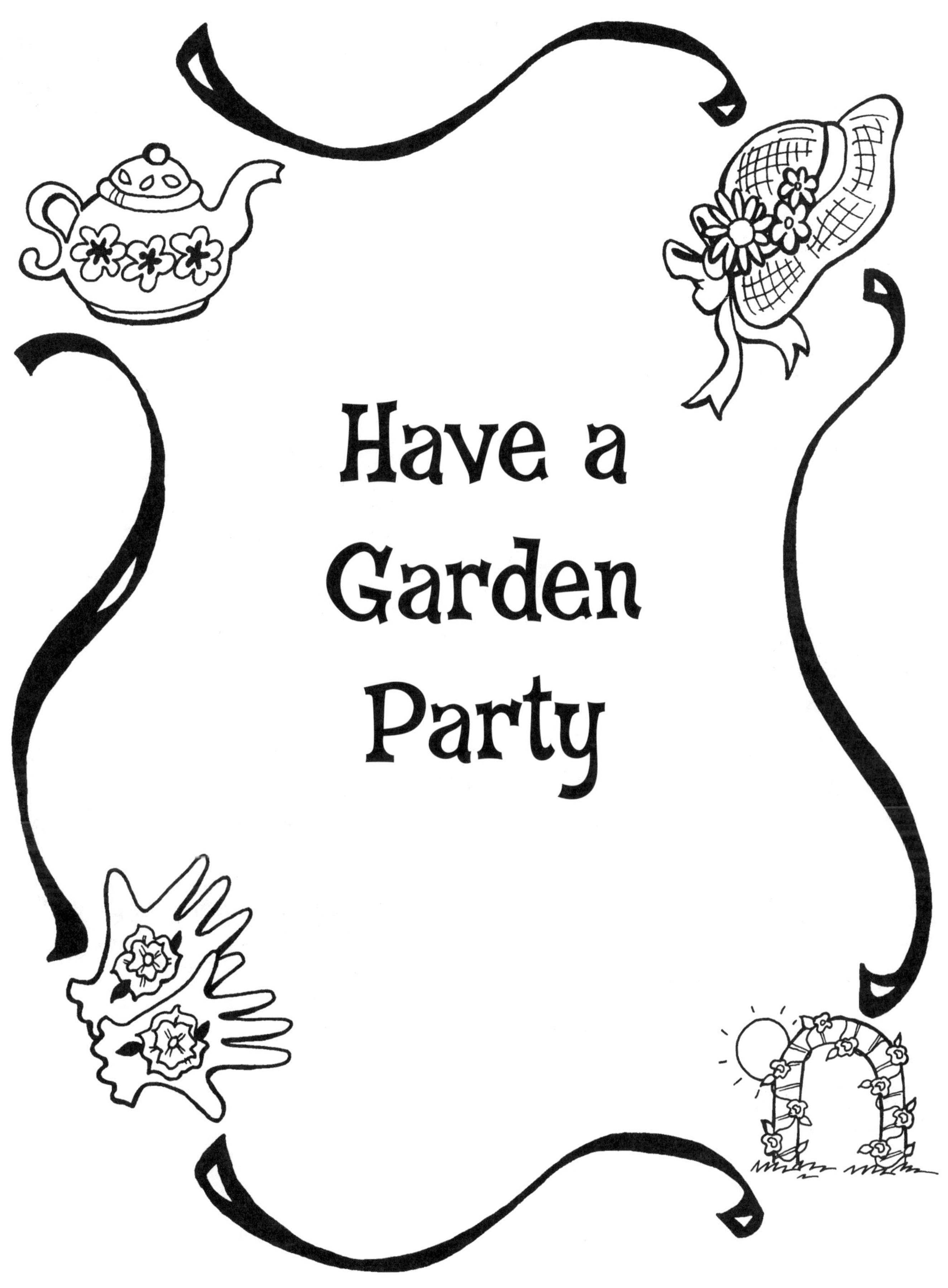
Have a
Garden
Party

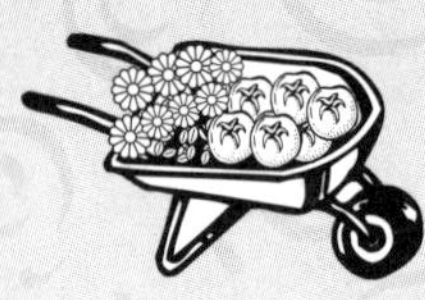

Planning

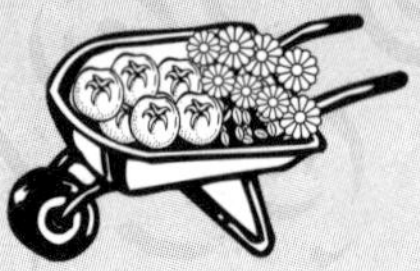

Have a party for your friends to share your beautiful flowers and the delicious vegetables you have grown in your garden. Good planning and preparation help make a party a success. Here are some suggestions.

Materials

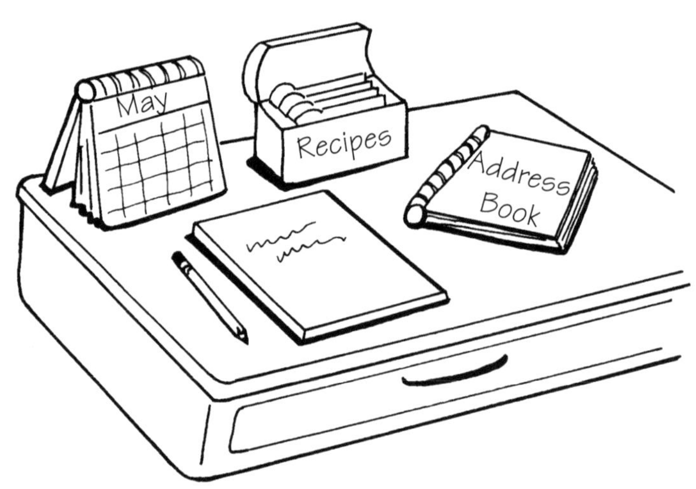

- paper
- pencil
- calendar
- names and addresses of your guests
- recipes

Let's Do It !

1. Decide on a date for your party and mark your calendar. Choose a time when it's not too hot.
2. Decide on a location for the party, and be sure to think about what you will do if it rains.
3. Use the chart on page 153 to make a guest list and plan a menu.
4. Use the instructions and forms on pages 155–158 to choose and create your party invitations.
5. Send invitations 1–2 weeks before the party.
6. Plan and arrange for decorations and entertainment.
7. Make a list of things you will need to buy at the store.
8. Plan where people will sit and how you will serve the food.
9. Decide what you will wear.
10. Who will help you get everything ready for the party? What will they do? When?
11. Allow plenty of time to prepare the flower arrangements for the party.

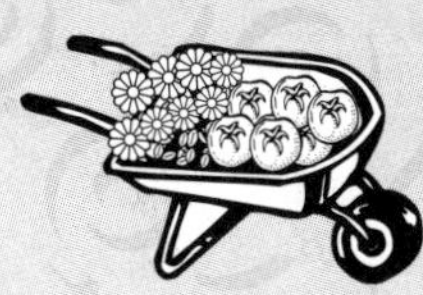

Planning

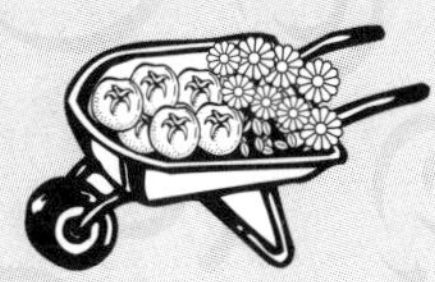

Whom I Will Invite

Response Yes/No	Name	Address

What I Will Serve ______________________________

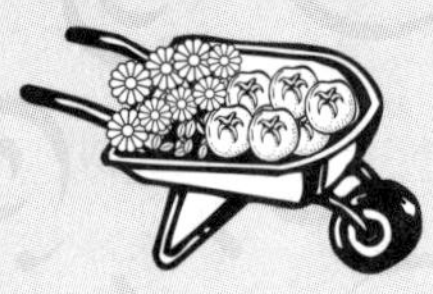

Invitations and Envelopes

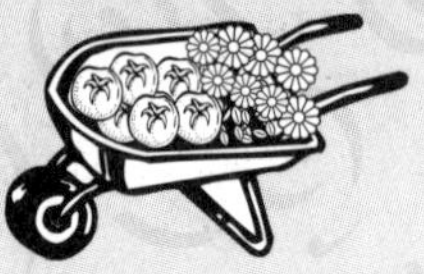

Materials

- copies of the invitation card and envelope (pages 156–157) or one-step invitation (page 158)
- colored and white paper $8^1/_2$" x 11"
- scissors or paper cutter
- rubber cement or a glue stick
- list of guests and addresses
- pen
- colored pencils or markers
- fun stickers—party, vegetables, or flowers
- postage stamps

Let's Do It !

1. Decide whether you will hand-write the invitations or duplicate them with the information already on it.
2. Reproduce an invitation and envelope or a self-mailing invitation for each guest. Make a few extra to allow for practice and mistakes.
3. Reproduce them on colored paper if there are too many to hand color. Reproduce them on white paper if you plan to color each invitation individually. You may wish to reproduce the self-mailing invitation on sturdier paper.
4. Carefully read and follow the directions on page 155.
5. As guests respond to your invitation, keep track of who is coming and who is not so you know how much food and beverages to plan for.

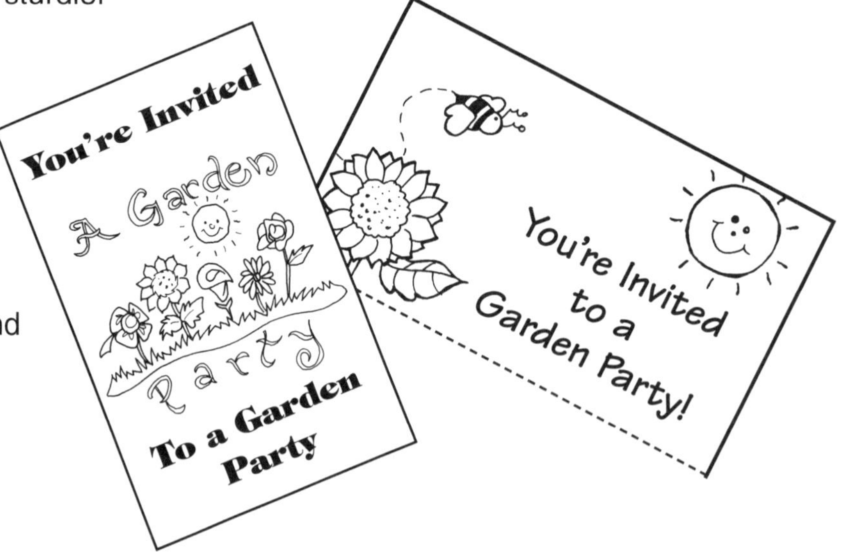

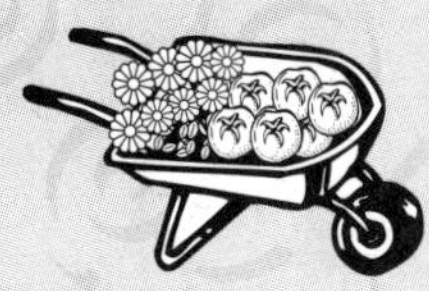

Invitations and Envelopes

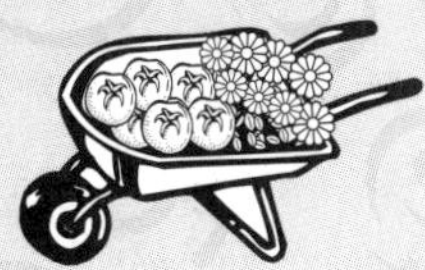

Invitation

Cut out the invitation (page 156) on the solid lines. Fold the card in half twice on the dashed lines so the picture is on the front and the information is on the inside. Fill out the information on the card.

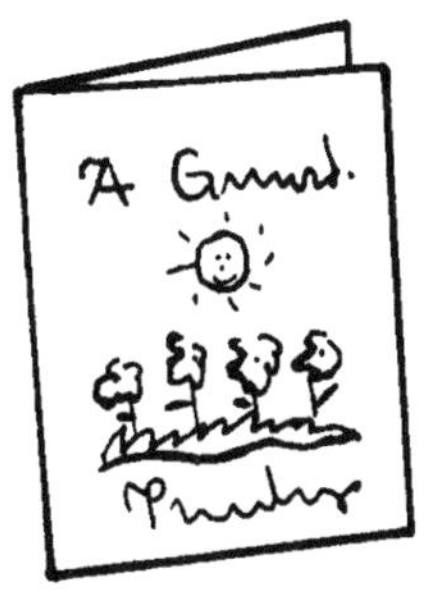

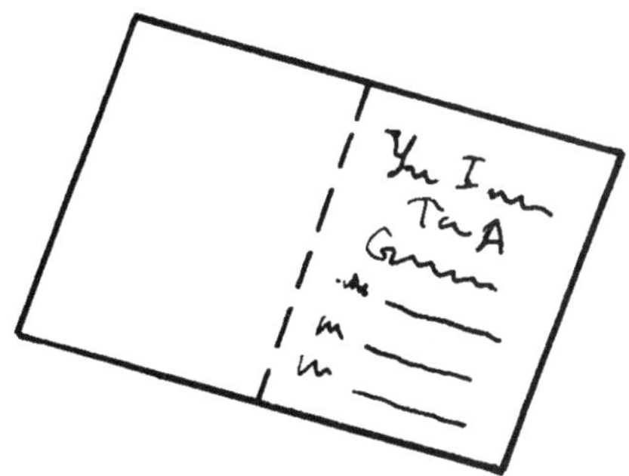

Envelope

Cut out the envelope (page 157) on the solid lines. Fold the sides inward on the dotted lines and glue the folded-over tabs. Fold the bottom up to the dotted line under the flap and press the sides together. When the glue is dry, insert an invitation and seal the flap with a fun sticker. Address the front of the envelope to your guest, and include your address in the upper left-hand corner. Stamp and mail the invitation.

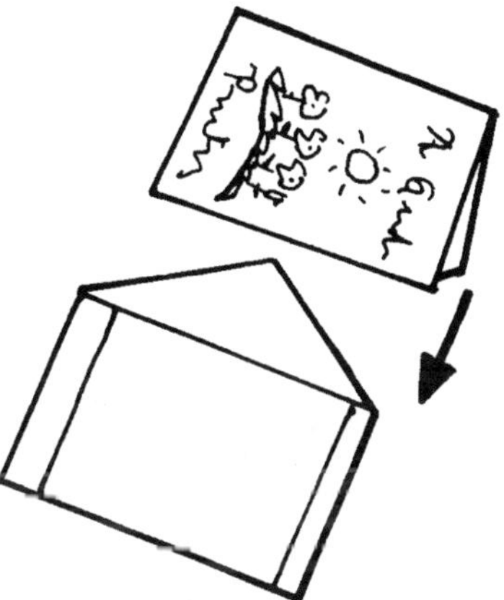

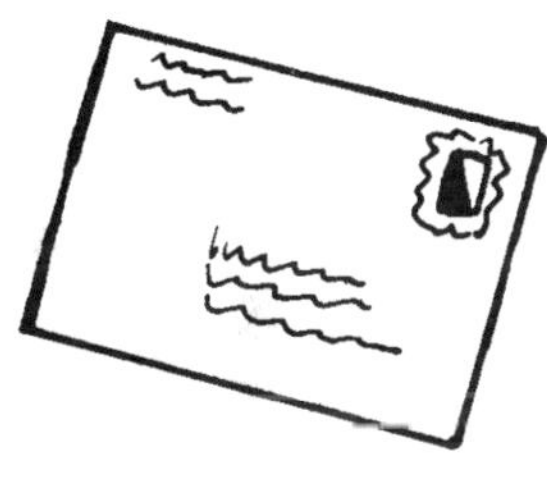

One-Step Invitation

Cut out the invitation (page 158) on the solid lines and fill out the information. Use the dashed lines as a guide. Fold the bottom of the invitation up about one-third. Fold the top of the invitation down and seal it with a fun sticker. Turn the invitation over and address it to your guest. Include your address in the upper left-hand corner. Stamp and mail the invitation.

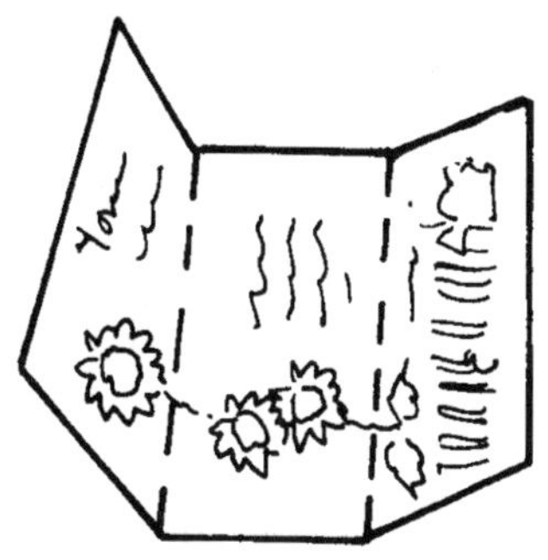

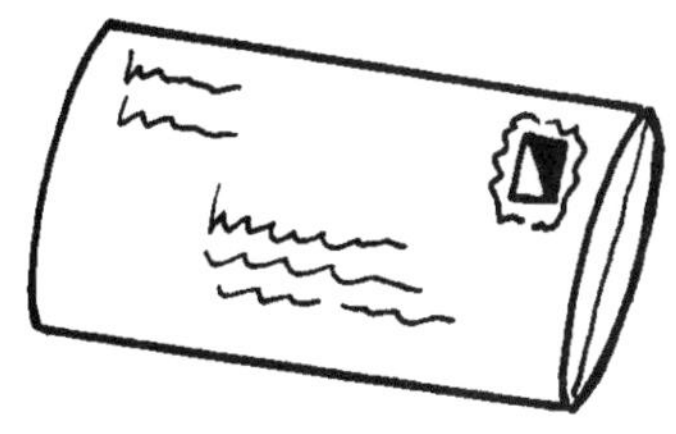

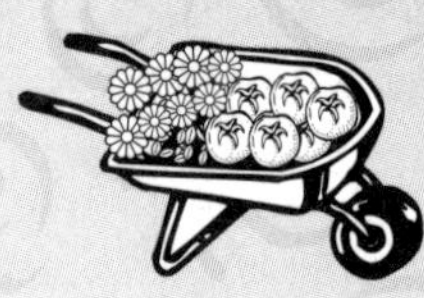

Invitation

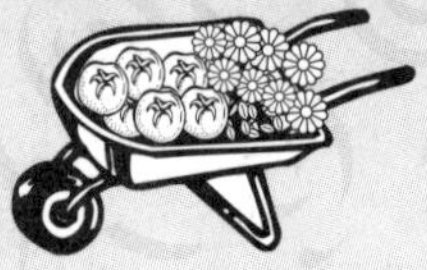

Given by ____________

Date ____________

Time ____________

Address ____________

____

____

Phone ____________

Please reply by ____________

You're Invited To

A Garden Party

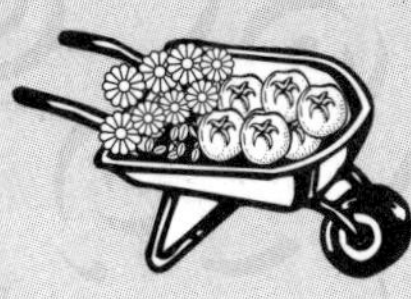

Envelope

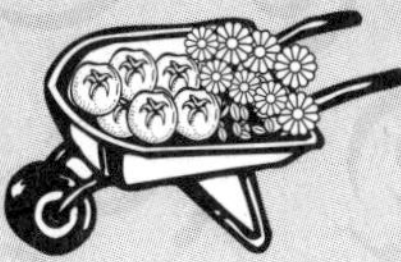

Cut out on the solid lines.

Fold on the dashed lines.

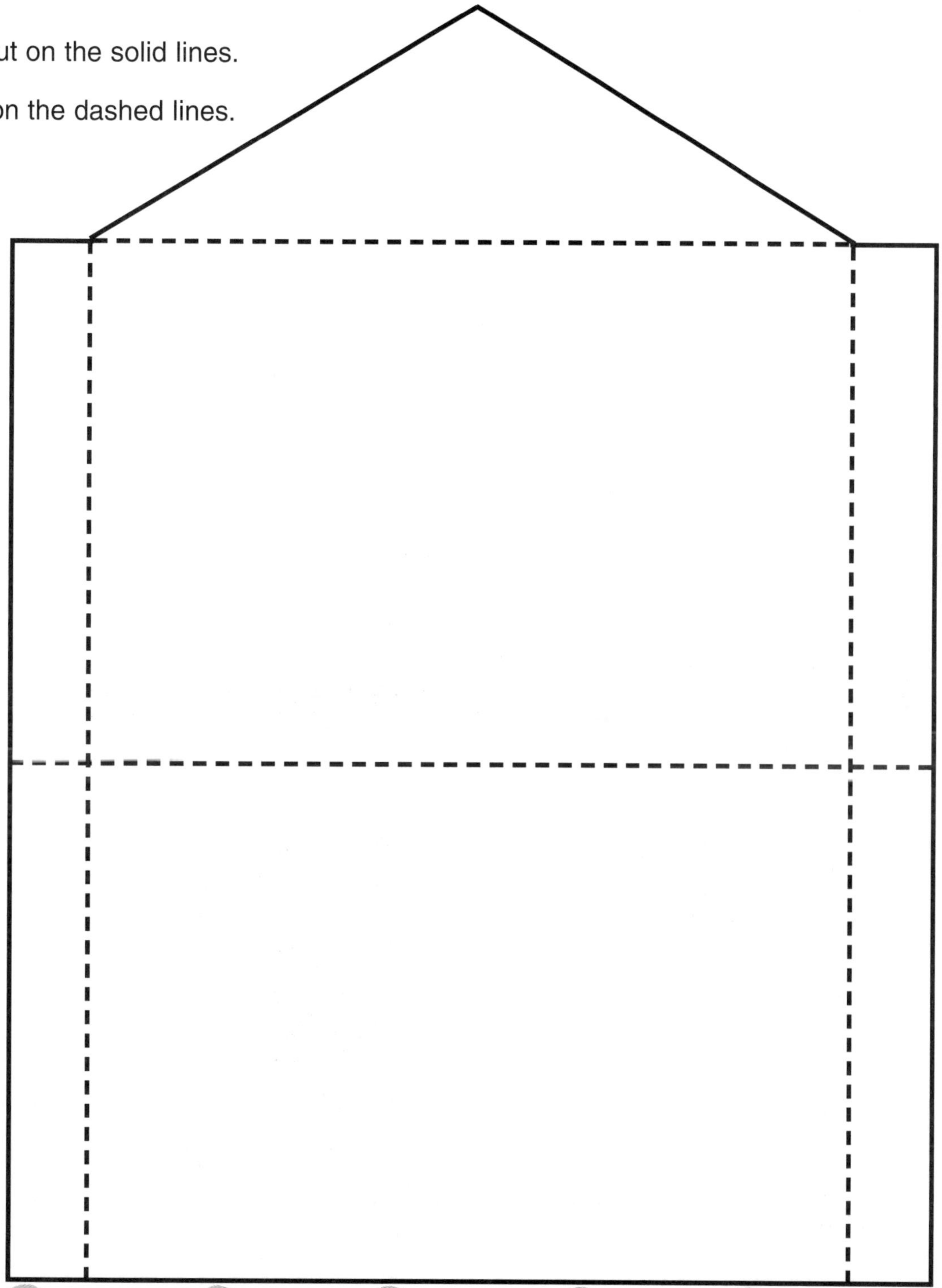

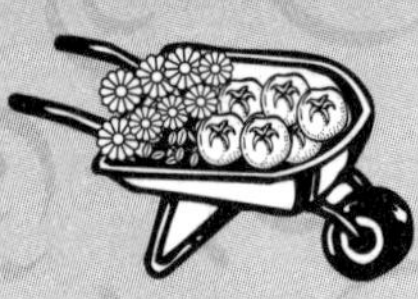

One-Step Invitation

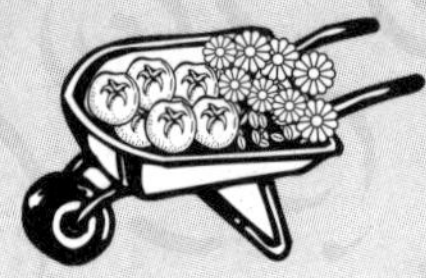

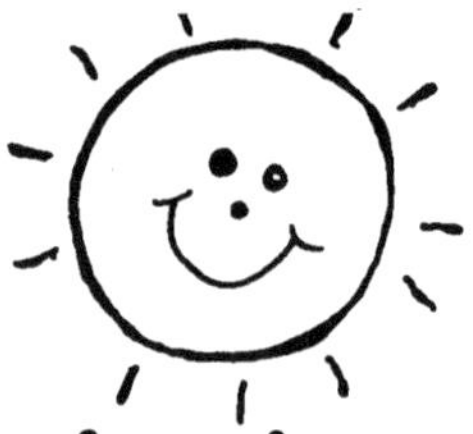

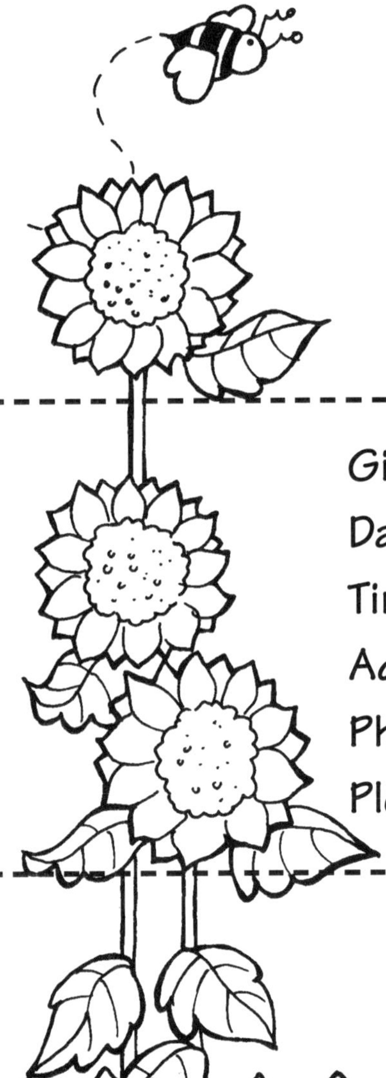

You're Invited to a Garden Party!

Given by ____________________

Date ________________________

Time ________________________

Address ____________________

Phone _______________________

Please reply by _____________

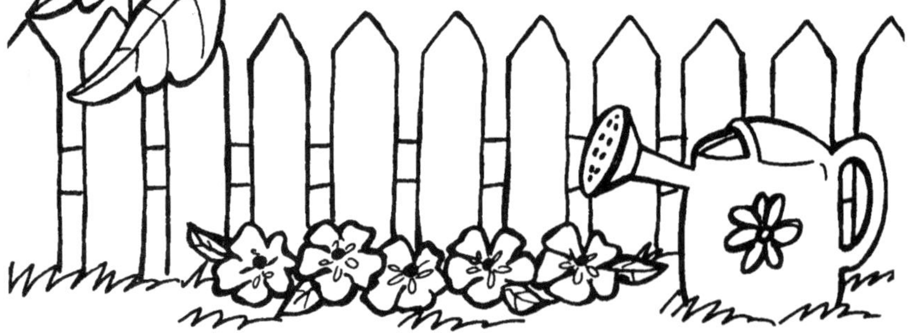

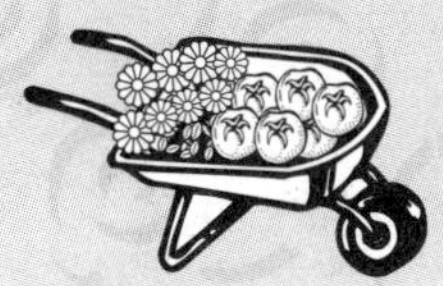

Index

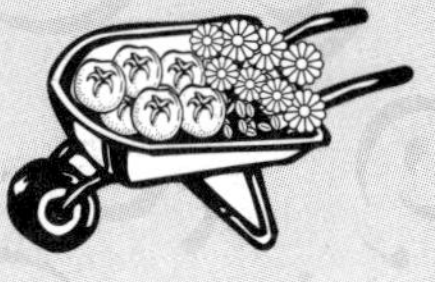

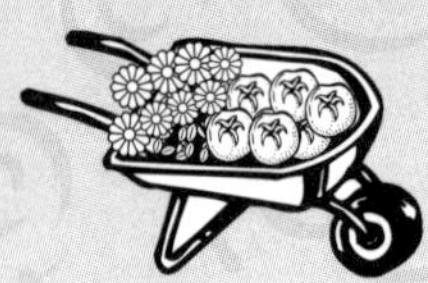

Index

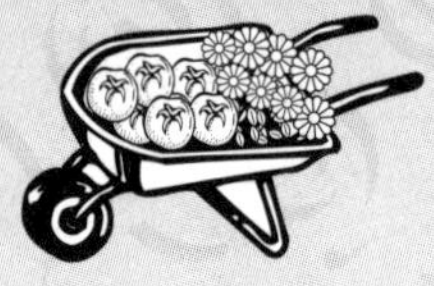